LIVING WATER

THE POWER OF
THE HOLY SPIRIT
IN YOUR LIFE

CHUCK SMITH

THE WORD
FOR TODAY

P.O. Box 8000, Costa Mesa, CA 92628 • Web site: www.twft.com • E-mail: info@twft.com

Except where otherwise indicated, Scripture quotations are taken from the New King James Version Copyright © 1979, 1980, 1984 by Thomas Nelson, Inc., Publishers. Used by permission.

Verses marked KJV are taken from the King James Version of the Bible.

Verses marked RSVB are taken from the Revised Standard Version of the Bible, Copyright © 1946, 1952, 1971 by the Division of Christian Education of the National Council of the Churches of Christ in the U.S.A. Used by permission.

Verses marked NIV are taken from the Holy Bible, New International Version ®, Copyright © 1973, 1978, 1984 by the International Bible Society. Used by permission of Zondervan Publishing House. The "NIV" and "New International Version" trademarks are registered in the United States Patent and Trademark Office by International Bible Society.

Cover by The Word For Today Graphics Deptartment

Cover Photo by Digital Stock © 1996

LIVING WATER

Copyright © 1996, 2001 by Chuck Smith
Published by The Word For Today
Santa Ana, California 92704

ISBN 0-936728-77-9

All rights reserved. No portion of this book may be reproduced in any form without the written permission of the Publisher.

Printed in the United States of America.

*Dedicated to all
who hunger and thirst after righteousness,
and who desire the fullness of the Holy Spirit's power
working in their lives.*

Contents

A Glorious Walk with the Spirit

Part One:

Who Is the Holy Spirit?

Part Two:

What Does the Holy Spirit Do?

Part Three:

What Are the Gifts of the Spirit?

Part Four:

How Should We Respond to the Spirit?

A Glorious Walk with the Spirit

While Jesus was upon the earth, He was the Person of the Godhead with whom man most closely related. Jesus was here to represent God to man, which He did wonderfully—to such a degree that He could tell Philip, "He who has seen Me has seen the Father. . . . I and My Father are one" (John 14:9; 10:30). Jesus was God in flesh upon the earth.

At first the disciples didn't recognize this. But over time they came to realize that when they walked with Jesus along the road, in fact they were strolling alongside of God. Eventually they saw that when they laid their hand upon His shoulder, in reality they were laying their hand on the shoulder of God. They recognized that when Jesus talked to them, they were hearing the very words of God. They understood that when they saw Jesus and His compassion for the sick, they glimpsed the heart of God and His desire to make right that which was wrong. When they saw Jesus take the scourge and drive the money changers out of the temple, they witnessed the determination of God to bring purity to man's religion—or more accurately, to purge man of religion and bring him into a pure relationship with God. When they saw Jesus weeping over Jerusalem because its people had failed to understand the opportunity for salvation that God had given, they watched the heart of God breaking over man's lost chances.

During His roughly 30 years on the earth, Jesus taught the disciples thoroughly and gave them many commandments. But on the day He ascended into heaven, He told His friends He would thereafter give them commandments and direct their activities in a new way. From that day on, He would guide and direct them through the Holy Spirit.

It's critical that we understand this. *The Holy Spirit is the primary agent of the Godhead working in the world today.* He is the person of the Godhead to whom we relate most closely. He is the One who is gathering a body of believers—the bride of Christ—to present unto the Lord. And the church through the Holy Spirit is doing the work of God in the world.

The Holy Spirit is called the *Paraklete*, "one called alongside to help." He has come alongside to help us in every situation. He is here to be our strength. He is here to be our provider. He is here to take care of the emergencies that arise in life. Anytime that we need help in any kind of situation, we can know that the Holy Spirit is here to be our helper. He is the One who has been called to come alongside to help us.

The Holy Spirit desires a personal, loving relationship with all of us. He wants to come alongside of you and help you in and through every situation you may face. That is why it is so vitally important that each of us come to know the person of the Holy Spirit, to know Him in His fullness. Only in that way will we be able to experience the comfort, help, and strength that He provides and which all of us so desperately need.

My Hope for This Book

The purpose of this book is to help you get to know the Holy Spirit so that you might enjoy a full, rich relationship with Him. It is my earnest desire to so present His glory and beauty that you will seek to yield your life fully to Him, knowing and personally experiencing His grace, His love, His power, and His gifts.

God wants us to know Him not merely as some eternal creator or as some force or power that fills the universe, but as a loving, caring Father who sent His Son to die for our sins. Jesus made it possible for us to enjoy this intimate relationship through the agency and the power of the Holy Spirit.

I am praying that by God's grace and through this book the Lord will develop in you an insatiable hunger for and thirsting after the Spirit. I pray that you will come into a deep, personal, intimate relationship with Him so that your life will be transformed by His power.

I pray that you will come to depend upon Him for guidance, for health, for strength, for comfort, for wisdom, and for power. And I pray that He will become closer to you than any person you have ever known—that you will be bathed in His glory and thus fashioned into the image of Christ.

Some exciting times lie ahead in these pages! But, of course, you don't have to wait for the end of the book to gain great blessing. You can yield yourself to the Holy Spirit even now, giving yourself over to His control and to His filling. I urge you to make up your mind even now to yield and surrender your life to Him. Then you can begin, even at this moment, to enjoy a glorious walk in the Spirit, delighting in the fullness that God desires for each of us.

Who is the Holy Spirit?

1

Personality Plus

I will pray the Father, and He will give you another Helper, that He may abide with you forever, even the Spirit of truth, whom the world cannot receive, because it neither sees Him nor knows Him; but you know Him, for He dwells with you and will be in you.

—JOHN 14:16,17

Jesus was a great One to have around while He walked upon this earth. People learned to trust in Him as the master of every situation. When you had Him around, you didn't worry about something going wrong; you knew He would take care of everything. Those who had been with Him for very long knew that He could handle any situation that might come up.

A tax collector giving you a bad time, trying to collect taxes that aren't really due? No problem; Jesus is here. "Go down and catch a fish," the Master tells Peter. "Take the coin out of his mouth and pay the taxes."

What a handy One to have around!

Or suppose you've attracted a big crowd of people and you're short on food. Not to worry. Here's a little boy with five loaves and two fish. Sit the people down in companies, and Jesus will take care of them all. And when it's all over, you find you've collected 12 baskets full of leftovers.

As I said, a handy One to have around.

Or maybe the Pharisees are trying to trip you up and stump you with some kind of technical question. Don't sweat it; Jesus will handle them. Don't give it another thought. Just leave it to the Master.

OK, but what if you're out in a stormy sea in danger of sinking? What then? Same song, fourth verse. Jesus has the power to still the storm and to bring you safely into His desired haven.

As I said, it's always great to have Jesus around.

That's the lesson the disciples learned over and over for three wonderful years. They discovered that Jesus was an amazingly handy Person to have around. They never had to worry when Jesus was present. They learned to relax and be confident because they knew the Lord was there to help.

Changes in the Wind

But by the fourteenth chapter of John, the winds of change have begun to blow. Jesus is making it plain that He is about to go to the cross to be crucified. Although His disciples don't understand everything He says, nevertheless they are deeply disturbed by His words. They don't want Him to go away, and their hearts quickly fill with fear and turmoil. The very fact that Jesus said, "Let not your heart be troubled," indicates that His men *were* troubled and they *were* afraid. *What will we do without Jesus?* they wondered. So Jesus answers their unspoken question:

> I will pray the Father, and He will give you another Helper, that He may abide with you forever, the Spirit of truth, whom the world cannot receive, because it neither sees Him nor knows Him; but you know Him, for He dwells with you and will be in you (John 14:16,17).

This is a pivotal point in the Gospel of John. Jesus is saying to His friends, "It's true that I'm going away and that where I'm going you can't come right now. But don't be worried! I'm going to prepare a place for you, and in time I will come again and receive you unto Myself. But in the meanwhile, I will not leave you comfortless. I will not leave you without any help. I will ask the Father to give to you another to come alongside of you to help you. I will not abandon you; I will not leave you comfortless."

The Greek word translated "comfortless" in John 14:18 is *orphanous*, literally "orphans." "I will not leave you as orphans," Jesus promised His friends. And to keep that promise, the

Master said He would pray to the Father and ask Him to give the disciples another "Comforter."

In Greek, the word translated "Comforter" is *parakletos*. *Para* is the Greek preposition for "with" or "alongside of," while *kletos* is the word for "called." So Jesus is telling His friends that He will ask the Father to send another Helper who will come alongside of them to help them. And the help they will receive would be the Helper Himself!

God's Special Agent

The Holy Spirit is God Himself, a Person with whom you can enjoy a personal relationship. He is not merely an impersonal force or power or essence within the universe, but He is rather a Person who can speak to you and to whom you can speak. He is a Person who can guide you, who can help you, who can strengthen you, who can teach you the truth of God.

The Holy Spirit is the agent through whom God works today in the world, within the church and in individual believers. That is why we need to become well acquainted with the Holy Spirit, for He is the One whom the Lord has placed over the church to guide, direct, and empower its activities.

When Jesus told His disciples, "I will pray the Father, and He will give you another Helper, that He may abide with you forever" (John 14:16), He was encouraging His men to prepare for a new way in which God would thereafter be relating to them. A new way, but not a totally foreign way.

In Greek, the word *another* in the phrase "another Comforter" is *allos*, which means "of the same kind or equal quality; another of the same order." A second Greek word, *heteros*, can also be translated "another," but it means "of a different quality." For example, suppose you were going to rent a car from Hertz. When you approach the counter, they say, "We're sorry, sir. You reserved a little compact Geo, but we happen to be out of that model right now. We can give you *another* car, a Lincoln Town Car, for the same price. Would that be acceptable?" That *another* in Greek would be the term *heteros*. It isn't the same or of the same quality. On the other hand, suppose you had reserved the Town Car and they said, "I'm sorry, we can't give you the Town Car, but we'll give you a Cadillac instead." That would be another vehicle of more or less the same quality as the one you reserved (*allos*).

So when Jesus says the Holy Spirit is of the same quality as Himself, He means the Spirit possesses the same essential qualities that He Himself does, especially those of divinity and personality. In essence He tells His men, "I have been with you, but now I am going away. But I will not leave you alone. I will ask the Father to give you another Comforter—*allos*, of the same quality, the same kind, as Myself. Just as I was with you and took care of every situation for you, so now the Holy Spirit will be with you and will take care of every situation for you."

Is the Spirit a Person?

There are certain things we need to know about the Holy Spirit in order to fully appreciate and understand Him and His work. The first thing is that the Holy Spirit is indeed a Person, and we need to recognize this if we are to have a personal relationship with Him.

If you think of the Holy Spirit as only an essence, as only a force, as only a power, you will find it impossible to have a personal relationship with Him. You cannot have a meaningful relationship with an essence or a force. Have you ever tried to get personal with an electric socket? How about with a steam turbine? An automobile engine?

Of course you haven't. The thought is absurd. And it's equally absurd to think of the Holy Spirit as an essence or a force or an impersonal power that permeates the universe, and yet hope to call upon Him in your time of need.

No, the Holy Spirit is a Person who has been sent by the Father at the request of Jesus to come alongside of you to help you. Jesus said, "I will pray the Father, and He will give you another Helper . . . the Spirit of truth."

Attacks on the Holy Spirit

Many cults attack the personality of the Spirit, just as they attack the deity of Jesus. The Jehovah's Witnesses are one such cultic group. The leaders of the Watchtower teach that the Holy Spirit is not a Person at all, but is merely an essence or an influence. These men say the Holy Spirit is not really a "He," but rather an "it." According to them, we shouldn't speak of *the* Holy Spirit, but of *a* holy spirit—an influence or power emanating from God, no more personal than a breeze flowing from a fan.

This is the same error as the early church heresy known as Arianism, so called because its chief exponent was named

Arius, a priest of Alexandria (A.D. 256-326). Arius taught that the Father alone was truly God; both the Son and the Spirit were inferior and created. Neither possessed by nature or by right any of the divine qualities of immortality, sovereignty, perfect wisdom, goodness, or purity.

The Jehovah's Witnesses have borrowed much of their heresy from this early Arian abomination. Thankfully, all of their arguments were anticipated and answered more than 16 centuries ago. More importantly, the Scriptures plainly declare and reveal that the Holy Spirit is indeed a Person.

Another group, called the Jesus Only sect, doesn't deny the personality of the Spirit but does deny He is a distinct Person within the Godhead. This sect is quite strong in the southern part of the United States and has spread as far west as Arizona. Its heresy is not Arianism but Sabellianism, which denies the separate persons of the Godhead. The Jesus Only sect insists that Jesus is the only God; He is the Father, He is the Son, and He is the Holy Spirit. It teaches that the three "personalities" of God are in reality only three masks that the one God wears.

But the Bible will have none of this. It clearly and firmly teaches that the Holy Spirit is a Person, the same in essence as the Father and the Son, yet separate in personality from them both.

Intelligence, Will, and Emotion

For a being to be considered a person, he or she must possess certain characteristics. First among these is intelligence; second is will; and third is emotion. All three are required if personality is to exist. Human beings possess all three and therefore can truly be considered persons. But rocks, bicycles, flowers, oak trees, and even computers all lack personality; they may be useful and pleasant and highly desirable, but none of them can be considered persons. They do not have intelligence, will, and emotion.

Yet when we consider what the Bible says of the Holy Spirit, it becomes clear very quickly that He is indeed a Person, possessing intelligence, will, and emotion. Let's consider each of these attributes in turn.

1. *Intelligence.* In 1 Corinthians 2:10,11, the apostle Paul writes of the Spirit's intimate knowledge of the "deep things of God"—inarguably a description of intelligence. He writes:

> But God has revealed them to us through His Spirit.
> For the Spirit searches all things, yes, the deep things
> of God. For what man knows the things of a man
> except the spirit of the man which is in him? Even so
> no one knows the things of God except the Spirit of
> God.

All the way through this passage, divine intelligence is ascribed to the Spirit. Paul insists that the Holy Spirit "knows" the things of God. Only a person with intelligence can "know" something. And not only does He know these "deep things," Paul says the Spirit also "teaches" us, helping us to compare "spiritual things with spiritual" (1 Corinthians 2:13).

Don't miss what Paul says about the Holy Spirit here. First, God "reveals" things to us by the Spirit. Second, the Spirit "searches" all things, even "the deep things of God." The deep things of God that man does not know, the Spirit *does* know. Third, the Spirit of God "teaches" us of the things that God freely gives us by helping us to compare one spiritual thing with another.

All of these activities manifestly require intelligence, one of the key components of personality. The Bible insists that the Holy Spirit possesses intelligence.

2. *Will.* The Holy Spirit is also said to have a will. In talking about the gifts of the Spirit in 1 Corinthians 12, Paul said that the Holy Spirit distributes "to each one individually *as He wills*" (verse 11). It is the Holy Spirit who decides what kind of spiritual gift each believer should receive. This act of choosing demands that He have a will. And in Acts 15:28, the apostles prefaced their judgment on a question of church doctrine by saying, "It seemed good to the Holy Spirit, and to us." In so saying they ascribed to the Spirit the same kind of judgment-making ability which they themselves possessed.

On some occasions, the Bible says the Spirit forbade His servants to visit certain areas, thus demonstrating His will:

> Now when they had gone through Phrygia and the
> region of Galatia, they were forbidden by the Holy
> Spirit to preach the word in Asia. After they had
> come to Mysia, they tried to go into Bithynia, but the
> Spirit did not permit them (Acts 16:6,7).

Only persons with a will are able to "forbid" men from taking a certain course of action or to disallow them from enacting another plan. Yet the Holy Spirit did both, making it clear He is a Person with a will.

3. *Emotion.* The Spirit has emotion. Paul warned the Ephesians, "Do not grieve the Holy Spirit of God" (Ephesians 4:30). Likewise in the Old Testament, Isaiah wrote, "But they rebelled, and vexed his holy spirit; therefore, he was turned to be their enemy" (Isaiah 63:10 KJV). You can vex the Holy Spirit.

Now, this would be impossible to say of a mere essence or a nonperson. It would be ridiculous to say, "Please, don't grieve that plant," or "You have vexed that plant. He's angry with you." You cannot say this of anything other than a person. The Holy Spirit is a Person who loves you, who can be grieved and vexed by you.

On the positive side, in the book of Romans, Paul speaks about the love of the Spirit (Romans 15:30). Now I wonder: Have you ever heard a sermon preached on the love of the Holy Spirit? I'm sure you've heard sermons on the love of Christ. Paul often talked about the love of Christ, and surely we've all heard many sermons on the love of God. But interestingly enough, the love of the Holy Spirit is seldom broached in sermons. Yet it is a biblical fact.

Again, only a person can love. You may adore a certain plant or flower in your home, but it would be nonsense to say, "My, how that plant loves you. It's just passionate about you!" But it would make perfect sense to say, "The Holy Spirit loves you. In fact, He's passionate about you." Better yet, it is true.

Personal Pronouns Are for People

Personal pronouns are also used for the Holy Spirit. While the word *spirit* itself is in the neuter (and that's why many people speak of the Holy Spirit as an essence rather than a person), it is a fact that personal pronouns are used to refer to the Holy Spirit. Some 16 times in the New Testament the Greek pronoun for the Holy Spirit is *echeinos*, which means "he," a pronoun in the masculine gender. We find it in John 14:26, which says, "But the Helper, the Holy Spirit, whom the Father will send in My name, He [*echeinos*] will teach you all things." We find the same thing in John 15:26: "But when the Helper comes, whom I shall send to you from the Father, the Spirit of truth who proceeds from the Father, He [*echeinos*] will testify of Me." And then again, in John 16:13: "However, when *He*, the Spirit of truth, has come, *He* will guide you into all truth." The same usage can be found in John 14:16,17 and 16:7-14.

All of these personal pronouns used in reference to the Holy Spirit can mean only that He is indeed a Person.

The Spirit Is Treated as a Person

Many personal treatments are accorded to the Holy Spirit. Allow me to give just three examples.

The Spirit can be *lied to*, as in the case of Ananias and Sapphira in Acts 5. Peter responded to these lies by saying, "Ananias, why has Satan filled your heart to lie to the Holy Spirit and keep back part of the price of the land?" (Acts 5:3).

The Spirit can be *resisted*. Stephen, in his defense recorded in Acts 7:51, said to his fellow Jews, "You stiff-necked and uncircumcised in heart and ears! You always resist the Holy Spirit; as your fathers did, so do you."

The Spirit can be *blasphemed*. Mark 3:28 records that Jesus said, "Assuredly, I say to you, all sins will be forgiven the sons of men, and whatever blasphemies they may utter; but he who blasphemes against the Holy Spirit never has forgiveness, but is subject to eternal condemnation."

Of course, it is impossible to lie to, resist, or blaspheme a non-person. And yet ungodly men do all three to the Holy Spirit.

The Spirit Acts as a Person

The Holy Spirit *speaks*. Again, it's hard to think of something other than a person speaking. Yet Acts 13:2 says, "As they ministered to the Lord and fasted, the Holy Spirit said, 'Now separate to Me Barnabas and Saul for the work to which I have called them.'" And in 1 Timothy 4:1, Paul writes, "Now the Spirit expressly says that in latter times some will depart from the faith." Revelation 2:7 likewise says, "He who has an ear, let him hear what the Spirit says to the churches."

Second, the Spirit *intercedes*. Paul writes in Romans 8:26, "Likewise the Spirit also helps in our weaknesses. For we do not know what we should pray for as we ought, but the Spirit Himself makes intercession for us with groanings which cannot be uttered." And in John 15:26 Jesus tells us, "But when the Helper comes, whom I shall send to you from the Father, the Spirit of truth who proceeds from the Father, He will testify of Me." So the Spirit testifies of Jesus.

Third, the Spirit of God *teaches*. "But the Helper, the Holy Spirit, whom the Father will send in My name, He will teach you all things, and bring to your remembrance all things that I said to you," says John 14:26. And Nehemiah 9:20 tells us, "You also gave Your good Spirit to instruct them, and did not withhold Your manna from their mouth, and gave them water for their thirst."

Fourth, the Spirit *communes* with us. Paul said, "The grace of the Lord Jesus Christ, and the love of God, and the communion of the Holy Spirit be with you all. Amen" (2 Corinthians 13:14).

Fifth, the Spirit *strives* with men. Genesis 6:3 says, "And the LORD said, 'My Spirit shall not strive with man forever.'"

Sixth, the Spirit *works miracles*. Paul wrote that the gospel was proclaimed "in mighty signs and wonders, by the power of the Spirit of God, so that from Jerusalem and round about to Illyricum I have fully preached the gospel of Christ" (Romans 15:19).

Last, the Holy Spirit *guides* us. What a wonderful, glorious truth this is! We can know for ourselves the divine guidance of the Spirit, even as Paul and his companions experienced it: "Now when they had gone through Phrygia and the region of Galatia, they were forbidden by the Holy Spirit to preach the word in Asia. After they had come to Mysia, they tried to go into Bithynia, but the Spirit did not permit them" (Acts 16:6,7).

Only a person could do all these things. But this is not a matter for mere intellectual speculation. Because the Holy Spirit *is* a Person, we can enjoy a relationship with Him graced with all of these loving, personal attentions!

Where Is He Leading You?

When you walk with the Spirit, develop in your relationship with Him, and respond to His work in you, it is very likely that you will begin to have all kinds of glorious, supernatural experiences. Sometimes there will be no response more appropriate than weeping. At other times there will be tremendous joy or overwhelming love. Many kinds of responses are possible as we walk in the Spirit and allow ourselves to be led by Him.

It's always glorious to realize that God's hand is upon you, guiding you along the right route. Of course, at the time you may not always recognize His Spirit's guiding hand; but as the event begins to come together, it suddenly dawns on you: *God is leading me!*

Several years ago I was called to visit a lady from Calvary Chapel who had broken her back in a serious car accident. I went to St. Joseph's Hospital to pray for her, and soon discovered that in her six-bed ward there were two other ladies also from our church. God had planned it so that I was able to minister to all three of them. I didn't know the other two were there, but when I walked in each of them got excited and thought I had come to visit her. (I prayed for them all.)

As I was leaving the room and walking back to the elevator, I couldn't contain my excitement. "Lord, I love Your efficiency," I said. "I don't know how many rooms there are in St. Joseph's Hospital, but there are an awful lot. But You're so efficient, Lord—You put the three ladies from Calvary in the same room so that I could get all three with one visit! This is great, Lord. I love it."

I got in the elevator and pushed the button for the ground floor, but when the door opened and I looked out, I knew I was lost. I had arrived at the nurses' station, not the lobby. So I stepped back in, thinking someone else must have stopped the elevator on that floor. But when I looked up at the indicator light, the "G" for ground floor was lit up. I was really confused then. A nurse saw my confusion and said, "Are you looking for the lobby?"

"Yes, what did they do with it?" I replied.

"You took the service elevator," she said. I looked up, and there was the sign, as big as life: "Service Elevator, Employees Only."

"Oh, I'm so sorry," I said. "I wasn't paying any attention upstairs."

"That's all right," she reassured me.

"Well...how do I get to the lobby?" I asked.

"It's very simple," she replied. "Just go down to the first hallway, turn right, and then you'll be right in the lobby."

I thanked her, and as I walked away I thought, *Oh, what a stupid mistake!*

As I turned down a short corridor, there was a girl, standing and weeping. She looked up, saw me, and screamed, "Chuck!" Immediately she came running up to me and began to sob almost hysterically. When I finally got her calmed down sufficiently, I asked, "What's wrong? What can I do? Tell me— let's pray. What can we pray for?"

"Chuck," she replied, "my dearest friend in the whole world—the man who led me to Jesus Christ—is this very moment having brain surgery. This man is such a wonderful Christian. He's been a missionary in Africa and was sent home to have this surgery. The doctors give him very little hope for being able to walk again. He has a brain tumor that they think has already affected his walking ability, and they feel that..." She broke off, in tears. "Chuck, I can't bear the thought of such a beautiful man of God being crippled. I'm just devastated."

God enabled us to pray together. I gave her some Scripture and pointed her to Jesus. "I was so desperate," she told me after we had finished. "I was just here praying, 'God, I can't handle this. Please send someone along to help me, to pray with me.'" She stopped for a moment, then continued. "And when I looked up, here you came walking down the hall."

Right then the light went on for me. My mistake wasn't merely a stupid error. God had prepared the whole scenario. And I suddenly had the realization: *God's hand is on me! He's leading me by the Spirit.*

Talk about a rush, about *real* excitement! I had been so excited about God's efficiency that on my way down to the lobby I hadn't paid any attention to the signs over the elevator. But God used my oversight to get me down a certain corridor. Had I used the main elevator, I would have walked through the lobby and been gone. But God's Spirit directed me to a certain corridor to meet the need of a certain young girl who in utter desperation was crying out to God for help.

He will do the same thing for you. As you walk in the Spirit and continue in the things of the Spirit, you too will be blessed with exciting experiences that will thrill you to the core of your being. You'll see the power of God as you witness the various manifestations of the Spirit. It's always thrilling to be a part of what God is doing.

As exciting as they are, however, they aren't what we are to look for. Ecstatic experiences can be wonderful, but they can never be our goal. Our goal—yours and mine—must always be to want more of God, and for Him to have more of us.

That's what the Spirit wants, as well. He wants a personal relationship with you that is warm, intimate, and growing. He wants to know you and be known by you.

So what do you say?

2

The Mystery
of the Three in One

And without controversy great is the mystery of godliness: God was manifested in the flesh, justified in the Spirit. . . .

—1 TIMOTHY 3:16

Everybody loves a good mystery. You curl up in a comfortable chair, suspend disbelief, immerse yourself in an exotic world full of odd twists and turns, and try to figure out whodunit before you reach the last, satisfying page. Most often your guess is off the mark, but sometimes you actually get it right. And then you can't help but think triumphantly, *Sherlock Holmes, beware!*

The Scripture has its own mysteries—just as intriguing, just as captivating as any mystery crafted by the latest bestselling author, yet they are infinitely more baffling. No human mind can plumb their depths. Who can fully explain how God can be sovereign and yet give men and women free will? How could Jesus be both 100 percent human and 100 percent divine? A thousand such puzzles confront us throughout the pages of the Bible. But perhaps the greatest biblical mystery of all is the Trinity.

The Greatest Mystery of All

As we consider the Trinity (or the triunity) of God, we first of all must recognize from the Scripture that it is indeed a mystery. In 1 Timothy 3:16, Paul declared, "Without controversy great is the mystery of godliness: God was manifested in the flesh, justified in the Spirit...."

So great is this mystery that our minds can't fully wrap themselves around its reality. We simply can't understand the mystery of the Godhead. But this should be no surprise. We must remember that we are dealing with an infinite God, and when we try to understand Him with our finite minds, we are bound to run into insurmountable difficulties. How can we talk about one God and yet three Persons of the one God? Yet that is what the Scriptures present to us.

I have no intention of trying to explain the Godhead. It is beyond the capacity of the human mind to fully comprehend. We must simply accept what the Scriptures tell us: There is one God who is manifested in three Persons, the Father and the Son and the Holy Spirit.

G. Campbell Morgan explained a big part of our problem in understanding the Trinity. He declared, "The idea of one essence subsisting after a threefold manner and in a trinity of relationships finds nothing in the phenomenon of nature upon which it can fashion as a sufficient symbol." That is, there isn't any symbol in the physical universe that can adequately picture the triunity of God.

Yet we do try to find one. We're always attempting to find some kind of symbol by which we can make an analogy describing the Godhead. But as Morgan said, there just isn't anything in nature that can adequately depict the triunity of God. Paul called it a mystery and, because it is a mystery, we cannot expect to reduce it to logical precepts.

Our finite minds rebel against this. They say, "The Trinity is a contradiction; how could there be one God and yet three Persons in that one God?" Because of the difficulty of comprehending the Trinity, there will always be those who jump in and deny the three Persons of the one Godhead. But beware! Denial of the Trinity *always* brings the denial of the deity of Jesus Christ and the personality of the Holy Spirit.

Some people have suggested that the Trinity is a mathematical absurdity. One plus one plus one, they point out, equals three. But this proves nothing. One *times* one *times* one equals one. You can't disprove the Godhead mathematically.

No, we must stick to what the Bible declares about the nature of God. And it says the Holy Spirit is God. It teaches us there is one God, manifested in three Persons: the Father, the Son, and the Holy Spirit.

The Westminster Confession says it like this: "There is but one living and true God. In the unity of the Godhead there are three persons. One God of one substance, power and eternity. God the Father, God the Son, and God the Holy Spirit."

In the Old Testament

The triunity of God is not nearly as clear in the Old Testament as it is in the New. Nevertheless, in the Old Testament we surely have indications, hints, and declarations of the three Persons of the Godhead.

The Holy Spirit is mentioned just under 80 times in the Old Testament, most often by the names "the Spirit of the LORD," "the Spirit of God," or "the Holy Spirit."

The first mention of the Holy Spirit by name comes in Genesis 1:2: "The earth was without form, and void; and darkness was on the face of the deep. And the Spirit of God was hovering over the face of the waters." Already by the second verse in the Bible we are introduced to the Holy Spirit.

But there may be a hint of the Spirit's existence even in the very first verse of the Bible. Genesis 1:1 says, "In the beginning God." The Hebrew word translated "God" is *Elohim*, a plural form (the singular is *El*). It is interesting that the first mention of God in the Bible uses a plural rather than a singular form.

Some have sought to explain this plural *Elohim* by calling it a "plural of majesty" or the "plural of emphasis." But that explanation appears to have no basis in either grammar or usage. Just a few verses later, the Scripture tells us, "Then God [*Elohim*] said, 'Let *Us* [plural pronoun] make man in *Our* image, according to *Our* likeness'" (1:26). Just who was God talking to? God said let "*Us*," after "*Our*" image and "*Our*" likeness. The plural pronouns used here concerning God should effectively wipe out any need for a concept such as "plural of majesty."

Other equally intriguing hints about the Trinity may be found in the Old Testament. I believe the rallying cry of ancient Israel points to the Trinity. Deuteronomy 6:4—"Hear, O Israel: The LORD our God, the LORD is one!"—is called the Shema by the Jews (*shema* is the Hebrew word for "hear"). It was chanted over and over during worship at the temple, especially during feast days. Worshipers would cry out repeatedly, "*Shema Ysrael*

Yahweh Elohim achad Yahweh." Over and over they affirmed that "the LORD our God is one Lord." The oneness of God was the foundation of the whole Hebrew religion.

Yet the very wording of the Shema is telling. *Yahweh* is the covenant name of God used by the Jews, while *Elohim* is the plural form of *El*, which means "God." Now, the word *achad* indicates a compound unity, not a singular unity. For example, when God created Eve out of Adam, He said, "And they shall become one [*achad*] flesh" (Genesis 2:24), a compound unity.

A different Hebrew word—*yachad*—is required when a singular unity is meant. Had this term been used in the Shema instead of *achad*, we would have no basis from the Old Testament to accept the idea of a Trinity. But the fact that the plural *Elohim* is paired with the *achad*—even within the monotheistic chant of the Hebrews—suggests the triunity of God.

Later, when Moses instructed Aaron on how to place the blessings of God upon the people, he was instructed to say, "Yahweh bless you and keep you; Yahweh make His face shine upon you, and be gracious to you; Yahweh lift up His countenance upon you, and give you peace" (Numbers 6:24). Notice the threefold declaration of Yahweh. One Yahweh—but why should the name be repeated three times? The Lord had said, "You will put my name on the children of Israel and I will bless them." This is the trinity of blessing in unity.

Centuries later when Isaiah saw his vision of the Lord, high and lifted up and sitting on the throne, he heard the seraphim say, "Holy, holy, holy is the LORD of hosts; the whole earth is full of His glory!" (Isaiah 6:3). Why repeat the "holy" three times? Once more it is a threefold witness, this time to God's holiness.

In the prophecy of Isaiah 48:16, the Messiah says, "Come near to Me, hear this: I have not spoken in secret from the beginning; from the time that it was, I was there. And now the Lord GOD and His Spirit have sent Me." The Revised Standard version reads, "The Lord God has sent me and his Spirit," which more literally reflects the original Hebrew. Notice that the Messiah, Jesus, is saying that the Lord God and His Spirit have sent Him. This is a prophecy of the coming of the Messiah, and later the coming of the age of the Holy Spirit.

In the New Testament

In the New Testament, of course, the triunity of God is taught from Matthew to Revelation. Matthew 3:16 says, "When

He had been baptized, [Jesus] came up immediately from the water; and behold, the heavens were opened to Him, and He saw the Spirit of God descending like a dove and alighting upon Him." While Jesus was being baptized and the Spirit of God descended upon Him like a dove, a voice from heaven said, "This is My beloved Son, in whom I am well pleased." Jesus was baptized, the Spirit descended, and the Father spoke from heaven. All three members of the Godhead are clearly at work here.

In John 14:16,17, Jesus said, "And I will pray the Father, and He will give you another Helper, that He may abide with you forever, even the Spirit of truth, whom the world cannot receive, because it neither sees Him nor knows Him; but you know Him, for He dwells with you and will be in you." At the request of Jesus, the Holy Spirit was to be sent from God. This same promise is repeated in John 14:26: "But the Helper, the Holy Spirit, whom the Father will send in My name..." Note again, all three members of the Godhead are clearly present.

When Jesus commissioned His disciples to go and teach all nations, He told them to baptize new converts "in the name of the Father and of the Son and of the Holy Spirit" (Matthew 28:19). Notice that they were to baptize these new disciples in "*the* name" (singular) of the Father, Son, and Holy Spirit. Again, all three are included.

When Peter spoke in Acts 10 to the group that had gathered at the house of Cornelius, he declared "how *God* anointed *Jesus* of Nazareth with *the Holy Spirit* and with power" (verse 38). Note once more, all three are mentioned.

In his letter to the Ephesians, Paul said, "There is one body and one *Spirit*, just as you were called in one hope of your calling; one *Lord*, one faith, one baptism; one *God and Father* of all, who is above all, and through all, and in you all" (Ephesians 4:4-6). Once more the Trinity is being proclaimed: one Spirit, one Lord, one God. One times one times one equals one.

It's interesting that in passages such as those just cited the Spirit usually is mentioned third, behind the Father and the Son. This explains why He is commonly referred to as the third Person of the Trinity. But in case anyone might be tempted to think that this practice implies inferiority, in the Ephesians passage the normal order is reversed. The Spirit is mentioned first, Jesus second, and God the Father third.

In a similar way, Paul in Romans 15:30 said, "Now I beg you, brethren, through the Lord *Jesus Christ*, and through the love of the *Spirit*, that you strive together with me in your prayers to *God* for me." Here we see the three members of the Trinity once more, but this time Jesus is mentioned first, the Holy Spirit is second, and the Father is third.

Allow me to give one more example proving that order of mention has nothing to do with superiority or inferiority. In Paul's benediction to Second Corinthians, the apostle writes, "The grace of the Lord *Jesus Christ*, and the love of *God*, and the communion of the *Holy Spirit* be with you all. Amen" (13:14). Here he mentions Christ first, God the Father second, and the Holy Spirit third. The order is irrelevant.

The weight of evidence allows us to say with confidence that the New Testament teaches one God, manifested in three coequal Persons. The Father, the Son, and the Holy Spirit are one, yet are distinct and separate. This means that the Spirit is every bit as divine as the Father and the Son.

Attributes of Deity

Another way to see the deity of the Spirit is to note the many divine attributes the Scriptures declare Him to have.

He is eternal. Hebrews 9:14 says, "How much more shall the blood of Christ, who through *the eternal Spirit* offered Himself without spot to God, purge your conscience from dead works to serve the living God?" Notice that the blood of Christ through the eternal Spirit purges your conscience from dead works to serve the living God. Once more, a reference to the Trinity.

The Holy Spirit is omnipresent. David asked in Psalm 139:7-10:

> Where can I go from Your Spirit? Or where can I flee from Your presence? If I ascend into heaven, You are there; if I make my bed in hell, behold, You are there. If I take the wings of the morning, and dwell in the uttermost parts of the sea, even there Your hand shall lead me, and Your right hand shall hold me.

> The Spirit of God is everywhere present. In heaven He is there; in hell He is there; in the uttermost parts of the sea He is there. We cannot flee from the Spirit because He is everywhere.

The Spirit is omniscient. Paul tells us in 1 Corinthians 2:10,11:

But God has revealed them to us through His Spirit. For the Spirit searches all things, yes, the deep things of God. For what man knows the things of a man except the spirit of the man which is in him? Even so no one knows the things of God except the Spirit of God.

The Spirit knows all things, even the deep things of God. Whatever God knows, the Spirit knows. And since God knows everything, so does the Spirit. He is omniscient.

The Holy Spirit is omnipotent. When an angel announced to Mary that God had chosen her as the vessel to bring the Messiah into the world, she asked how that could be, since she was a virgin. The angel answered her, "The Holy Spirit will come upon you, and the power of the Highest will overshadow you; therefore, also, that Holy One who is to be born will be called the Son of God" (Luke 1:35). The angel made it clear that the Holy Spirit is the power of the Highest. All three members of the Godhead worked together in what has been called "the immaculate conception." And the result was the incarnation of the Son of God.

Divine References

Divine references also are made concerning the Holy Spirit. For example, in Acts 5:3, Peter first accuses Ananias of lying to the Holy Spirit, then quickly adds, "You have not lied to men but to God."

Peter reasons that if someone has lied to the Spirit, he has lied to God. The two are equal; the Spirit is God.

In 2 Corinthians 3:18, Paul speaks of our being transformed from glory to glory "by the Spirit of the Lord." The newer translations have more correctly and literally rendered the phrase, "By the Lord, the Spirit" (in Greek, *hupo kurios pneumatos*). He means the Lord is the Spirit, or the Spirit is the Lord. They are one and the same.

Works of Deity

Works of deity also are ascribed to the Holy Spirit.

The Scriptures teach that all three Persons of the Godhead were active in the creation. In Genesis 1:1 we learn, "In the beginning God created the heavens and the earth," and in verse 2 we further learn that "the Spirit of God was hovering over the face of the waters." And in John 1:3 we discover that Jesus was also involved: "All things were made through Him [Christ], and without Him nothing was made that was made." Paul adds in Colossians 1:16,17:

> For by Him [Jesus] all things were created that are in heaven and that are on earth, visible and invisible, whether thrones or dominions or principalities or powers. All things were created through Him and for Him. And He is before all things, and in Him all things consist.

In the Psalms we read more about the Holy Spirit's part in creation: "By the word of the LORD the heavens were made, and all the host of them by the breath of His mouth" (Psalm 33:6). The word *breath* in Hebrew is *ruach*, which means "wind," or "spirit." So Psalm 33:6 could very well be translated, "By the word of the Lord [and Jesus, of course, is the Word of the Lord] were the heavens made, and all the host of them by the Spirit [or breath, *ruach*] of His mouth."

God Speaks in the Spirit's Voice

Another line of evidence that the Holy Spirit is God may be found in noting how the New Testament uses some Old Testament texts. Very often an Old Testament scripture about God is ascribed to the Holy Spirit in the New Testament, thus making the Holy Spirit and God one.

Consider Isaiah 6:8,9, which reads, "Also I heard the voice of *the Lord*, saying: 'Whom shall I send, and who will go for Us?' Then I said, 'Here am I! Send me.' And He said, 'Go, and tell this people: "Keep on hearing, but do not understand; keep on seeing, but do not perceive."'" Paul quotes this passage in Acts 28:25,26, where he says, "*The Holy Spirit* spoke rightly through Isaiah the prophet to our fathers, saying, 'Go to this people and say: Hearing you will hear, and shall not understand; and seeing you will see, and not perceive.'" Here Paul quite clearly attributes to the Holy Spirit an Old Testament scripture ascribed to God.

In Jeremiah 31:31,32 the prophet said, "Behold, the days are coming, *says the Lord*, when I will make a new covenant with the house of Israel and with the house of Judah—not according to the covenant that I made with their fathers in the day that I took them by the hand to bring them out of the land of Egypt, My covenant which they broke, though I was a husband to them, *says the Lord.*" Yet in Hebrews 10:15 the writer says, "*The Holy Spirit* also witnesses to us; for after He had said before, 'This is the covenant that I will make with them after those days, says the Lord.'" The New Testament declares it was the Holy Spirit who inspired Jeremiah, even though the prophet himself said it was the Lord who spoke these things. In other words, the Holy Spirit is the One who inspired the writing of the Bible.

That is why in 2 Timothy 3:16 we read, "All Scripture is given by inspiration of *God*," and yet Peter says in 2 Peter 1:21, "For prophecy never came by the will of man, but holy men of God spoke as they were moved by *the Holy Spirit.*"

Notice: Paul says all Scripture is given by the inspiration of *God*, yet Peter declares that holy men spoke as they were moved by *the Holy Spirit*. Is there a problem? No, none at all. Why not? Because the Holy Spirit is God.

That is why Jesus in Mark 12:36 could say, "For David himself said by *the Holy Spirit*..." And it is why Peter, speaking about a fulfilled prophecy of David, said, "Which *the Holy Spirit* spoke before by the mouth of David" (Acts 1:16). When God spoke, it was the Holy Spirit talking. The Holy Spirit is God. He is the third member of the Godhead.

Here to Help

The Holy Spirit, the blessed third Person of the Trinity, is the great gift God has given to you and to me. He has come to be our Comforter, our *paracletos.*

He is ready to come alongside of you to help you in your Christian walk.

He is ready to come alongside of you to guide you in the way of truth.

He is ready to come alongside of you to strengthen you.

God, in the Person of the Holy Spirit, has been sent by the Son to indwell you so that you might be empowered to be conformed into the image of Jesus Christ.

Such is the marvelous gift that God has freely bestowed upon you and me. We will never receive a better gift. Other gifts may thrill us, delight us, even astonish us. But no other gift will ever supersede this gift—because the gift is God Himself.

What Does the Holy Spirit Do?

3

At Work
in the World

*Nevertheless I tell you the truth. It is to your advantage
that I go away; for if I do not go away, the Helper will not
come to you; but if I depart, I will send Him to you. And
when He has come, He will convict the world of sin, and of
righteousness, and of judgment: of sin, because they do
not believe in Me; or righteousness, because I go to My
Father and you see Me no more; of judgment, because the
ruler of this world is judged.*

—JOHN 16:7-11

Jesus was always full of surprises. Have you noticed that? Just when His men thought they had Him figured
out, He would throw them a curve. Just when His opponents
thought they had Him cornered, He would spring His own
trap and leave them drop-jawed and red-faced.

And just when we think we know what He's about to say, He
zigzags and astonishes us with words we never expected to hear.

The Master's teaching on the work of the Holy Spirit in
the world is like that. Jesus tells us that the Spirit's work is to
reprove the world of sin, of righteousness, and of judgment.
But in each case we discover that His work is vastly different
from what we would have expected.

The Spirit Convicts of Sin

When we talk about sin, what do we normally think

about? Lying, stealing, cheating, pornography, fornication, and murder all come to mind. Often we think of breaking the Ten Commandments. And so when the Lord tells us the Spirit will reprove the world of sin, we might expect Him to say He will convict sinners of all their cheating and dishonesty and corruption. But that is not what Jesus says. He says, "... *of sin, because they do not believe in Me.*"

Does God Have a Video?

Jesus says the Holy Spirit reproves the world of sin because they do not believe in Him. That and that alone is the sin for which a person will be judged. No other charges need be brought.

I've often heard it said that God has a kind of video in heaven, and one day He will show on a giant screen all your ungodly thoughts and deeds. But Jesus says the Spirit will convict the world "of sin, because they do not believe in Me." In other words, it boils down to a single issue: What have you done with Jesus? Do you believe in Him for your salvation?

The very name "Jesus" speaks of His mission. The angel said to Joseph, "You shall call His name Jesus, for He will save His people from their sins" (Matthew 1:21). *Jesus* is the English transliteration of the Greek word *Iesous*, which was taken from the Hebrew name *Yeshua*, which is a contraction of *Yahwehshua*, or "Yahweh is salvation." Jesus Himself described His mission like this: "The Son of Man has come to seek and to save that which was lost" (Luke 19:10). That was His mission, and the Holy Spirit testifies to the world of this. He reproves the world of sin because it does not believe in Jesus.

In John 3, Jesus told Nicodemus that God did not send Him into the world to condemn the world, but that the world through Him might be saved. He also said that whoever believed in Him was not condemned, but whoever did not believe in Him was condemned already because he did not believe in the only begotten Son of God. They are condemned because they refuse to believe in Jesus. Thus the Holy Spirit convicts people of sin because they do not believe that Jesus is the Son of God sent by the Father to save the world.

The Scripture testifies, "He who believes in the Son has everlasting life; and he who does not believe the Son shall not see life, but the wrath of God abides on him" (John 3:36). At the end of John's life, the apostle wrote that if we do not believe, we are making God a liar. By our refusal to believe in Jesus Christ as the Son of God who bore the sins of the world, we are blaspheming the Holy Spirit. If we refuse to believe, we call the Spirit a liar, for we reject the record that God gave of His Son (see 1 John 5:10-12).

This is no light matter. As the writer of Hebrews warned us:

> Anyone who has rejected Moses' law dies without mercy on the testimony of two or three witnesses. Of how much worse punishment, do you suppose, will he be thought worthy who has trampled the Son of God underfoot, counted the blood of the covenant by which he was sanctified a common thing, and insulted the Spirit of grace? For we know Him who said, "Vengeance is Mine, I will repay," says the Lord. And again, "The Lord will judge His people." It is a fearful thing to fall into the hands of the living God (Hebrews 10:28-31).

There is only one way to avoid such a horrible sin. The apostle Paul spelled it out when he wrote, "If you confess with your mouth the Lord Jesus and believe in your heart that God has raised Him from the dead, you will be saved" (Romans 10:9).

Of course, such a confession must be genuine. A false confession never saved anyone. There are many who make false confessions about the Lordship of Jesus Christ. In fact, Jesus tells us that one day many will come to Him and say, "Lord, Lord, open to us!" But He will reply, "I do not know you" (Matthew 25:11,12). He insisted that "not everyone who says to Me, 'Lord, Lord,' shall enter the kingdom of heaven, but he who does the will of My Father in heaven" (Matthew 7:21).

How can you tell if a confession is true or false? Any true confession that Jesus Christ is Lord will be manifested by submission to Jesus Christ and to His Lordship. Any confession not followed by such submission is false and is therefore powerless to save.

Where Do You Stand?

Jesus Himself put it like this: "He who believes in Him [Jesus] is not condemned; but he who does not believe is condemned already, because he has not believed in the name of the only begotten Son of God" (John 3:18).

This is the issue. Do you believe in God's provision for your sin? Do you believe that God sent His only begotten Son to bear your sin, to die in your place? Have you accepted or rejected Jesus Christ? That's the only issue, an individual issue. What is your relationship with Jesus Christ? Did you accept Him and the redemption that He purchased, or did you reject it by rejecting Him?

When you stand before God at the final judgment, He will ask you but one question: "What did you do with My Son?" It all comes down to your personal relationship with Jesus Christ.

The testimony of the Holy Spirit to the world is that all of us need to receive Jesus Christ as Savior and let Him become the Lord of our life. The whole issue is believing in Jesus Christ. That makes the difference in being forgiven or being condemned. It's the only issue.

The Spirit Convicts of Righteousness

The second task of the Holy Spirit in the world is to reprove the world of righteousness. The Spirit not only reproves the world of sin, but also of righteousness. Now, sin is doing the wrong thing; righteousness is doing the right thing. Sin is missing the mark; righteousness is hitting the mark.

What Happens to the Unrighteous?

Paul tells us that "the unrighteous will not inherit the kingdom of God" (1 Corinthians 6:9). In Galatians 5 the apostle lists for us the works of the flesh and adds, "I also told you in time past, that those who practice such things will not inherit the kingdom of God" (verse 21). He says that those who do these things are unrighteous; they are not right. And if you do these things, you're not going to inherit the kingdom of heaven.

In the book of Revelation we are told that God will not allow anything to enter heaven that would defile it. In Ephesians 5:5, Paul tells us that "no fornicator, unclean person, nor covetous man, who is an idolater, has any inheritance in the kingdom of Christ and God." And in Hebrews we are exhorted to "pursue peace with all men, and holiness, without which no one will see the Lord" (12:14). In all these verses the Holy Spirit is speaking to us about a holy life, about a righteous life, about denying the flesh life.

Jesus said to His disciples, "Unless your righteousness exceeds the righteousness of the scribes and Pharisees, you will by no means enter the kingdom of heaven" (Matthew 5:20). What a shocker that must have been to the disciples! The scribes and Pharisees were known for their righteousness; they were the fellows who were always straining at gnats and swallowing camels. They were always so careful to demonstrate their righteousness before the people, to keep every little jot and tittle of their own interpretation of the law. But inwardly they were breaking the law all the time. So Jesus told His men that "unless your righteousness exceeds theirs, you're not going to enter the kingdom of heaven."

Solving the Puzzle

It's clear that righteousness is a prerequisite for entering heaven. So what did Jesus mean when He said the Spirit would reprove the world of righteousness "because I ascend to My Father?" It doesn't seem to follow. The logical question is, What does the ascension of Jesus Christ testify to us of righteousness? How does the Holy Spirit put the two together?

He does it like this. When Jesus ascended into heaven, God bore public witness to the world that this was a man who lived such a holy life that His righteousness granted Him entrance into the kingdom of heaven. Jesus exemplified the kind of righteousness that God will accept, and by His ascension into heaven God was saying, "This is it. This is the standard of righteousness that will gain you entrance into heaven—greater than that of the scribes and the Pharisees. Nothing short of this righteousness can grant you entrance into the kingdom of heaven."

Don't believe the lies of Satan that somehow God will be persuaded to let all kinds of people into heaven who are basically sincere and good, but who never accepted the Spirit's witness about Christ. Don't believe that God will tolerate evil in the kingdom of heaven, just as long as it's not too bad. Don't believe that God will give you some kind of special dispensation to live after the flesh while on earth, but still grant you entrance into the kingdom.

Read the lists in Galatians 5 and Ephesians 5 again and consider the warnings. "We know that they which do such things *shall not* inherit the kingdom of heaven," Paul insists.

But maybe that's not your problem. Maybe you don't live like that. Maybe you're counting on making it to heaven on the basis of your good life. Then you must consider what Jesus says in John 16:10. The witness of the Spirit is this: If you want God to accept you on the basis of your own righteousness, then you will have to be as righteous as Jesus Christ. For His ascension into heaven is God's witness to the world that such righteousness is the only righteousness that the Lord will accept.

How Righteous Was Jesus?

And just how righteous was Jesus? The Bible tells us that God "made Him [Jesus] *who knew no sin* to be sin for us" (2 Corinthians 5:21). First John 3:5 declares, "In Him *there is no sin.*" And Hebrews 4:15 tells us, "We do not have a High Priest who cannot sympathize with our weaknesses, but was in all points tempted as we are, *yet without sin.*" Jesus could truthfully say of Himself, "I always do those things that please Him [the Father]" (John 8:29).

Because Jesus lived a sinless life, always doing the things that pleased the Father, God received Him up into glory. By doing so, He proclaimed to the world the only righteous standard that He will accept.

Do you want to be accepted into heaven apart from Jesus Christ? Then the Spirit's witness is that you must be sinless, for that is the only righteousness that God will accept. If you can't meet that standard, don't expect God to accept you. Unless you are perfect and always have been perfect, you will be rejected.

Despite this clear-cut witness of the Spirit, many people today still seek to offer to God their own righteousness as the basis of their salvation. "Lord," they say, "I do such good things and I give to the poor. I am kind and considerate, and I do my best to live an honest life. I try to live by the Golden Rule. I want You to accept me, and therefore I will do, as best I can, all of these good works. Then, surely, You will love me and accept me for everything I have done!"

I hear this line of reasoning quite often when a person has died. The family of the deceased will tell me of all the good things the person did, then ask me to commend their loved one to God because of all of his or her good works.

But what did God say about man's works of righteousness? Through Isaiah the prophet, the Lord said that our works "are like filthy rags" in His sight (Isaiah 64:6).

A Strange Case of Reasoning

Now, some people reason like this. "Do you believe that it is possible for you to be perfect for one minute?" they ask. If I don't think too hard, I can say yes. So they reply, "If you can be perfect for one minute, then you could be perfect for two minutes. And if you could be perfect for two minutes, then you could be perfect for four minutes. And if you could be perfect for four..." They keep extending the argument and finally conclude it is possible for a man to live in sinless perfection.

For the sake of argument, let's say you could do this. I'll grant it to you—I can't grant it to myself. I'm too honest. I'm so far from perfect that I just thank God for Jesus and for grace. But let us say that you could make a resolve right now: "I am going to be perfect from this moment on. I will never think one single thought that is outside of God's will. I will never act in a critical or prideful way. I'll not do anything for myself. I will live completely for others and for God. I will be perfect." And let us suppose that you could pull it off.

Then imagine that an earthquake unexpectedly hit and the building you were standing in started to collapse, crashing down on you in huge chunks. You're hit by one of the biggest pieces. As you're lying on the shattered floor, dying, I come by and say, "Congratulations! You did it! You set your heart and your mind and your resolve on living a holy life, and now you have reached the stage of sinless perfection. Congratulations!" As I congratulated you for this splendid job, if even the tiniest bit of pride arose and you thought, *Yes, I am wonderful!*—uh-oh! You've been wiped out because God hates pride.

But again, for the sake of argument, let's suppose you took even that kind of compliment in stride. Let's say you're truly one humble guy. Nevertheless, you still have a big problem. What about what you *already* did before you resolved to live sinlessly? What about the sins you committed before your oath? Here's the bad news: *You were disqualified before you started!* Therefore, if you want to come before God on the basis of your own righteousness, you might as well forget it. It's too late.

You say, "But, Chuck, aren't you closing the door to all of us?" Yes, as far as our own righteousness and efforts are concerned. If you're thinking that you can get to heaven on the basis of your good works or your good intentions or your own efforts, forget it. You'll never make it. There's only one way that any of us will gain entrance into the kingdom of heaven, and that is through the righteousness of Jesus Christ, imparted to us by our faith and trust in Him. There is no kind of service or duty to God we can perform for which He will accept us into heaven. Only by faith in Jesus Christ can we ever make it to the kingdom.

That is the Holy Spirit's witness to us through the ascension of Christ. The Spirit reproves the world of righteousness by pointing to Jesus Christ. He is the example; He's what God would have us to be. And if you can't meet that standard, then your only hope is to place your faith in Him.

The Spirit Convicts of Judgment

Finally, the Holy Spirit reproves the world of judgment. Now again, we might have expected Jesus to say, "... of the judgment to come against all sinners." And there *is* a day of judgment coming, the final day of reckoning when everyone will give an account of himself to God. So we might have expected Him to talk about that future judgment. But again, Jesus throws us a curve. He said, "... of judgment, *because the ruler of this world is judged.*" The judgment that Jesus speaks about isn't some *future* judgment; rather, it is a judgment that *already* has taken place. The prince of this world, Satan, was judged.

And where was the prince of this world judged? There is only one possible answer: At the cross. There was the ruler of the world judged; there was sin judged. God brought His judgment against sin upon Jesus at the cross.

Getting the Big Picture

Perhaps we should back up for a moment here to get a fuller understanding of what's going on. It's important to remember that, for a time, Satan had a rightful claim to this world. He gained it when Adam forfeited that right to him in the garden. That's why Jesus calls him "the ruler of this world."

Originally the earth was the Lord's and the fullness thereof. He created it. When God created man and placed him upon the earth, He gave Adam dominion over the earth. But Adam surrendered his dominion to Satan when he disobeyed the commands of God and obeyed the devil's suggestion to eat the forbidden fruit. When Adam yielded himself to Satan, he became his servant and thus the devil gained dominion over the earth. As Paul said in Romans 6:16, "Do you not know that to whom you present yourselves slaves to obey, you are that one's slaves whom you obey, whether of sin to death, or of obedience to righteousness?" Adam obeyed Satan and thus became the slave of sin.

Long centuries later when Satan took Jesus up to a high mountain to show Him the kingdoms of the world and their glory, he offered to give them to Him—if only Jesus would bow down and worship him. "This has been delivered to me, and I give it to whomever I wish," Satan boasted in Luke 4:6. Amazingly, Jesus did not dispute the devil's audacious claim. He recognized that Satan was the prince of this world and called him such (John 12:31; 14:30; 16:11).

But Jesus was unwilling to let the situation stand. He had come to redeem the world back to God, and by His death upon the cross He paid the price for our redemption. For we are not redeemed with corruptible things, as silver and gold, from our vain manner of living, but with the precious blood of Jesus Christ, who was slain as a lamb without spot or blemish (see 1 Peter 1:18,19). Jesus Christ came to judge Satan through the cross so that the devil's dominion over the earth might be brought to an end.

The Triumph of the Cross

It was at the cross that Satan was judged. On the cross the power of Satan was broken, his hold over the earth canceled. Paul tells us in Colossians 2:13-15,

> And you, being dead in your trespasses and the uncircumcision of your flesh, He has made alive together with Him, having forgiven you all trespasses; having wiped out the handwriting of requirements that was against us, which was contrary to us. And He has taken it out of the way, having nailed it to the cross. Having disarmed principalities and powers, He made a public spectacle of them, *triumphing over them in it.*

On the cross Jesus Christ defeated those principalities and powers of darkness which were against us. The resurrection was the proof of His victory.

Thus, the prince of this world has been judged. The authority and power that he once had over us has been broken through the death and resurrection of Jesus Christ. Therefore let not sin reign in your body, that you should obey the lusts of the body (see Romans 6:12).

Now, it is true that God has not yet taken control of the world. We are waiting and longing and praying for that day. Jesus told us to pray, "Your kingdom come. Your will be done on earth as it is in heaven" (Matthew 6:10). Oh, how I long to see the day when God's will instead of Satan's is being done on this earth! Believe me, it will be a far different world than what you see now. For righteousness will cover the earth "as the waters cover the sea" (Isaiah 11:9). The lion will eat straw like an ox and lie down with the lamb, and a little child will lead them (see Isaiah 11:6,7; 65:25). There won't be any physical or mental disabilities, for the lame will be leaping and the mute will be praising God, and the blind will behold God's glory and wonder (see Isaiah 35:6).

But until that glorious day, the witness of the Holy Spirit is this: We don't have to live under the dominion of sin any longer. We don't have to live under the rule of Satan, for he has been judged. He has no rightful claim over our lives. We can be set free because Jesus died to liberate us from the powers of darkness.

Because Satan has been judged, you, through Jesus Christ, can be freed from his dominion and his control. You can live a life in fellowship with God, being accounted righteous through your faith in Jesus Christ.

The world is still under the power of Satan, but the Holy Spirit bears witness that no one has to be chained by sin any longer. We don't have to be a captive and be held by the enemy in darkness. The prince of this world has been judged and thoroughly defeated. Now he holds people in bondage only by usurped authority and power. Jesus died for the sins of the world. And we can be set free from the power of sin.

I am a child of God through my faith in Jesus Christ, and God sees me as righteous for the righteousness of Jesus Christ has been imputed to me. God will accept me into heaven. Sin no longer rules my life. Because I am in Christ, I have been set free. Satan no longer has dominion over me because he was judged at the cross.

The same can be true of you. You don't have to be ruled by sin anymore; the prince of this world has been judged. His power has been broken and you, through Jesus Christ, can have victory over the powers of darkness.

What About You?

Such is the witness of the Holy Spirit to the world—a beautiful witness indeed. Sin can be brought to an end in your life when you believe in Jesus Christ and the righteousness of Christ is imputed to you. The power of Jesus' sinless life makes it possible for you to live with God forever in heaven. And even while living on earth, you don't have to live under the power and bondage of darkness anymore. Satan has been judged at the cross.

What a glorious witness! What a glorious truth!

The Spirit testifies that we have been enabled to enjoy a loving relationship with God by believing in Jesus Christ. That's the issue that one day will determine your eternal destiny—that, and only that. Do you believe in Jesus Christ? Did you receive Him as your Savior and Lord, or did you reject Him for whatever reason?

Let me ask you a question. Do you know where you stand as you consider your own relationship with Jesus Christ? If you have not yet made that commitment to believe and trust in Jesus Christ, to confess Him as the Lord of your life, I pray that God would speak to your heart right now, before you turn another page. Allow God's Holy Spirit to speak to you of sin, of righteousness, and of judgment. And then accept the marvelous gift of eternal life that God has provided for you through the sacrifice of His sinless Son, Jesus Christ.

It's true that Jesus delights in throwing curveballs, but this is not one of them. It's not even a fastball. It's a slow, graceful pitch that God wants you to hit out of the ballpark. For in this most important game of all, God doesn't want you out; He wants you *in*. He wants you to arrive safely home with Him in heaven.

Jesus has already won the championship. But it's up to you to join His team.

4

Keeping
the Lid On

*For the mystery of lawlessness is already at work; only He
who now restrains will do so until He is taken out of the
way.*

— 2 THESSALONIANS 2:7

We live in difficult days. But according to Scripture, it will get worse before it gets better.

The apostle Paul sounded this ominous warning almost 2000 years ago. He revealed that a day was coming when evil would run rampant across the face of the earth. Mankind would rebel against God in a way unparalleled since time began, swiftly bringing on itself fearsome plagues and terrors that would signal the end of this world system. Even in his own day, Paul could see the signs of the coming destruction. He wrote, "For the mystery of lawlessness is already at work" (2 Thessalonians 2:7).

Today this "mystery of lawlessness" is not hard to detect. We see the decaying effect of sin everywhere. The spirit of the Antichrist surrounds us. Jesus Christ is being mocked, scorned, ridiculed, and derided.

Beware of the "Religious Fanatics"

It's gotten so bad that a "cultist" is now being defined in some governmental circles as "one who believes that the Bible is the inerrant Word of God, and that Jesus is coming again."

Do you believe these two ideas? If so, you are now being classified as a cultist. You own the title of "religious fanatic."

Watch for this term, "religious fanatic." It will be used more and more as we draw ever closer to the end. Globalists—those who push relentlessly for a one-world government—freely acknowledge that religious fanatics represent the greatest hindrance to their move toward absolute control of the planet. Members of many groups are being labeled as religious fanatics, and religious fanaticism has been branded as one of the greatest evils in the world today. What's holding back the New Age, according to a growing number of authorities? Their answer: Religious fanatics.

Several powerful men who enjoy the media spotlight have for years been waging a bitter war against born-again believers—a group they consider among the worst of the religious fanatics. Men such as Steve Allen, Carl Sagan, Ed Asner, and Norman Lear have been seeking to subvert the faith of many and make viable, believing Christians look like half-wits bereft of their senses. They are out to eradicate sincere religious belief so that nothing will hinder the coming of the New World Order.

The sobering truth is that the powers of evil have a master plan to remove a good portion of these religious fanatics. Only then, they believe, will they have their day.

And you know what? They're right!

Restraining Until the Time

The Scripture makes it clear that one of the Holy Spirit's primary tasks is to restrain evil *until the time set by the Father*. At that time He will be removed and Satan will be allowed to rule the earth for seven horrible years. As Paul wrote:

> Let no one deceive you by any means; for that Day will not come unless the falling away comes first, and the man of sin is revealed, the son of perdition, who opposes and exalts himself above all that is called God or that is worshiped, so that he sits as God in the temple of God, showing himself that he is God. Do you not remember that when I was still with you I told you these things? And now you know what is restraining, that he may be revealed in his own time. For the mystery of lawlessness is

already at work; only He who now restrains will do
so until He is taken out of the way (2 Thessalonians
2:3-7).

The Holy Spirit is the One who is restraining this "mystery of lawlessness." He is the One who is holding the lid on the world's boiling kettle of violence. Once the Holy Spirit is removed and no longer restrains evil, the powers of darkness will take over. But unbridled evil cannot last long; a society sunk in immorality and wickedness cannot exist for any length of time. It will be a quick plunge into the darkest hour of the history of man, and then straight down into the abyss.

Oh, how the powers of darkness long to take over complete control of the world! But they can't—not yet. The Holy Spirit in the church is restraining them. He is that restraining force in the world today, holding back the tide of evil that is even now welling up and ready to flood the earth.

The Battle Is On

Because we Christians are redeemed and yet live in a world still under the power of Satan, we find ourselves in the midst of spiritual warfare, engaged in a conflict that is becoming more pronounced every day. Satan is mustering his forces for one final battle, and he is manifesting his power as never before. The devil is determined to destroy all of the influence of Jesus Christ from this earth. That necessarily entails the destruction of Christians and their righteous influence.

Modern technology has brought the darkness of the world right into our homes by way of television and radio and on-line computer services, and many Christians have unwisely allowed themselves to be molded and shaped by the ungodly philosophies of the wicked. Tragically, the church of Jesus Christ has been extremely weakened by compromise with the world.

Somehow we have largely forgotten that Jesus said to His disciples, "You are the salt of the earth." He intended for us to be a purifying influence; we are to vent the stench of rottenness that surrounds us. "But if the salt loses its flavor," Jesus warned, "how shall it be seasoned? It is then good for nothing but to be thrown out and trampled underfoot by men" (Matthew 5:13). Jesus meant the church to be a purifying influence on the world until the rapture, when all born-again believers will be removed from this earth and taken to heaven.

Jesus told His faithful church at Philadelphia (the church that represents the true church in the latter days), "You have a little strength" (Revelation 3:8). That's all the strength we have. We're not a great, mighty force, an irresistible power for righteousness. How I wish to God we were! But we're not; compromise in the church has extremely weakened our position as a witness and as a purifying agent to the world.

Nevertheless, Jesus said, "I will build My church, and the gates of Hades shall not prevail against it" (Matthew 16:18). The church of Jesus Christ, though weak, shall still prevail through the power of the Holy Spirit. The church will prevail because of the restraining influence of the Holy Spirit in her midst.

The Time of the End

And what exactly is the Spirit through the church restraining? The Bible tells us there is one final, great battle to be fought before Satan is forced to return control of the earth to the Lord. Even now Satan is mustering his forces for this final conflict, which I believe the devil is deceived into thinking he is going to win.

In Revelation 19:19, John wrote, "And I saw the beast [the Antichrist], the kings of the earth, and their armies, gathered together to make war against Him [Jesus Christ] who sat on the horse and against His army." This conflict is the last to erupt before the Lord establishes God's kingdom upon the earth. Before this battle takes place, Satan will create a one-world government with his own representative at its head.

It is Satan's strategy to bring all of the governments of the earth under the control of one man, whom the New Testament refers to variously as "the man of sin," "the son of perdition," "the Antichrist," or "the beast." He is the one man whom Satan will vest with his powers, his throne, and his authority. He is Satan's instrument to rule the world and through whom the devil will be worshiped. In Revelation 13:2, John said of the Antichrist, "Now the beast which I saw was like a leopard, his feet were like the feet of a bear, and his mouth like the mouth of a lion. And the dragon [Satan] gave him his power, his throne, and great authority."

When the beast has been vested with the powers of Satan, he will be able to work all kinds of supernatural signs and wonders by which he will astound the world. In Matthew

24:24, Jesus declared, "For false christs and false prophets will arise and show great signs and wonders, so as to deceive, if possible, even the elect." In 2 Thessalonians 2:9 Paul said the Antichrist's coming would be "according to the working of Satan, with all power, signs, and lying wonders."

The Antichrist will not work alone in this lying masquerade. Revelation 13:11-13 speaks of "the false prophet" who will work together with the Antichrist:

> Then I saw another beast coming up out of the earth, and he had two horns like a lamb and spoke like a dragon. And he exercises all the authority of the first beast in his presence, and causes the earth and those who dwell in it to worship the first beast, whose deadly wound was healed. He performs great signs, so that he even makes fire come down from heaven on the earth in the sight of men.

Daniel confirms that the Antichrist's "power shall be mighty, but not by his own power." It will be the power of Satan, the power of darkness:

> He shall destroy fearfully, and shall prosper and thrive; he shall destroy the mighty, and also the holy people. Through his cunning he shall cause deceit to prosper under his hand; and he shall exalt himself in his heart. He shall destroy many in their prosperity. He shall even rise against the Prince of princes; but he shall be broken without human hand (Daniel 8:24,25).

The Antichrist will be a violent enemy of God. He will speak blasphemies against the Lord: "He shall speak pompous words against the Most High" (Daniel 7:25). A few chapters later, the prophet writes,

> Then the king [the Antichrist] shall do according to his own will; he shall exalt and magnify himself above every god, shall speak blasphemies against the God of gods, and shall prosper till the wrath [the Great Tribulation period] has been accomplished; for what has been determined shall be done (Daniel 11:36).

Paul adds that this man of sin "opposes and exalts himself above all that is called God or that is worshiped, so that he sits as God in the temple of God, showing himself that he is God" (2 Thessalonians 2:4). And Revelation 13:5,6 says:

> And he [the Antichrist] was given a mouth speaking great things and blasphemies, and he was given authority to continue for forty-two months. Then he opened his mouth in blasphemy against God, to blaspheme His name, His tabernacle, and those who dwell in heaven.

The Two Witnesses Appear

God will not leave Himself without a witness, however, even in these dark days. The Bible describes two witnesses whom God is going to send to the Jews after the church is gone. Quite possibly they are Moses and Elijah. We are told how they will be hated by the world, and that if someone seeks to hurt either of these two witnesses, fire comes from their mouths and destroys that person.

Do you remember how when Elijah was on the earth the king sent out a captain with 50 men to bring the prophet in as a prisoner? "Man of God, the king has said, 'Come down!'" the captain said in 2 Kings 1:9. The prophet replied, "If I am a man of God, then let fire come down from heaven and consume you and your fifty men" (verse 10), and fire did come down and consume him and his 50 men. So the king sent out another captain with 50 soldiers, who said the same thing: "Man of God, thus has the king said, 'Come down quickly!'" (verse 11). Elijah answered, "If I am a man of God, let fire come down from heaven and consume you and your fifty men." And it was so. A third fellow sent to the crusty old prophet was a little smarter. In essence, he said, "I'm a family man, sir. And I'm under orders of the king. Please—would you mind? Have mercy on me." This time, Elijah went down.

This story, coupled with Malachi 4:5 where God promises to send Elijah before the coming of the great day of God, is one of the chief reasons why some believe Elijah will be one of the two witnesses. Another reason is the fact that he never died but instead was taken up into heaven in a whirlwind, along with the appearance of a chariot and horses of fire (see 2 Kings 2).

In the Great Tribulation, anyone seeking to hurt the two witnesses is destroyed by fire flashing out of their mouths. Yet the Scripture says when they have completed their testimony, then the beast will make war against them and overcome them and put them to death. He can't do that, however, until they've completed their testimony.

War Against the Saints

We also read that the Antichrist will make war against the Jews, who in that day will be known as "the saints" and God's "elect." Revelation 13:7 says, "It was granted to him [the Antichrist] to make war with the saints and to overcome them. And authority was given him over every tribe, tongue, and nation" (Revelation 13:7). Daniel 7:21 adds, "I was watching; and the same horn [the Antichrist] was making war against the saints, and prevailing against them."

Daniel 7:25 further says of the Antichrist, "He shall speak pompous words against the Most High, shall persecute the saints of the Most High, and shall intend to change times and law. Then the saints shall be given into his hand for a time and times and half a time [three and one-half years]."

When the Antichrist comes on the scene, he will fight against the saints and overwhelm them. He will prevail against them, thus showing that those saints cannot be the church since Jesus said the gates of hell *will not prevail* against the church. These "saints" are sometimes called tribulation saints and include both Gentiles and Jews who turn to Jesus Christ during this awful period of great tribulation.

A Cashless Society

On seizing power, the Antichrist will inaugurate a new system of extremes. As Daniel said, he "shall intend to change times and law." One of the most notable changes will be his elimination of money. The Antichrist will usher in a cashless society.

A few years ago when I talked about a cashless society, everybody shook their heads and said, "A cashless society— who ever heard of that?" Well, who hasn't heard of that today? If you read the business section of your local newspaper or occasionally scan publications such as *Forbes Magazine*, surely you've read of this. We are hearing more and more about a cashless society.

I noticed just this past week a sign in the grocery store where I shop. It said, "We accept VISA, MasterCard, Discover cards." More and more I find people standing in line who use their cards instead of cash. They run their cards through a special register, sign a little receipt, pick up their groceries and are on their way—all without cash. It is amazing how quickly we are rushing toward a cashless society.

The Bible anticipated all this. It says of the Antichrist,

> He causes all, both small and great, rich and poor, free and slave, to receive a mark on their right hand or on their foreheads, and that no one may buy or sell except one who has the mark or the name of the beast, or the number of his name (Revelation 13:16,17).

Be warned: That day may not be as far away as you think. Recently some in our government have been touting a national identity card, primarily to assist providers of health care. And already children in this country are given Social Security numbers at birth. It's all happening at an unbelievable rate.

At home in a drawer I have a little plastic device that looks something like a squirt gun. It has a little needle which is able to inject tiny transmitters under the skin. These microchip transmitters are about half an inch long and a fraction of an inch wide (some are even smaller). People "tagged" with these devices can be tracked anywhere in the world by orbiting satellites, which triangulate their position. This microchip, of course, can also be programmed with all kinds of personal information: your bank balance, address, driver's license number, whatever.

Banks are calling for a cashless society. Businesses are moving toward a cashless system. The government wants a cashless society. Why? Because it would be so much cheaper—there would be no money to print. And printing money is expensive.

I have in my office a 500 billion-dollar bill. It's the largest bill ever printed. Five hundred billion dollars—of course, it's Serbian. It is becoming a collector's item and is worth all of eight U.S. dollars. But it illustrates how quickly currency is becoming outdated.

So far, I have resisted this move to cashless transactions. I'm one of those rare individuals who still pays cash. It usually shocks the clerk.

"Do you want to put this on your charge card?" I'm asked.

"No, I'll pay cash," I reply.

"Cash?"

"Will you still take it?"

"I guess so."

Still, much about a cashless society makes good sense. With the crime rate rising out of control, the only way to effectively stop robberies and drug-dealing is to get rid of money. It also has been estimated that the government is losing billions of dollars every year in uncollected taxes. But if all economic transactions were made by computer, authorities would able to trace everything that was bought or sold. Such a system would eliminate the theft of money because money would be worthless.

Even now, because crime has exploded, people are becoming reluctant to carry cash. The move to computerized transactions is an ideal solution. There won't be any cash to steal, and every transaction will be recorded.

To a limited degree, we are already dabbling in the cashless society. Today we are using cards, but it would be a simple step to move to an identification chip affixed to a person's body. (How about on the forehead or the right hand?)

Things are definitely in place to eliminate money as a means of exchange. It could happen any week. You could pick up the morning paper at any time and read that you have two weeks to turn in all of your cash. After two weeks, it would have no value. Cash will disappear. If you were to turn in more than 5000 dollars, you would be required to fill out forms to show why you had that much cash.

This isn't science fiction; in fact, it is being proposed even as you read this. Everything is in place.

Ready for a One-World Government

The die already is cast for a global surrender to the one-world system. In the media we constantly hear terms such as "global community," "global economy," "world bank," "global actions." We hear of the necessity of global cooperation and, for example, of the necessity of united efforts to stop regional wars. We are told how essential a global peace force is.

Even in the United States there are powerful forces which have global government as their goal. The two best-known groups are the Council for Foreign Relations and the Trilateral Commission, both of which are attempting to move our nation first into cooperation, and then into submission, to the global authority. More and more powers are to be given to the United Nations, including laws that supersede those of our own nation. Bit by bit the United States is surrendering control of its troops to the United Nations and its secretary-general.

The reason for all this is not hard to imagine. With the awesome weapons of mass destruction that modern technology has devised, the world's leaders realize that mankind's only hope for survival is through global government. And they're working feverishly toward that end.

What's Holding Them Back?

So what's the delay? What's holding back these powers and forces of darkness that want to take full control of the earth? The Bible's answer is simple: This is a part of the work of the Holy Spirit in the world, restraining these powers of darkness and hindering them from installing their final man of power.

That's what Paul meant in 2 Thessalonians 2:7,8 when he wrote:

> For the mystery of lawlessness is already at work; *only He who now restrains will do so until He is taken out of the way.* And then the lawless one will be revealed, whom the Lord will consume with the breath of His mouth and destroy with the brightness of His coming.

The Holy Spirit is hindering, standing in the way, restraining these powers of evil until the day He is taken out of the way. As soon as He leaves, the wicked one shall be revealed and begin his reign of terror.

Now, it is actually the Holy Spirit *in the life of believers* that is the hindering force. Some might say, "No, it's just the Holy Spirit," but it isn't; it is the Holy Spirit *in the church*, in the life of the believers, that restrains the coming evil.

We are here to be a restraining force to evil through the power of the Holy Spirit. We are not called to restrain evil through the political process; that will never work. This is a spiritual battle, and it is only through spiritual weapons that we have any hope of success.

Satan loves to draw Christians into the physical arena because he can make mincemeat out of them there. Jesus said, "The sons of this world are more shrewd in their generation than the sons of light" (Luke 16:8). If you try to fight evil through the political process, look out. You're going to get taken care of, but good.

God has given us spiritual weapons, and those are what we need to use. They are the only things we have that bring any real force to this conflict. And God will preserve us until we have finished our testimony, just as He has promised to preserve the two witnesses in the tribulation until they finish their testimony. And when the church has finished its testimony, then the Lord will remove it and Satan will take over.

On that day the powers of darkness will be in full control. There will be no more restraining force to oppose evil. Gone will be the voices raised against wickedness. Immediately after the church is removed, the man of sin will take over through the powers given to him by Satan. And then the world will be plunged into darkness such as it has never seen nor will see again (see Matthew 24:21,22). It is only the presence of the Holy Spirit in the church that is keeping Satan from this final thrust to gain absolute control over the earth, when the world will be plunged into its darkest hour.

How I thank God for the work of the Holy Spirit in our lives! And I pray that we might be the purifying influence we were meant to be while we remain here. Let us be a strong witness for Jesus Christ, bearing a faithful testimony to the truth.

May the Lord hasten the day when we might complete our testimony and be received out of this dark, black world. Then will the powers of sin have their final day, a horrible seven years before Jesus returns to establish His kingdom of righteousness, light, joy, and peace.

What's Your Testimony?

While the consummation awaits, the forces of darkness are in control *even now*. From the fall unto this very day, the world has lain in the power of the wicked one. God, for His own reasons and purposes, has left Satan's forces in control over the present evil world system. I personally believe that they cannot quite understand why their whole program can't be instituted. They've been attempting to set in motion their demonic plans, but they just can't manage it.

I think they're beginning to realize the culprit, however; that's why they've begun to talk about the religious fanatics who are holding back world progress and peace.

During this time when Satan is still in control, those who desire to serve God can be a part of the restraining force which is even now holding back evil. They can be redeemed from the power of sin through Jesus Christ, sealed with the Holy Spirit, and empowered by the Spirit to live in obedience to the Lord Jesus Christ.

Until the day the Spirit is removed from this earth—and the church with Him—Satan will be unable to fully institute his hateful program of world domination. His servants will be unable to set in motion their wicked plans. But they're ready to move.

Me, too. Even so, come quickly, Lord Jesus.

5

The Church's Divine Helper

They were all filled with the Holy Spirit, and they spoke the word of God with boldness. Now the multitude of those who believed were of one heart and one soul; neither did anyone say that any of the things he possessed was his own, but they had all things in common.

—ACTS 4:31-33

The church exists as a result of the Holy Spirit; it was He who gave birth to the body of Christ on the day of Pentecost when He was poured out upon the disciples. Since that day, the Spirit has been at work in the church in a multitude of vital and mighty ways. Without the Spirit in its midst, the church would be nothing more than a social club or a service organization. But when the Spirit is given His proper place, the body of Christ becomes a dynamic force of change in a sick and dying world. If nothing else, that is the lesson that the book of Acts should teach us.

The Work of Direction

While Jesus was here on earth, it was He who directed the ministry of the apostles. Jesus told them what to do, where to go, and what to believe. When the Master ascended into heaven, He continued to direct the church, only now He did so through the Holy Spirit. Through the Holy Spirit, Jesus continues to guide His people.

In the book of Acts we see how the Holy Spirit directed the activities of the early church. There we see the tremendous success the church enjoyed and observe how well a church can function when it is directed by the Holy Spirit. On the other hand, as we look at the church today, we see how poorly it functions when it isn't directed by the Holy Spirit. When the church is directed by the genius of men and the committees they create, it quickly becomes inept and ineffective.

If we who are called to lead the church wish to know success and enjoy effectiveness in our ministry, we must strive to be led by the Holy Spirit in everything we do. That is what the first-century church learned very early on.

An Exclusive Institution

In the beginning, the church was an exclusively Jewish institution. It began in Jerusalem and its initial converts were all Jews. Most Jews were uncertain if a Gentile could even be saved, so they kept the good news to themselves. There was no thrust into the world, despite Jesus' commands to take the gospel to every creature in all the nations over the entire face of the earth (see Matthew 28:19; Acts 1:8).

That all began to change one day when Peter went down to the city of Lydda and there found a paralytic by the name of Aeneas who had been bedridden for eight years. Peter prayed for him, the man was healed, and "all who dwelt at Lydda and Sharon saw him and turned to the Lord" (Acts 9:35).

A fellowship had been meeting in nearby Joppa. One of the key members of the fellowship was a lady named Dorcas who was one of those delightful women who is always doing nice things for others. She was continually making clothes for the needy and was one of those special persons who are so important and vital within the church. But Dorcas died, and the church sent couriers to Lydda. They were to tell Peter, "Come quickly to Joppa." When Peter returned with them he was led to the room of Dorcas, where by faith he commanded Dorcas to arise from the dead. And she did! It was a tremendously exciting moment in the fellowship at Joppa.

Unclean to Clean

Peter stayed some time at the house of Simon, a tanner who lived by the beach. One day about noon as the others began to prepare lunch, a hungry Peter went up on the roof to spend some time in prayer. While he was praying he had a strange vision. A sheet tied at all four corners came down from heaven, loaded with all kinds of animals, including unclean animals that Jews were prohibited to eat. Peter heard the voice of the Lord saying to him, "Rise, Peter; kill and eat." Being a good Jew, Peter objected: "Not so, Lord! For nothing common or unclean has at any time entered my mouth." But the Lord said to Peter, "What God has cleansed you must not call common" (Acts 11:7-9).

This vision was repeated three times for emphasis. And then the Lord said to Peter, "Behold, three men are right now knocking at the gate. Go with these men—and don't ask any questions." Just as the Lord had said, three men were at the gate. Peter went down, invited them in, and they explained that they served a Roman centurion 20 miles up the coast in Caesarea.

They said that this Roman centurion—a good and just man who feared God—was praying one day when an angel appeared to him and told him to send his servants to Joppa. By the beach they would find the house of a man named Simon the tanner. They were to inquire for another man named Peter and invite him to come with them.

Did you notice in this story that the Lord always speaks on both ends? I like it that way. I get a little suspicious when someone says to me, "The Lord told me to tell you . . ." if the Lord hasn't already told me Himself. Sometimes when a person says this, it comes as confirmation of a word that God already has shown me. But if the Lord hasn't been dealing with me on that issue, then I don't jump to respond just because someone says he has a word from the Lord for me. I will judge it and wait upon the Lord, but I'm not going to rush off just because someone believes God has instructed him to tell me something.

In this story, the Lord told Peter what He wanted him to do. Now, this is a radical departure for Peter (and it's going to get even more radical as he gets into it). Notice that the Spirit is setting it all up on both ends.

When these men told Peter they were instructed to come and get him, Peter replied, "Stay with us tonight and tomorrow we will go with you." So the next day they began the journey up the beach toward Caesarea, arriving in the late afternoon. Cornelius invited Peter into his home, and Peter asked, "What do you want?" Cornelius then told him about the vision, pointed to his friends who had gathered at his house, and said, "We are here to hear what you have to tell us." So Peter began to preach Christ to them. As he did so, the Holy Spirit fell upon them.

Peter had wisely taken some Jews along with him to be eyewitnesses of his adventure, because he figured it was going to get him in trouble... which it did. When Peter returned to Jerusalem, he was confronted by the believers there. "What's this we hear of you," they demanded. "That you went to the Gentiles? That you actually ate with them?" So Peter described his vision, how the Lord had told him not to call that unclean which the Lord had cleansed. "The Spirit told me to go," he explained. In other words, Peter had gone to Caesarea under the direction of the Holy Spirit. It was the Spirit who directed his activities, even though those activities departed radically from Jewish tradition.

Prophets and Circumstances

Peter's experience is just one example of the Holy Spirit leading the church. In Acts 13, we read that as the leaders of the church at Antioch "ministered to the Lord and fasted, the Holy Spirit said, 'Now separate to Me Barnabas and Saul for the work to which I have called them'" (verse 2). Just before this verse we're told that in that church there were certain prophets and teachers, including Barnabas, Simeon, Lucius, Manaen, and Saul. They comprised the church leadership. As they fasted and waited upon the Lord, the Holy Spirit spoke to them.

How did the Spirit speak to them? I believe He spoke to them through the gift of prophecy, inasmuch as this statement about the Spirit speaking immediately follows the mention of these prophets. I believe it was a word of prophecy that said, "Separate to Me Paul and Barnabas for the ministry to which I have called them." In any case, after the leaders had fasted and prayed further, they laid their hands on Barnabas and Saul and sent them away. These two men, summoned by the Holy Spirit, departed to Cilicia and then to Cyprus. In this way the Holy Spirit guided the ministry of Saul and Barnabas very directly, calling them by name and then sending them to specific locations.

Further on in Acts we are told: "Now when they had gone throughout Phrygia and the region of Galatia, they were forbidden by the Holy Spirit to preach the word in Asia" (Acts 16:6). The Holy Spirit forbade them to visit a particular area where they had planned to go. So they came to Mysia and intended to go into Bithynia, but the Spirit would not allow them to enter.

It's interesting to compare Acts 13 with Acts 16. In the first incident it appears there was a spoken word of the Spirit which guided the apostles' actions. But in chapter 16 we are not told how the Spirit forbade the apostles to go to Asia or how He prevented them from visiting Bithynia. We get some clues, however, when we read Paul's epistle to the Galatians. There we discover that when Paul visited Galatia, he got so sick that he could barely move. So it would appear that the Spirit forbade them to go into Asia by allowing Paul to become so ill that he couldn't get out of bed. And when they intended to go to Bithynia, he was still too weak to travel.

This should be instructive for us. I think we make a mistake when we expect the Holy Spirit to lead or guide us only in some extraordinary, supernatural way. Surely, when the Spirit instructed the church to "separate to Me Barnabas and Saul," that was an example of supernatural guidance. When Peter had his vision and the Spirit audibly told him to go, that was pretty spectacular. That was direct. But the Spirit also leads in other ways; there are times when He leads us by putting hindrances in our path. Many times the Lord will cause circumstances to arise that prevent us from doing a certain thing we were planning to do. The Spirit often directs that way, as Paul's letter to the Galatians seems to indicate. He was so sick in Galatia that he was simply unable to travel any farther, yet he recognized this circumstance as the guidance of the Holy Spirit. He and Barnabas had planned to go on to Asia, but the Lord wanted to lead them in another direction. And they followed His leading.

Visions and Dreams

As Paul and Barnabas passed by Mysia, they came to Troas, where Paul had a vision. Once more the Spirit would lead them in a very supernatural way. Now He directs them through a vision. In the vision, a man of Macedonia cries to Paul, "Come over to Macedonia and help us" (Acts 16:9). Sometimes the Spirit directs the activities of the church through visions.

Years ago I knew a man named Dr. Edwards. He was a bank president in San Jose when he committed his life to Jesus

Christ. As he totally dedicated his life to the Lord, he felt God calling him to go into the ministry. He began to study the Word and went to school to prepare for his new career. One night he had a vision of an old, gray-haired man using an old-fashioned plow being pulled by an ox. The field was only half-plowed, and this old man was saying, "Come and help me." Dr. Edwards didn't understand what it meant.

Soon God began to place upon his heart a desire to go to Panama as a missionary. He left America and established a church in Panama City, as well as other churches in the area. He was very successful, sharp, well-educated, and doing a tremendous job. One day he got a call from a hospital saying, "Dr. Edwards, we have an old man here who is dying. Nobody seems to know him, but there should be a minister here to be with him. He will soon be dead." And so Dr. Edwards left for the hospital to visit this man and to pray with him. To his amazement, the dying man was the old, gray-haired figure he had seen in his vision. You might say it was Dr. Edwards' own Macedonian call—or, should we say, Panamanian call? The Spirit had used a vision to direct Dr. Edwards' work.

After the old man's death, Dr. Edwards began looking into his story and discovered he had been a Cumberland Presbyterian missionary in Panama for some 30 years. Dr. Edwards wasn't able to find any work the man had established; his had been a ministry of planting seeds. But Dr. Edwards built on the man's foundation and was able to establish an extremely strong missionary work in Panama.

I have never had a vision in this sense, nor do I think I have ever had a dream of spiritual import. Yet I do not at all discount them or consider them invalid for today. Doesn't Peter quote the prophet Joel as saying, "Your young men shall see visions, your old men shall dream dreams" (Acts 2:17)? I'm too old for a vision, but I'm still open to dreams.

Sometimes in the middle of the night I reach a state in which I'm unsure if I'm awake or asleep. In that state, sometimes thoughts come to me. Maybe I am dreaming or maybe God's working and I don't even realize it. The other night something came to me very strongly. I don't know where it came from—I wasn't even thinking on the subject—but I recognized it as the word of the Lord to me.

The Lord said, "There are churches and ministries which lead people to a greater appreciation and love for themselves. You are leading the people into a greater appreciation and love for Me." It impressed me so strongly. In the middle of the night, I was blessed with that word from the Lord to my heart. And I thought, *Lord, that's exactly what I want to do. I don't want to bring the people to a greater appreciation of themselves. I want to bring them into a greater appreciation of You and of Your love for them and what You have done for them.*

How thankful I am for the guidance of the Holy Spirit, whether He directs us by means of prophecy, dreams, visions, or more ordinary circumstances. If you're young, I pray God will give you some visions. And if you're old, I pray He will give you some dreams. And if you don't know which you are, you'll find out when you get the visions or the dreams.

As we allow the Spirit to lead us, the church grows and flourishes, just as it did in the first century. If we will but obey, their glorious experience can be ours as well.

The Work of Protecting the Church

The Holy Spirit also works to protect the church from hypocrisy and corruption. We see this especially in the first few years of the early church.

The Curse of the Church

Acts 4 describes a time when "the multitude of those who believed were of one heart and one soul" (Acts 4:32). No one laid claim to their own possessions, but everyone held all things in common. They shared the wealth, and no one lacked anything. "For all who were possessors of lands or houses sold them, and brought the proceeds of the things that were sold, and laid them at the apostles' feet; and they distributed to each as anyone had need" (Acts 4:34,35).

But a man named Ananias, along with his wife, Sapphira, sold a parcel of land and kept back part of the price for themselves; the rest they laid at the apostles' feet. But Peter said, "Ananias, why has Satan filled your heart to lie to the Holy Spirit and keep back part of the price of the land for yourself? While it remained, was it not your own? And after it was sold, was it not in your own control?" (Acts 5:3,4). In other words, "Ananias, no one told you to sell it. It wasn't a requirement of the church. The land belonged to you before you sold it, and the money belonged to you after you sold the land. No one asked you to bring the cash and lay it at our feet."

Notice that the sin of Ananias wasn't in bringing only part of the money; his sin was *hypocrisy*, the curse of the church. Ananias was pretending that he had brought all of the money in order to impress other people. He was acting as though he were giving everything, when he wasn't. He was trying to appear more committed than he really was.

In those days, there was such power in the church that you couldn't get by with such a sin. Peter said to Ananias, "Why have you conceived this thing in your heart? You have not lied to men, but to God" (Acts 5:4). As soon as Ananias heard these words, he fell dead on the spot—and "great fear came upon all those who heard these things" (5:5). The Spirit of God was seeking to protect the purity of the church from this dread, horrible, ugly cancer that has been such a scourge through the years. The Spirit was jealous to purify the church of this kind of hypocrisy.

Today's church is greatly weakened in comparison with its first-century counterpart. There isn't nearly the power in the church today that there was then. In one way, I suppose we should be thankful for this. I wonder how many in the pews would survive the third verse of the old hymn: "Take my life and let it be consecrated, Lord, to Thee. Take my silver and my gold. Not a mite would I withhold . . ." And pop! pop! pop! They're gone. No one left.

But in the early days, the Holy Spirit sought to protect the church from the dreaded curse of hypocrisy. The Spirit's purpose was to keep the church holy, to maintain a standard of purity, and to protect it from corruption.

He's Not for Sale

In Acts 8 we read that Philip went to the city of Samaria and there preached Christ. A multitude of people responded to his message, and the Holy Spirit worked miracles and wonders through this deacon in the early church. Unclean spirits were being cast out, and many who were paralyzed and lame were healed. As a result, great joy spread throughout the city.

A man named Simon also believed and was baptized. Before his conversion, Simon had been a magician, skilled in the art of sorcery. Prior to the coming of Philip, Simon had bewitched the people of Samaria into thinking he controlled some great power of God. But as Philip preached, Simon himself believed, was baptized, and accompanied Philip through the city. As he beheld genuine miracles performed by the Spirit through Philip, he probably wondered, *How does he do that?*

When the apostles in Jerusalem heard that the Samaritans had received the gospel, they sent Peter and John to investigate. They soon discovered that the Holy Spirit had not yet come upon any of the Samaritans, so the apostles laid their hands on them and they received the Holy Spirit. Now when Simon saw that the Holy Spirit was imparted by the laying on of the apostles' hands, he offered them money, saying, "Give me this power also, that anyone on whom I lay hands may receive the Holy Spirit" (Acts 8:19).

That practice later became known as "simony," the buying of positions of power in the church. This sin became a curse to the church. Here Simon was seeking to buy the Spirit's power. So Peter said to him:

> Your money perish with you, because you thought that the gift of God could be purchased with money! You have neither part nor portion in this matter, for your heart is not right in the sight of God. Repent therefore of this your wickedness, and pray God if perhaps the thought of your heart may be forgiven you. For I see that you are poisoned by bitterness and bound by iniquity (Acts 8:20-23).

The Holy Spirit was revealing these things to Peter in order to protect the church from those who would seek to buy their way into power. Corruption could not be tolerated.

The Work of Edification, Exhortation, and Comfort

Another crucial work of the Holy Spirit in the church is His activity of edifying, exhorting, and comforting the body of Christ.

As Paul compares the gift of speaking in tongues with prophecy in 1 Corinthians 14, he writes, "He who speaks in a tongue edifies himself.... If I pray in a tongue, my spirit prays, but my understanding is unfruitful" (verses 4,14). On the other hand, "He who prophesies speaks edification and exhortation and comfort to men.... He who prophesies edifies the church" (verses 3,4).

This makes it plain that a key work of the Holy Spirit in the church is to edify the body, to build it up. Exhortation and comfort both play a key role in this. The Spirit wants to bring you to a greater appreciation of God and of God's love for you, to reveal Jesus Christ and His work for you, to urge you to do what you know you should, and to bring healing to your painful wounds. He does all this so that you might be built up in the Lord.

In chapters 2 and 3 of the book of Revelation, Jesus addresses Himself to the seven churches of Asia Minor. In each of His seven messages, Jesus said, "He who has an ear, let him hear what the Spirit says to the churches." In each case, the Spirit spoke the words of Jesus to the anointed teachers and ministers of each local church. In some cases words of edification predominated; in others, words of exhortation and warning were more necessary; and in a few, words of comfort were needed. In each congregation, Jesus exhorted those who had an ear to hear, to heed what the Spirit was saying to the church.

A big part of achieving an effective ministry is identifying the right human leaders to minister edification, exhortation, and comfort to the people of God. This, also, is a work of the Holy Spirit. Remember that it was the Spirit who told the church at Antioch, "Separate to Me Barnabas and Saul for the work to which I have called them" (Acts 13:2). Later on we find that Paul tells the elders of the church at Ephesus, "Take heed to yourselves and to all the flock, among which *the Holy Spirit has made you overseers,* to shepherd the church of God which He purchased with His own blood" (Acts 20:28). The Holy Spirit often ministers His edification, exhortation, and comfort to us through human leaders.

The Holy Spirit has been sent to build us up, to exhort us to holy living and trusting God, and to comfort us. How glorious are all these works of the Holy Spirit! Every one of us needs to be edified, exhorted, and comforted. And the Holy Spirit provides all three in boundless measure.

The Road to Success

Do you know why the early church was so successful? It enjoyed God's favor because the Holy Spirit directed all its activities.

The early church allowed the Holy Spirit to direct where it should go and what it should do. He was in charge. The Spirit ordained and established the leadership of the church. As a result, we read that angry opponents of the gospel confronted the apostles with this charge: "You have filled Jerusalem with your doctrine" (Acts 5:28). Similarly, when the apostle Paul and his party came to Thessalonica, certain Jews warned the magistrates, "These who have turned the world upside down have come here too" (Acts 17:6).

What a tremendous witness for the early church! It was filling whole cities with the doctrines of Jesus Christ and turning the world upside down.

Would to God that I could be arrested and charged with filling my city with the doctrine of Jesus Christ! Then I would say, "Throw the book at me, judge. Praise the Lord!"

When Paul wrote his letter to the Colossian church some 30 years after its birth, he could say, "The word of the truth of the gospel ... has come to you, as it has also in all the world, and is bringing forth fruit" (Colossians 1:5,6). How amazing this is! The early church, directed by the Holy Spirit, was able to reach *the entire world* with the gospel of Jesus Christ. Be astonished at what they accomplished. Unlike us, they had no planes. No helicopters. No trains. No automobiles. No telephones. No fax machines. No televisions. No radios. No recording devices. No computers. No magazines. No newspapers. No printing presses. In fact, they had none of the modern transportation and communication systems that we take for granted—*and yet they brought the gospel to the entire world!*

The tragic mistake of the modern church is its declaration of independence from the Holy Spirit. We have declared that we no longer need the Spirit to direct our activities. Instead, we follow respected committees of learned men who have been to seminary and who have made in-depth sociological, demographic, and ethnographic studies of the world. We know how to go into a community, poll it, and determine the best methods to reach the people there. We have a thousand high-tech programs, but the tragic fact is that the church is failing to reach this world with the gospel of Jesus Christ. And no wonder. God said, "'Not by might nor by power, but by My Spirit,' says the Lord of hosts" (Zechariah 4:6).

We need a church that will return the Holy Spirit to His rightful place as Director of activities; a church where the Holy Spirit roots out hypocrisy and corruption; a church where the Holy Spirit edifies, comforts, and exhorts His people; in short, a church where the Holy Spirit is *in charge.*

Let us again acknowledge that Jesus Christ is the head of the body, the church. Let us gratefully acknowledge our dependency upon the Holy Spirit and earnestly desire that the church be a reflection of what the Lord wants it to be. Let us ask Him to give us His wisdom and guidance and direction in every decision that is made regarding the church's function, operation, leadership, expenditures, and outreach.

Despite all our failures and all our foolishness and all our bumblings, the Holy Spirit stills desires to guide and direct the activities of the church. We must be thankful for the opportunities that He still gives to us to reach this world with the gospel of Jesus Christ.

May it be our earnest desire and prayer to become all that God wants His church to be—a light to the world, sharing God's love through Jesus Christ. Then we will fulfill the Spirit's own vision for "a glorious church, not having spot or wrinkle or any such thing, but ... holy and without blemish" (Ephesians 5:27).

6

The Manifold
Grace of God

But the Helper, the Holy Spirit, whom the Father will send in My name, He will teach you all things, and bring to your remembrance all things that I said to you.

—JOHN 14:26

There is a wonderful phrase in the King James version of the Bible that sadly disappears from nearly all the modern translations. Peter is describing the many gifts of the Holy Spirit which God grants to us for our blessing, and he urges us to be good stewards of "the manifold grace of God" (1 Peter 4:10).

"The manifold grace of God." What a glorious phrase! It captures so beautifully the rich array of spiritual blessings that God lavishes on His dearly beloved children. And I do mean "lavish." For God spares no effort in His holy desire to bestow upon us His very best.

We can only scratch the surface in this chapter, but I hope it is enough to convince you of the staggering nature of "the manifold grace of God" poured out upon you by the Holy Spirit of God. His work in the life of the believer is simply astonishing in both its depth and its breadth.

Sealed with the Spirit

One of the greatest works of the Holy Spirit in the lives of believers is His special work of sealing. Paul tells us that after we believed, we "were *sealed* with the Holy Spirit of promise, who is the guarantee of our inheritance until the redemption of the purchased possession, to the praise of His glory' (Ephesians 1:13,14).

That's Mine!

In the days of Paul, the city of Ephesus was one of the major seaports of Asia. Most of the goods coming from the east to be sold in the west came through the port of Ephesus. It was the merchandising center of the world. Great caravans would come from the east bringing their wares. Merchants from Rome would gather in Ephesus to purchase these articles and pack them for shipping to Puteoli, the great port city of Rome. From there they would be distributed throughout the empire. The goods would be stamped with a wax seal and then imprinted with a signet ring bearing a unique mark of ownership. Then the cargo would be loaded on the ships and sent to Rome.

When the merchandise arrived at Puteoli, servants of the merchantmen used the seals to identify their master's goods as they were unloaded. The seal was the mark of ownership.

Paul uses this picture when he says God has put His stamp of ownership on us. And what is this stamp of God's ownership? His Holy Spirit! Having the Holy Spirit gives us the assurance to say, "I belong to God. That's His seal on my life, to prove His ownership of me."

You once were a slave to sin, in the bondage of corruption, but Jesus purchased you from the slave markets. Now you belong to Him. Paul wrote to the Corinthians, "Do you not know that your body is the temple of the Holy Spirit who is in you, whom you have from God, and you are not your own" (1 Corinthians 6:19)? Our body is the temple of the Holy Spirit; we are not our own. We have been bought with a price. Therefore, let us glorify God in our body and in our spirit, which are His.

Peter wrote, "Knowing that you were not redeemed with corruptible things, like silver or gold, from your aimless conduct received by tradition from your fathers, but with the precious blood of Christ, as of a lamb without blemish and without spot" (1 Peter 1:18, 19).

We're like merchandise aboard a ship headed for home port. When we arrive He's going to say, "Yes, he's Mine. He has My stamp on him. There's My seal. They're all Mine." And Jesus will acknowledge us as His.

An Amazing Down Payment

But that's not all. The Holy Spirit is also called "the guarantee" or "the earnest" of our inheritance. We still use the phrase "earnest money," which refers to the cash we put down on a purchase to show we are earnest about our intent to pay the whole amount. Earnest money says to the seller, "I don't have all the money with me right now, but I'm going to give you a deposit to prove the sincerity of my intentions. This money indicates that I intend to complete the transaction."

Suppose you advertise a car for sale and someone comes to look at it. He takes it for a ride and says to you, "I love it, I want it, I'm going to buy it. Save it for me. I don't have the money, but I'm going to the bank and see if I can negotiate a loan. Please don't sell this car to anybody. Save it for me, because I really want this car." If you are wise you will say, "OK, give me a deposit. Show me that you are earnest about this." If you merely say, "OK, it's yours," and the person leaves, you may never see him again. In the meanwhile, other people may come by and say, "Oh, that's just what I'm looking for; I want to buy it." You'll have to say, "I've already sold it," and you may pass up a lot of buyers for someone who may never return. Maybe while he is on his way to the bank, he passes a used-car lot and sees another vehicle in better shape than yours at a cheaper price, and so he grabs the car without telling you. He feels he has no obligation to you; after all, he didn't give you any earnest money.

God wants you to know that He's sincere about redeeming you. He intends to complete this transaction. He doesn't plan to back down. To show His intent, He has given you a deposit on the future glory He has promised you. That deposit is the Holy Spirit.

The Spirit Teaches Us

While Jesus was on earth, He wanted His disciples to know that the Holy Spirit would be alongside them to help them understand the ways of God and the Word of God, even as He had taught them and brought them understanding.

In John 14:26, Jesus said, "But the Helper, the Holy Spirit, whom the Father will send in My name, He will teach you all things, and bring to your remembrance all things that I said to you." A little later, in John 16:13, the Master adds, "However, when He, the Spirit of truth, has come, He will guide you into all truth." We enjoy that same promise today.

Looking for Nuggets

To study the Bible is a tremendous privilege. It is a marvelous book. The more I study it, the more it amazes me. And to aid and assist in the study of the Bible, it is helpful to dig into the original languages. In that way one can milk some of the nuances out of the text, the little nuggets that don't translate well into English.

I'm grateful that my own study of Greek has enabled me to occasionally find these blessed nuggets of truth. I say I *studied* Greek; I don't say I *learned* Greek. I am not a natural linguist. Languages are extremely difficult for me. I enjoy a natural aptitude in other areas, but not in linguistics. Nevertheless, I've had enough Greek that I can dig into it, and it's worth digging to find these nuggets every once in a while. I believe the phrase that says, "Raking is easy, but all you get is leaves; digging is hard, but you might find diamonds."

And yet, I have discovered that folks sometimes find diamonds without digging!

When I was pastoring years ago in Huntington Beach, we had a blessed saint of God in the church who made it only through the sixth grade. Oh, how she loved the Lord! I would be studying in Galatians and digging through the Greek and trying hard to find some of these little nuggets of truth. Finally I would get hold of one of them and I would think, *My, how wonderful it is to know a little Greek!* But before I could share my nugget, this dear woman would often say, "Brother Smith, I was reading the other day in Galatians, and I thought, "You know, this must mean...'" and she would expound the same truth I had worked so hard to dig out. And I thought, *God, it's not fair. Here I burn the midnight oil to try to maintain a grade in Greek, and here she gets it without any Greek at all!*

Yet this is what Jesus means when He says the Holy Spirit will teach us. He is saying to the disciples, "You don't have to worry about not understanding the Scriptures. As I have taught you, so the Spirit is now going to teach you."

A Spirit-filled child of God, in love with the Lord and in love with His Word, is a truer guide into the truth of God than some fellow with a Ph.D. who is not born again but who knows the original languages. Trying to understand the Bible apart from the help of the Holy Spirit will only get you into all kinds of weird things.

First John 2:27 says, "But the anointing which you have received from Him [the Holy Spirit] abides in you, and you do not need that anyone teach you." This is interesting because practically every cult insists that you *do* need man to teach you. These cults are strong on selling you their books and getting you to read their materials. Why is this so necessary? Because you would never come to their screwy interpretations unless you were led to them by their books.

I am not at all afraid of what someone will come to believe if he reads only the Bible. I have no qualms about saying, "Just read the Word." I believe that as we read the Bible and ask the Holy Spirit to teach and instruct our hearts, He will lead us into all truth.

Of course, God has given teachers and pastors to the church "for the equipping of the saints for the work of ministry" (Ephesians 4:12). But even though a gifted teacher may be truly explaining the truth of God's Word, unless the Holy Spirit bears witness to the truth in your own heart, you will not learn. It is the Holy Spirit who teaches us the Scriptures. How marvelous it is to have the Author of the Scriptures Himself to help us understand what He wrote!

Refreshing Our Memory

Jesus also promised that the Holy Spirit would bring to our remembrance verses and passages needed at the moment. This certainly happened with the disciples. In John 2:22 we read, "Therefore, when He had risen from the dead, His disciples remembered that He had said this to them; and they believed the Scripture and word which Jesus had said." Jesus told them the Holy Spirit would quicken their memory, and He did. John 12:16 says, "His disciples did not understand these things at first; but when Jesus was glorified, then they remembered that these things were written about Him and that they had done these things to Him." At first they didn't understand what Jesus was talking about. But later on, after Jesus was glorified, the Holy Spirit brought to their remembrance what the Master had said. He helped them put the whole thing together.

How grateful I am that the Spirit continues this ministry today. Have you ever been talking with someone, when suddenly you began quoting Scripture you didn't even know you knew? It often happens to me. I'll start to quote a passage of Scripture, and it just keeps rolling out, even though I didn't realize I had memorized these verses. Yet in that moment the Holy Spirit brings to memory that particular passage.

He does the same thing in our special times of need. Perhaps you're going through a heavy trial and feel overwhelmed and pressed down, when suddenly a scripture comes into your mind that fits the situation perfectly. The Holy Spirit brings to your remembrance the things of God and the ways of God. He is there to help you, teaching you. It is a remarkable and glorious work.

The Spirit Prays for Us

In Romans 8:26,27 Paul opens up another area in which the Holy Spirit is a tremendous help:

> Likewise the Spirit also helps in our weaknesses. For we do not know what we should pray for as we ought, but the Spirit Himself makes intercession for us with groanings which cannot be uttered. Now He who searches the hearts knows what the mind of the Spirit is, because He makes intercession for the saints according to the will of God.

The weakness that Paul is talking about here is our weakness in knowing the will of God. We don't always know how we should pray. As we size up a situation, we may judge it one way and start praying that way, but it may be just the opposite of what God wants to do.

Suppose you know a person who is careless with his finances and as a result is in a real bind. Though he didn't have the money, he rang up 127 dollars in long-distance charges. He doesn't have the money to pay the bill, and his phone's going to be disconnected. How shall I pray? Should I pray, "God, send him the money so he can pay the phone bill?" But what if God wants to teach him how to be wise and prudent in the expenditure of his money? If I pray that his phone bill will be paid for him, perhaps I will be short-circuiting what God is trying to teach him.

It's dangerous to get insistent with God and start demanding that He do certain things. There are foolish people who say, "God, if You don't answer this prayer, then I just can't trust You and I'm not going to serve You or believe in You anymore. If You don't succumb to my will and my desire in this issue, I'm through. I'm walking away." How ridiculous. How utterly ludicrous. God says, "My ways are not your ways. My ways are beyond your finding out" (see Isaiah 55:8, 9).

I have discovered through the years that many of my prayers were completely out of the will of God. There were things I was almost insisting that God do, but in His love and goodness to me, He didn't do them. Today I am as thankful for the prayers that God did *not* answer as I am for the prayers that God *did* answer.

Can We Change God's Mind?

It is important to realize that the purpose of prayer is not to change the mind of God or to convince God to see things our way. Many people mistakenly think that their prayers will change the mind of God. But that's not the purpose of prayer at all. You wouldn't *want* to change the mind of God. God said, "I know My thoughts toward you. They are good, not evil. I desire to bring you to a blessed, glorious, desirable end" (see Jeremiah 29:11). God's plan for you is much better than anything you could devise for yourself, so for you to think that you can improve upon the plan of God is sheer folly. Prayer is not designed to change the mind of God.

You may ask, "If prayer isn't to change the mind of God, then why should we pray? What is the purpose of prayer?" The purpose of prayer is to open your heart to allow God to do the things He wants to do, the things that He knows are best for you.

I am convinced that every good and right thing you have ever prayed for, God intended to give to you before you bowed your head. Jesus said our heavenly Father knows that we need all these things even before we ask Him (see Matthew 6:31, 32). Prayer opens the door of our will, thereby allowing God to do what He desires to do for our benefit and for our good.

The Cycle of Prayer

True prayer moves in a cycle. It begins in the heart of God, with the purposes and desires of God. Then God places those desires in your heart. "It is God who works in you both to will and to do" (Philippians 2:13). As the psalmist said, "Delight yourself also in the Lord, and He shall give you the desires of your heart" (Psalm 37:4). God puts His desire in your heart, and then you express it back to Him in prayer. It begins with God, it moves down, touches your heart, and then returns to God. Thus the cycle is complete and the door is now open; God has the opportunity to do those things for you that He so wants to do.

Second Chronicles 16:9 says, "For the eyes of the Lord run to and fro throughout the whole earth, to show Himself strong on behalf of those whose heart is loyal to Him." God is looking for people whose hearts are in harmony with His. That's all He wants—hearts in harmony with His own. God is looking for instruments through which He might accomplish His work and through which He might pour out His resources to a needy world.

The key thing is to discover the will of God. Get your heart beating in harmony with God's heart. "Now this is the confidence that we have in Him," John wrote, "that if we ask anything according to His will, He hears us. And if we know that He hears us, whatever we ask, we know that we have the petitions that we have asked of Him" (1 John 5:14,15). If we are praying according to the will of God, we can pray in confidence that our petitions will be answered because we have opened the door for God to do what He desires to do. The key is asking according to His will. And keeping in step with the Spirit enables us to know what that will is.

The Spirit Helps Us Witness

A big part of "the manifold grace of God" is the power to be a bold and effective witness. In Acts 1:8, Jesus declared, "But you shall receive power when the Holy Spirit has come upon you; and you shall be witnesses to Me in Jerusalem, and in all Judea and Samaria, and to the end of the earth."

Who, Me?

It's important to see just who Jesus was commissioning. In the eyes of the world, these people were nothing and nobodies. Five of them were fishermen; all of them lived in one inconsequential province on the eastern side of the Mediterranean. It was a turbulent, insignificant little province, and these people were insignificant even within that unimportant region. But Jesus told them that their mission was to take His message into all the world and to declare it to every creature.

Immediately we see the total impossibility of the mission from a human standpoint. How could this tiny, insignificant group ever carry this message to all the world?

But God never commands us to do anything unless He also gives us the capacity to accomplish it. Yet too often we give Jesus a thousand reasons why we *can't* do it. We tell Him of all of our past failures. We argue with His commands rather than obey them. It's so foolish. When will we discover that the Lord never commands us to do anything unless He also gives us the power to do it, if we will but obey?

"But, Lord, we're so few. Lord, who's going to listen to us? Lord, we're nobody." But Jesus promised them the power by which they were to do it. He told them to wait in Jerusalem until they had been "endued with power from on high." And then they would be made into mighty witnesses of the resurrection of Jesus.

That was the heart of the message of the early church. Because Jesus rose from the dead, anyone who repents of his sin and places his faith in Jesus can have remission of sins. Jesus commissioned the first disciples to spread this message, and they did so remarkably, witnessing to the resurrection of Jesus in word, life, and deed. Let's briefly look at each of these.

The Place of Words

First, these believers were to witness through their *words*. They were to preach this gospel, to communicate the good news in words and sentences comprehensible to their audience.

Our task is the same. It has not changed. It is important that we, too, witness through words. As Paul asks, "How shall they believe in Him of whom they have not heard? And how shall they hear without a preacher" (Romans 10:14)? Paul knows that they cannot believe without first hearing about Jesus, and that they will not hear of Him unless someone preaches to them. That is why we must continue to use words to witness of the saving work of Jesus Christ.

Thank God, there are some people who are extremely gifted in verbalizing their witness for Christ. They just have the gift. They never meet a person without speaking up for Christ. Wonderful! I love it! My father was one of those people.

But as Paul rhetorically asked at the end of 1 Corinthians 12, "Are all apostles? Are all prophets? Are all teachers?" The obvious answer is no. Not everyone has that gift. Yet unfortunately, many times we can get very discouraged if we are pressed into verbalizing our witness for the Lord when we aren't gifted as an evangelist. We feel a duty and an obligation to witness verbally, but we cringe and have a horrible time whenever we try it. Then we feel constant guilt when we fail to verbalize our faith to everyone we meet.

The Place of a Godly Life

But witnessing is far more than giving people an invitation or telling them about Jesus Christ. An even more powerful witness is *living* the life of Jesus Christ before them.

What a powerful witness it is when your life agrees with your testimony and others see your words worked out in your life! That's why Paul said to Timothy, "Be an example to the believers" (1 Timothy 4:12). It's why he reminded the elders at Ephesus that he had been careful to back up his preaching with the way he lived (see Acts 20:18-35). And it's why he told Titus that some would "profess to know God, but in works they deny Him" (Titus 1:16).

The way we live becomes a witness of what we believe. To be an effective witness for Jesus Christ, we must live in such a way that His character shines through.

Recently I spent a wonderful day at a high school camp with some beautiful young people. What a thrill to see the work of God's Spirit in their lives. A young girl came up to me just as I was leaving and said, "Pastor Chuck, I want to witness to my brother and I don't know how to do it." I told her the best way was to live the Christian life before him. "Let him see what Jesus has done in your life," I told her. "That is the strongest witness you can possibly give to him."

Did you know that the name *Christian* was coined in Antioch by *unbelievers* as they observed the lives of Jesus' followers? *Christian* originally meant "a follower of Christ." It is wonderful when the world gives you that title. It isn't something that you have to declare: "I'm a Christian!" Well, are you? Are you Christlike? If a person should say to you, "Oh, how I would love to see Jesus Christ," you ought to be able to say, "Well, if you have seen me..." Such would be a faithful and true witness.

Unfortunately, oftentimes what we say is thoroughly discredited by what we are and by what we do. It's possible to witness to someone verbally and tell how wonderful the work of Jesus Christ is in your life, even while your life denies your own words. "He gives me such glorious peace, and you need to know this peace of Jesus Christ," you might say. But if some little irritant comes along and you blow up and yell at everything and everybody, how effective will your witness be? Or suppose you're talking about the joy of the Lord, yet you're always grouchy and grumpy and snapping at everybody. What you say will be meaningless because of what you are. Those who talk a lot about the Lord but don't live the life succeed only in mocking Christianity.

Jesus wants you to be a witness of Him. He wants your life to be so like His that it bears witness to Him. Then people will know what He is like as they observe the Spirit at work in your life.

The Place of Deeds

The third way believers are to witness is through *deeds* wrought by the Holy Spirit in their lives. Hebrews 2:4 declares, "God also bearing witness both with signs and wonders, with various miracles, and gifts of the Holy Spirit, according to His own will." Notice that we can't make these things happen. These signs and wonders and miracles do not appear according to my will; I do not control the operation of the Holy Spirit. He divides to each man severally as He will. Beware of those who would pretend to control God, who claim to manipulate the works of God or force His hand! They cannot. The Spirit is sovereign.

Paul wrote to the Romans, "For I will not dare to speak of any of those things which Christ has not accomplished through me, in word and deed, to make the Gentiles obedient—in mighty signs and wonders, by the power of the Spirit of God, so that...I have fully preached the gospel of Christ" (Romans 15:18,19). Mighty signs and wonders may have come through the apostle, but it wasn't he who produced any of them. God's Spirit chose to make him a vessel, and he was content with that. This is also why he told the Corinthians, "My speech and my preaching were not with persuasive words of human wisdom, but in demonstration of the Spirit and of power, that your faith should not be in the wisdom of men but in the power of God" (1 Corinthians 2:4,5).

So, too, our testimony and our witness will be effective only as it results from the Holy Spirit working through us. It is only as we are filled with the Spirit and yielded to Him that we can be bold, powerful witnesses.

The Spirit Helps Us Become Like the Son

The primary work of the Spirit in the life of every believer is to conform him or her into the image of Christ. Everything He does in our lives is intended to serve this goal.

In His Likeness

When God first created Adam, He created him in His own likeness and in His own image. Tragically, man fell from the image of God and became selfish, cold, indifferent, and vengeful. It is impossible to look around today at humanity and understand what God had in mind when He created mankind. All of us have sinned and have fallen short of the glory of God. None of us can set himself up as an example of what God intended when He created Adam and Eve.

If we want to understand what God had in mind when He created mankind, we have to look at Jesus Christ. Jesus expressed God's ideal for man. He lived in the image of God to such an extent that He could say, "He who has seen Me has seen the Father" (John 14:9).

Jesus lived as God would have us live. The Bible tells us that Jesus was the brightness of God's glory and the express image of His person (see Hebrews 1:3). In 2 Corinthians 4:4 Paul called Christ "the image of God," and in Colossians 1:15 he said that Jesus "is the image of the invisible God."

Jesus lived in the image of God. He was all that God wants us to be. He established the model. Peter tells us that He was an example for us, that we should follow in His footsteps (1 Peter 2:21). Jesus is the model God uses as He works in my life to conform me into His image, and it is God's desire and purpose to restore us fallen creatures back into His image. God wants to nullify the effect of sin and the fall of man and to restore us once more into the image of His Son, Jesus Christ.

Our Biggest Mistake

The mistake we often make at this point is to look at the model and say, "That's what I want. That's the way I want to live. That's the way I want to be. I hate myself when I get angry and lose my temper. I hate myself when I fly off and say ugly things to people. I hate myself when I stumble and go after the flesh. So I'm just not going to do that anymore." We see the ideal and understand what God intended for us to be, and in our heart we desire to live a life of love and purity, righteousness, truth, and peace. But then somehow we imagine we can achieve that goal by sheer effort and brute resolve.

Yet the mere desire to be like Jesus doesn't itself create the reality. It doesn't enable us to realize our goal. We do not become like Christ by imitation, which is where a lot of people go awry.

Jesus once said to Peter after he had failed yet again, "The spirit indeed is willing, but the flesh is weak" (Matthew 26:41). I am certain that all of us have found this to be true in our own experience. We don't lack desire; it isn't that our spirit is unwilling. The problem is that our flesh is weak. That's why mere imitation will never work.

We can try to be like the little engine chugging up the hill that kept saying, "I think I can, I think I can, I think I can"—but there's no way. I can't. I cannot bring myself into conformity with the image of Jesus Christ.

Yet the purpose of the Holy Spirit in my life *is* to conform me to the image of Jesus Christ, and hence back into the image of God in which man was originally made. In Romans 8:29, Paul tells us that God has predestined us to be conformed to the image of His Son. In Ephesians 4:13, he insists that God desires for us to come "to the measure of the stature of the fullness of Christ." God wants to conform us to the image of His Son. That's the work He is doing in our lives through the Spirit.

But *how* does He do it?

Becoming Like His Son

In writing to the Corinthians, Paul said, "But we all with unveiled face, beholding as in a mirror the glory of the Lord, are being transformed into the same image from glory to glory, just as by the Spirit of the Lord" (2 Corinthians 3:18). That's the key. As we with unveiled faces begin to see the glory of the Lord, we begin to be transformed into His image. The Spirit of God reveals to us the glory of the eternal God. As we behold that glory, we are being changed, brought from glory to glory, as we are molded and changed into His image by His Spirit at work in us.

A few years ago I knew a retired naval officer. Through the years he had learned "Navy talk" and had a foul tongue. Then he accepted Jesus Christ. About six months after becoming a Christian, he was in his backyard mowing the lawn and whistling, "Love, love, love, love, Christian, this is your call." He wasn't paying close attention to what he was doing, and he failed to duck under a tree. A big branch caught him right in the forehead and laid him on his back. His self-propelled lawn mower just kept going until it hit the fence.

As he was lying on the ground, pain throbbing from his forehead, he jumped up, ran to his lawn mower, turned it off, sprinted into the house, and blurted out, "Honey, honey! Guess what happened?" She looked at the big welt rising on his forehead and said, "What *did* happen?" He said, "Oh, no, no. Not that. I hit a tree—*and I didn't cuss!*" She replied, "Oh, honey. Do you know I haven't heard you use a swear word in six months?" Amazed, he answered, "I haven't?"

It was just another example of "the manifold grace of God." The Spirit did it, and my friend wasn't even aware of it. But what rejoicing erupted when he realized what God had done! I think that's why God so often lets us struggle and see our weaknesses; that way we won't go around boasting or bragging when we enjoy victory. He lets us get to the place of hopelessness, recognizing our total inability, so that when He does the work we are careful to give Him praise and glory.

Thank God, the Spirit of God is conforming us into the image of Christ as He works within us day by day. And at last when the Spirit's work is done in my life and I have been thoroughly conformed into the image of Jesus, "I shall be satisfied when I awake in Your likeness" (Psalm 17:15). On that day I will again be what Adam was when God first created him. And so will you, as you yield and surrender to His Spirit working within you.

All We Need Is Ours Already

Everything that we need to live a successful Christian life is already ours through the work of the Holy Spirit. He sealed us unto the day of redemption and lives in us as the earnest of the priceless inheritance awaiting us in heaven. He helps us to understand and to know the Scriptures and the purpose and will of God. He prays for us when we don't know what to pray for. He empowers us to be bold in our witness in word, life, and deed. And He works unceasingly in our life to mold us into the image of Jesus Christ, who is the express image of God.

What a beautiful Helper the Holy Spirit is! And how we need His help to lead a successful Christian life. We need Him to indwell us, to lead us and empower us. We need His presence, we need His power, we need His leading. We need to walk in the Spirit so that we will not fulfill the lusts of our flesh. The flesh life is very strong; only God's Holy Spirit is stronger.

Let us ask the Holy Spirit to come and fill us until we overflow, until there pours forth from our lives rivers of living water. Let us hungrily receive "the manifold grace of God," and then give thanks as we yield ourselves to the Holy Spirit and to His power. What a glorious work He does in our lives to conform us to the image of His Son.

Truly, this is "the manifold grace of God."

What Are the Gifts of the Holy Spirit?

7

Unity in Diversity

I do not know of any subject concerning which there is greater ignorance in the church today than the gifts of the Holy Spirit. This ignorance occurs on both sides of the issue. On one side, some people lack the understanding that the gifts of the Holy Spirit are available for the church today. On the other side, some who revel in these gifts display a strong lack of knowledge concerning their proper scriptural exercise.

All the gifts of the Spirit seemed to be manifested at Corinth, yet they were being abused. That is why Paul wrote to the Corinthians—to correct these abuses. And for that, we can be very thankful because he left us with crucial guidelines for the proper use of the gifts.

In 1 Corinthians 12 Paul lists nine spiritual gifts, divided into triplets (of power, faith, and utterances). But after he produces this list, he says, "But all these worketh that one and the selfsame Spirit" (verse 11, KJV). In other words, he gives us nine manifestations of the Spirit, but he takes pains to remind us there is still just one Spirit. *There is unity in diversity.* That is a key thing for us to remember as we look at the various gifts of the Spirit.

Understanding Spiritual Gifts

Paul said, "Now concerning spiritual gifts, brethren, I would not have you ignorant" (1 Corinthians 12:1). Paul wanted the church to be knowledgeable of certain important spiritual truths; he knew they hadn't understood what they needed to.

And no doubt, because of the difficulty of understanding this subject, there remains a lot of ignorance to this day.

The overarching principle concerning the gifts of the Spirit is this: The true gifts of the Holy Spirit, when manifested in a scriptural and correct way, will always focus people's hearts on Jesus Christ. Jesus said the Spirit would not testify of Himself, but of Christ. The scriptural exercise of the gifts will always give you a fresh vision of Jesus Christ and His glory, causing you to fall in love with Him, and to be drawn to Him all over again. Your heart will almost explode with love and appreciation for what Jesus is and what He is able to do.

This is the chief way by which you can tell whether any gift is a true manifestation of the Holy Spirit. Is there a great deal of attention drawn to the person exercising the gift? In the magazines various ministries send out, whose picture is on every other page? To whom are they drawing attention? Who are they promoting? Who are they seeking to raise up in the eyes of the people? A true manifestation of the Holy Spirit will always exalt the person of Jesus Christ. That's what the Holy Spirit has come to do.

The first thing to understand, after that, is that there are *diversities of gifts*. In 1 Corinthians 12 Paul lists nine different gifts. Yet this is not a complete or exhaustive list; toward the end of the chapter Paul also mentions the gifts of helps and governments, and in Romans 12 he again adds to the list.

Paul says there are different gifts, yet only one Spirit. It is the same Spirit who distributes all of the gifts as He wills. These gifts complement each other; they do not compete with each other.

Second, there are *differences of ministries*. Some have the gift of apostleship, some the gift of prophets, some the gift of pastor-teachers. Others have the gift of government or the gift of helps. Some have the gift of exhortation, an important and valuable gift. My wife has this gift. After she speaks to and exhorts various groups, they're ready to go out and challenge the world. These are all different gifts of administration, but the same Lord directs them all. Though we may serve Him in different ways, we serve the same Lord.

Third, there are *diversities of operations*. I know how certain gifts operate in my life, but it doesn't follow that they will operate in the same way in your life. They might, but not necessarily. Why not? Because there are diversities of opera-tions. The Spirit works differently in our lives, according to our own unique personalities and idiosyncrasies.

Surely if you're a parent you've discovered that none of your children are exactly alike. Each one has a unique and distinct personality. Or, if you have 14 grandkids, you find that not two of them are alike. All of them are different, unique in the ways they act and react. God respects the differences that exist, and deals with us according to our need and according to who we are and how we respond.

Differences Are Good

I've noticed that testimonies can be exciting, thrilling, and beneficial—or harmful. When a person testifies of his experi-ence with God or his experience with a gift of the Spirit, many of us have a tendency to think, *But that's not the way it happened to me*, or *I've never had it happen like that*. If you haven't received a certain gift you may think, *I see—that's the way it's going to happen when I receive it*. We imagine that it's going to happen in the same way to everyone. But it doesn't.

Maybe you have the gift of prophecy. Before you exercise your gift, it may be that you hyperventilate and feel a tingling sensation. But someone else, who also has the gift of prophecy, may not feel any tinglings and doesn't hyperventilate. Rather, in a very calm way, he exercises the gift. You both have the same gift, but it operates in different ways for each of you. This is the way God designed it.

Our Lord is a diverse Lord, and He deals with each of us as individuals. God loves you individually and He deals with you individually, according to your own temperament and characteristics. How glorious it is that God can and does deal with each of us personally and individually!

That's why it's important that you not try to duplicate another person's gift. Don't try to copy the method of opera-tion that you see in others, believing that it's the only way the gift can operate. Don't try to follow some pattern. And espe-cially avoid such thoughts as, *If I don't do it like you do it, then I question whether I really have it*.

Don't try to receive the same experiences someone else received, or think that your experience isn't genuine because it didn't happen to you like someone else said it happened to him. I've heard people say, "It felt like there was hot oil poured on the top of my head. It began to run all over my body, just pouring down. I was engulfed in this glow." Or they describe it in other exciting ways: "It was like cold water down my back, just tingling" or "It was like a soft glow that seemed to fill the whole room." I wouldn't dream of invalidating any of their experiences—they're all wonderful!

If you had a hot-oil experience, great! If you had a cold-water experience, wonderful! If you had a soft glow experience, marvelous! But your experience is not necessarily going to be the same as the next fellow's. Don't look for the soft glow. If you do, your eyes will be upon the experience rather than on Jesus.

According to His Will

The Spirit wants to operate in our lives, sovereignly and according to His will. But He'll do so in different ways. A person may feel extraordinary sensations, or he may feel nothing at all. None of that discounts the fact that God's Spirit is at work in your life.

That was my problem for a long time. I didn't receive the kind of experience I heard people talking about, and, thus, I felt I didn't "have it." I heard people say, "When I came to, I looked and—my! It was 7 P.M. I don't know where that five hours went." Hearing these testimonies as a child, I understood the phrase "when I came to" to mean an unconscious state. I was certain that when a person was being baptized or filled with the Holy Spirit, he or she would be rendered unconscious. So I waited for years to be struck unconscious so I could "come to." But it never happened to me like that.

If you read through the book of Acts, you will see that every account of an empowering of the church by the Spirit is unique. No single pattern covers all; it didn't happen the same way in any two recorded cases.

Let's expect such differences, and not try to confine God to a pattern. Let's not put God in a box—let God be God and let Him be sovereign and move as He will.

For the Profit of All

Paul teaches that the manifestation of the Spirit is given to everyone for the profit of all (1 Corinthians 12:7). The purpose of gifts of the Spirit is to benefit the whole church; they are not given to us for our own personal profit. God doesn't give me the word of knowledge so that I can go to the race track and clean up.

There is a great evil today—men and women who seek to personally capitalize on the gifts of the Spirit. People have been touched by God through their ministries, and they take advantage of that fact. Maybe a friend or a child has been healed, and they are so thrilled and excited that they want to shower gifts of appreciation upon the person through whom God worked. Sadly, many a person has used God's gifts to personally enrich themselves.

But the gifts of the Holy Spirit are not given for personal enrichment. They are not toys for us to take and enjoy, to bring us satisfaction and pleasure as we're sitting in the solitude of our homes. They are given that the whole church might profit. God has given to each of us a gift that is to be used to bless the whole church.

There is only one gift intended to edify the person exercising it rather than the whole church—the gift of speaking in tongues. Paul said, "He that speaketh in an unknown tongue edifieth himself" (1 Corinthians 14:4). The exercise of the gift of tongues in one's own personal devotions edifies oneself. This is the only gift designed for personal edification. The body isn't edified through that gift unless there is an interpretation. Therefore, the general rule is that the gifts of the Spirit are for the profit of the whole body.

When Gifts Overlap

In the various manifestations of spiritual gifts there is often a crossover between gifts; they are not as independent as we sometimes think. For example, sometimes the gift of discernment overlaps with the word of knowledge, or the gift of prophecy crosses over to a word of wisdom.

Perhaps you are warning someone, and saying, "Friend, I think what you're doing is dangerous. And if you continue, this and this and this may happen." Then, sometime afterward, you find out that the scenario you suggested really did happen. In that way, prophecy became tied together with a word of knowledge.

When you spoke you weren't saying, "This *is* going to happen to you," but "This is what *could* happen." Yet, in the course of time it really did happen, so the word of knowledge became prophecy in a very natural way.

This reminds us that all of these gifts are from the Spirit, and He guides and directs their use as He sees fit. He orchestrates all things to accomplish His good purposes in our lives. And for that we should be extremely grateful.

Which Are the Best Gifts?

At the end of 1 Corinthians 12, Paul encourages the church to covet earnestly the best gifts. But "best" is a relative word. The best gifts for *what*? The best gifts for whatever ministry is most needed in the body of Christ at that moment.

I have many saws in my garage. What is the best saw I have? It depends on what you need to cut. If you have to cut a piece of pipe, you'd better not use my crosscut saw or you'll be in big trouble. The question is, What job needs to be done?

The same question should be asked about the gifts of the Spirit. What are the best gifts? The best gifts are those which can best accomplish the task at hand.

As we discuss each of the gifts, you'll see the value of each one in certain situations. Sometimes the best gift is that of speaking in other tongues. But at other times that would be of no value at all; it would only cause people to think you're insane. I can imagine when the working of miracles would surely be the best gift—for example, when you need to pay the rent and there's nothing in your account. Then the gift of tongues wouldn't do you much good—but the working of miracles would sure help.

As we investigate each of these gifts, we will see how each one could be "the best gift" under certain situations. Paul instructs us to covet earnestly the best gifts. He doesn't tell us to pray for them, but to covet them earnestly. That's an important distinction because the Holy Spirit divides to each person severally as He will. He is sovereign.

I didn't choose which gifts I should have. That was a sovereign work of God in my life. So are the callings and the various ministries. It's all God's sovereign work.

Fight the Right Enemy

Oh, that we could see the oneness of the body of Christ, that we would stop competing with or opposing others just because we do not agree with their particular doctrinal slant! What a tragedy that churches find themselves in an adversarial position with other churches, speaking against each other because they do things differently.

One of the great catastrophes of the church is her failure to properly identify who the real enemy is. So many times the church is divided against itself. Even within a church there comes conflict. Battle lines are drawn, divisions created—and that is tragic. How Satan loves to bring discord and division among the brethren!

We shouldn't be pitted against one another. We should be united in our effort to bring people into the kingdom of God and out of the kingdom of darkness. The real enemy is Satan, and it is our task to bring men and women out of his kingdom and into the glorious kingdom of God. Once that occurs, it really doesn't matter if these babes in Christ affiliate with us or join with someone else who loves and serves the Lord. It should never be our purpose to try to get people to come to our church. Our task is to bring them to the knowledge of Jesus Christ and to surrender to His will.

It may be that our church can't effectively minister to their needs. Someone may look at me and say, "That old bald-headed man—what does he know? I want someone who's really hip and can talk about my marriage and help me. I need someone who is more humorous and clever." Thus, I may not be able to minister to him—and that doesn't matter to me! The main issue is that we bring people out of their darkness in sin, and bring them to the glorious light of Christ. Then we must let them go wherever they can be ministered to and get help.

Some time ago I received a letter from a fellow who wrote, "I considered an affiliation with the Calvary Chapels, but this aspect was wrong and that doctrine was wrong and I don't know if I really understand what's going on there." I wrote back and said, "I don't think you do. And I would suggest you not pursue any further trying to affiliate with Calvary Chapel." He described his shock at one of the issues that was brought up, and I said, "If you stick around, you'll probably find a lot more shocking things. So maybe it's better that you not stick around."

The wise thing is to go where you feel comfortable. Fill your niche where God has called you. That's all.

I used to speak out against the ritualism of certain churches. "Those liturgical services with the incense and the robes," I would say disapprovingly, "how dead." I would also speak out against the overly demonstrative Pentecostals: "People are screaming and running up and down and doing wild things.

How foolish." In fact, I could find something wrong with just about everyone...but me.

There's at least one nice thing about aging: It does mellow a person. Through the years I have learned to respect and accept those who want to worship God in a liturgical setting. Their temperaments best allow them to worship God in that kind of setting. I also realize there are others who worship God best in a highly emotional setting. They want to be stirred up, to get up and shout, to have a lot of excitement and exuberance in their worship experience.

I now realize we are all serving the same Lord, though we may be doing it differently. Yet He is the same Lord and He loves us all. He loves those who love the formal ritualism and the smell of incense, and thus He has provided for them an environment where they are comfortable, and where they can sense and feel His presence. He also loves those wild, extreme people who have to do a lot of shouting and running around to get rid of their energy. He loves them, too, and He's provided an environment for them.

It's not that one way is wrong and another right. There are differences, but it's the same Lord. That's what we seem to forget. Because of our differences we often think, *We're serving a different Lord*, so we fight each other. But rather than judge others because of the way they worship, it's better that we accept that they're just different.

Paul said, "Who are you to judge another's servant? To his own master he stands or falls. Indeed, he will be made to stand, for God is able to make him stand" (Romans 14:4). When you judge someone because they are wild in their worship of God, you're judging God's servant. But they don't serve you—they're serving the Lord. God is able to hold them up (even though they may want to throw themselves down). He's able to make them stand.

Be Open to God

I want to be open to God. As I open myself unto God, I do so unreservedly, without any fears. I don't worry about the bogeyman stories that we so often hear, about some poor fellow who opened himself to God and they carried him away to the booby-hatch a blithering idiot. He made the mistake of saying, "God, I want to be filled with your Spirit," and that did it!

What a blasphemous concept of God and of Jesus! Jesus said, "If you then, being evil, know how to give good gifts to your children, how much more will your heavenly Father give the Holy Spirit to those who ask Him" (Luke 11:13)!

Our problem is that we have closed the door to God many times. We don't want Him to move. Or, if He does move, we tell Him, "Here are the parameters, and here are the guidelines. God, You'd better not step out of our little order here. We've got it all formulated on how it's supposed to work."

How sad. The Lord knows what is best for us. It's wisest to defer to Him and to the Holy Spirit to give us those gifts that can best be exercised for the benefit of the whole church. He divides to each person severally as He wills; it is our job to be open.

May nothing stand in the way of His imparting to us those gifts that might benefit us and edify the church. Let us commit ourselves and the exercise of these gifts of the Spirit to God. Then may God empower us, and use us, as He sees fit.

8

The Word of Wisdom

To one is given the word of wisdom through the Spirit.
—1 CORINTHIANS 12:8

I love the advice a poor mother gave to her young son: "Honey, when you ain't got no education, you just have to use your brain."

How rare a commodity is wisdom in these days! Before we begin to look at the word of wisdom, it would be worth our while to note that there is a definite, distinct difference between knowledge and wisdom. They are not the same thing.

Is Knowledge Part of Wisdom?

Knowledge is the accumulation of fact; wisdom is the proper application of the fact. Knowledge will tell you that the cute little black animal with the white stripe down its back is not a cat; wisdom will tell you to keep your distance. Knowledge will tell you that the coiled creature in front of you is poisonous; wisdom will tell you to avoid petting it.

There is a vast difference between knowledge and wisdom. Some of the most knowledgeable people in the world are some of the most inept. They have a lot of knowledge but don't know how to use it. People who are very intelligent and knowledgeable often do foolish things because they are not wise. For example, Timothy Leary, a brilliant man full of knowledge, destroyed himself with LSD and led countless others down that destructive path.

I marvel at the unintelligent things brilliant people believe and do, once they have rejected the truth of Jesus Christ.

Because "the fear of the Lord is the beginning of wisdom" (Psalm 111:10), people who reject God are prone to do and believe ridiculous things. In India, some of the most educated people in the world live in filthy and in unhealthy conditions—almost like animals—in order to spend time at the compound of a guru named Sai Baba. These brilliant people believe that one of the greatest honors is to be able to eat his excrement.

Such practices are so shocking that our minds almost can't conceive it. When people in rebellion against the truth are given over by God to reprobate minds, Satan always seems to reduce them to the worst kind of filth. This happens to brilliant people who reject the truth of God.

Paul tells us in 2 Thessalonians 2:10,11, "because they did not receive the love of the truth . . . God will send them strong delusion, that they should believe the lie." God allows them to believe a lie rather than the truth. Paul outlines the whole downward progression in Romans 1:28: "And even as they did not like to retain God in their knowledge, God gave them over to a debased mind, to do those things which are not fitting." They commit acts which are unspeakable, unthinkable. When a person rejects the truth of Jesus Christ, and gives his mind over to the impurities of darkness, Satan leads him down the path to the very bottom.

If someone does not have the fear of the Lord, he or she does not have true wisdom. In fact, that person hasn't even begun walking the path of wisdom.

Knowledge without wisdom can be extremely dangerous. Through knowledge, we have been able to create super weapons with the capacity to destroy mankind. We hope that wisdom will keep humankind from destroying itself through these weapons. Solomon said, "Wisdom is the principal thing; therefore get wisdom" (Proverbs 4:7).

The Gift of Wisdom

The Bible teaches that beyond wisdom in general, there is a specific gift of the Holy Spirit that is called the "word of wisdom." This is not a vast reservoir that you can draw upon at according to your own whim. It does not make you some kind of guru, that you can say, "Anything you want to know, just come to me and I will open up my treasures of wisdom." It doesn't work like that—it isn't a reservoir of wisdom that you can tap at will. Rather, it is an anointing of the Spirit that comes upon you in a time of need, and gives you the right words to say. A word of wisdom comes when critical issues arise and important decisions must be made. It is a wise word that is so right it brings divided factions together. When people hear it they say, "Oh, yes. That's good!"

The word of wisdom is so fitly spoken it can defuse tension. Suppose a heated argument or disagreement is going on. A person may receive a word of wisdom which resolves the issue and satisfies both sides. "Yes—I can buy that," the arguers say. This word of wisdom can be a glorious thing in resolving tough issues and problems. It settles people's differences and brings solutions to thorny problems. It removes the rancor between people, settles the issue, and brings a peaceful solution that everybody can be happy with.

Of course, as with all spiritual gifts, the word of wisdom remains under the control or operation of the Spirit. It isn't something to have whenever we want it. Rather, it is something the Spirit gives to us in answer to a particular need. It is more than wisdom in general; there are times when the Spirit directly gives us the right word.

The Word of Wisdom in Scripture

We see the word of wisdom manifested in King Solomon's life in the Old Testament. In one instance, two women came to him, both claiming that a little child was theirs. The women gave birth about the same time, but one woman's child had died. She claimed the dead child belonged to the other woman, so they brought their case to Solomon. Both women steadfastly affirmed, "That child is mine!" So Solomon said to his guard, "Take your sword and cut the child in two; then give them each half." The true mother pleaded, "No, no! Don't do that! Let her have it." The other woman said, "Hey, fair enough. We each get half." Solomon pointed to the child's real mother and said, "This is the true mother; give the child to her" (see 1 Kings 3:16-28). By the word of wisdom, he was able to resolve this difficult issue.

Jesus often demonstrated the word of wisdom. Perhaps the most classic case occurred when the Pharisees sought to trap Him in a catch-22 dilemma. They carefully crafted their question to leave no room for his escape; they thought there was no way He could get out of this one. "Is it lawful for us to pay taxes to Caesar or not?" they asked. They knew that if

Jesus said, "Yes, you should pay taxes to Caesar," He would lose every Jew in the crowd because they all hated paying taxes to the Roman government; it really galled them. On the other hand, if He were to say, "No, you shouldn't pay taxes to Caesar," the Pharisees could run down to the magistrate and say, "You have an insurrection. There's a rebel down here who's teaching the people not to pay taxes!" They figured they had him cornered with no way out. No matter which way he answered, they'd have Him.

Well, not quite.

Jesus said, "Show me a coin," so a fellow held up a coin. Jesus asked, "Whose likeness and inscription has it?" They said, "Caesar's." He replied, "Then render to Caesar the things that are Caesar's, and give to God the things that are God's" (see Luke 20:22-26 RSV). His word of wisdom baffled them and their trap blew up in their faces.

The gift of the word of wisdom also operated in the lives of the disciples. In Acts 6, a dispute arose concerning the welfare program of the church. Jewish believers who had adopted the Greek (or Hellenistic) culture thought their widows were not getting the same kind of treatment as were the more traditional, Hebraic Jews. When they came to the apostles and complained, the twelve called the church together and said, "It is not desirable that we should leave the word of God and serve tables. Therefore, brethren, seek out from among you seven men of good reputation, full of the Holy Spirit and wisdom, whom we may appoint over this business; but we will give ourselves continually to prayer and to the ministry of the word" (Acts 6:2-4). The postscript to this incident says their words "pleased the whole multitude." That's the word of wisdom.

Later in Acts 15, a problem arose among the Gentile believers in Antioch because of some legalistic Jews who had come down from the church in Jerusalem. These men saw the freedom that the Gentile believers had in Jesus, and said, "Look, you can't really be saved unless you keep the law of Moses and are circumcised. We in Jerusalem still keep the whole law."

Because these men represented themselves as officials from the church in Jerusalem, Paul said, "Come on, we're going to Jerusalem and get this issue resolved." So Paul and Barnabas came back with these fellows to the church in Jerusalem, where the elders of the church gathered to resolve the issue.

This was a sticky problem in the early church, causing sharp division that was dividing the church. On one side were those who were proclaiming that Gentiles were not subject to the law of Moses—Paul being one of these. On the other side were the Judaizers who said, "You can't be saved without keeping the law of Moses." As the church council in Jerusalem gathered to resolve the issue, there was the very real danger that the church might split in two.

Peter stood up and described how the Lord had called him to go to the Gentiles, and how they had received the Holy Spirit. Then he said, "I don't think we should put on them the yoke of bondage [referring to the law] that neither we nor our fathers were able to bear." Next Paul and Barnabas described their ministry among the Gentiles and the tremendous miracles God had wrought through them. Finally James spoke up. "Brethren," he said, "I suggest that we write to the Gentile believers and greet them, but let us not trouble them who have turned to God. Let us suggest that they abstain from polluting themselves with idols, from fornication and from things that are strangled and from blood." We are told that this suggestion—this word of wisdom from James—pleased the apostles and the elders and the whole church. Everybody said, "Great! Good idea!" and it was a settled issue. In this way the word of wisdom defused a potentially explosive situation. When the church in Antioch received the letter, they rejoiced over its encouragement (see Acts 15:1-31).

The Word of Wisdom Today

Oftentimes when I am asked a question about the Bible, I start to answer the question before I know fully what the answer is. As I start to give an answer, often there comes into my mind appropriate passages of Scripture and a sudden clarity of understanding. As I answer the person, I also learn because of the exercise of the gift of the word of wisdom.

This is the word of wisdom: You didn't know the answer before this moment, but even as you speak your heart testifies of its truth and it makes sense. The Spirit of God gives you the answer. It is something that you had not learned or studied or thought about, but it is so right, so on target, that you recognize it as a word of wisdom.

In exercising the ministry of pastor-teacher, I believe there are three spiritual gifts that operate, especially when we are teaching the word of God: prophecy, the word of knowledge, and the word of wisdom. Oftentimes as we minister, the Lord opens up passages to our own hearts and gives us wisdom and understanding of a particular passage. I often listen to my own teaching tapes and get blessed by them. Many times, as I listen, I say to myself, "Did I say that? That's good." It was good because it was the gift of the word of wisdom in action. I was saying things beyond my own wisdom—giving color, understanding, and enlightenment to the audience through the operation of the word of wisdom.

You Don't Get a Buzz

It's likely that you have exercised this gift without even realizing it. Can you remember a situation in which someone asked you a difficult question, and as you fumblingly started to respond, the answer just came to you? You were able to give the answer, it was clear, and it made sense, and it was good. That's the gift of the word of wisdom.

These gifts of the Spirit operate so naturally that often we're not even aware the gift is being exercised. Many times it is not until later, when we have more information, that we suddenly discover we were speaking words of wisdom beyond our own understanding. We didn't have all the facts, yet the wisdom was right on target.

You don't get some kind of a buzz or hear sirens when you exercise the word of wisdom. Bells don't go off and prompt you to say, "Hearken thou now unto me, for words of wisdom are about to flow from my lips." Somehow, many people have in their minds the belief that the only time the Spirit can move upon our lives is when we're in a trance, when we're spaced out. Some people think that when the Spirit makes contact, we walk around like zombies, and our words become powerful, dynamic words of God, delivered in a loud voice with tremolo.

Not so. It doesn't work that way. The word of wisdom operates in a very natural manner. Often we expect that supernatural things happen only in supernatural ways, but many times they occur in such natural ways that we don't recognize their truly supernatural character. Oftentimes we are not even aware that what we are saying is being inspired by the Spirit— but it is.

Surfing and the Leading of God

As I look back on my life and how God has led me, I see how He supernaturally led me in very natural ways. I had no idea God was leading me, but as I look back, I can clearly see the hand of the Lord. He is so good, leading us even when we don't know we're being led!

When I first began in the ministry, I tried to be an evangelist. All of my messages were evangelistic, even though I was pastoring a church. Always at the end of my message I appealed for the people to accept the Lord. Of course, if there were no pagans present (which was often the case), I would appeal for people to rededicate their lives, or to repent for not bringing pagans to church. I went down the list until I forced them to come down to the altar and repent. I always measured the success of my sermon by how many people came forward and how hard they cried.

I had collected two years' worth of topical sermons, and after I finished two years in a church, I would request a change of location. Then I'd go to a new church and preach my two years of messages there. That went on until I landed in Huntington Beach, California.

In those days, Huntington Beach was a lazy little beach community of about 6,000 residents, with the lowest tax burden in Orange County. Oil wells provided an abundant tax base which provided the city with the finest library and schools. The town was a sleeper; people didn't know how great it was to live there.

There weren't a lot of surfers back then, and the publisher of the local newspaper, the town pharmacist, and I used to meet down at the beach and go surfing every morning. It was wonderful; we were the only three people there. We would watch the surf to see if it was breaking best on the north or the south side, then go out and have it all to ourselves. We could be through by 10 A.M. and then attend to our various tasks. It was just perfect—but I had a problem, I'd run out of sermons. My two years were up and it was time to request a change . . . but this time I didn't want a change. I liked living in Huntington Beach. Our daughter had started school, and we wanted her to have all the advantages afforded by the city's tremendous school system.

At the time I was reading a book titled *The Apostle John,* by

Griffith Thomas. In chapter seven he includes some marvelous outline studies on First John. As I read them I thought, *This is tremendous sermon material. These are great outlines. My, I can get a sermon from every one of them.* There were 43 of them. *Wonderful!* I thought. *I can stay in Huntington Beach another year!* The following Sunday I announced we were going to do something different; we were going to start a study of a book of the Bible, First John.

By the end of the year, by heavily using Mr. Thomas' book and other commentaries, I was able to stretch the 43 sermons into 52. I stayed a whole year in first John. But the amazing thing was, in that year the church *doubled* in size. I baptized more people that year than I had in any previous year of ministry! Yet I wasn't preaching evangelistic sermons, I was teaching the people the Word of God, and evangelism was happening anyway.

After that year I still enjoyed living in Huntington Beach and still didn't want to move, so I remembered the words of one of my college profs who said that the book of Romans would revolutionalize any church. I had read it, of course, but it had never done much for me. Yet I'd heard the same thing from many others, so I decided that if it could cause a revolution, I'd teach it.

I wasn't ready for the revolution it caused; I never expected it to revolutionalize *me*! In Romans, I discovered the grace of God and a new relationship with Him. I spent two years in Romans and still didn't want to leave. Just then I came across a new edition of *Halley's Bible Pocket Handbook*. On the cover it said, "the most important page in this book is 748." So I turned to page 748 to find out what the author figured was the most important page in his great little book. He proposed that every church should have a systematic way of reading the Bible all the way through. Ideally, he said, the pastor's sermon would come out of the portion the people had read the previous week. It was then I realized, *Hey, I've got the whole Bible. I can spend the rest of my life here!*

That's the way God naturally did a supernatural work in my own life and ministry to lead me into expositional studies. I went from topical evangelistic messages to studying the Bible book by book. I became a teacher rather than a preacher.

It all seemed so natural. God took my natural love for the beach, my natural love for surfing, and He used them to guide me in His path to become a Bible expositor. God works in very natural ways His supernatural work in our lives.

Praying for Wisdom

It is sad but true that divisions within the church often arise. That's why it is so necessary for someone with the word of wisdom to offer a solution that will be acceptable and amenable to both sides so that division does not take place. Many churches have been severely divided because of the lack of the gift of the word of wisdom.

It's hard for me to understand why, when God has made available to us His wisdom, we would rely upon our own. Why would we make decisions without seeking His guidance and His wisdom? "In all your ways acknowledge Him, and He shall direct your paths," we're promised in Proverbs 3:6. That's the wisest thing we could ever do.

Have you ever made decisions that, afterward, you regretted? You thought, *Oh no! How could I have decided that? Look how it turned out.* And you might think, *God, why did you let me get in this mess?* Do you know why? Because you didn't ask for wisdom. Ask and it shall be given; seek and ye shall find; knock and it shall be opened (see Matthew 7:7).

Ask for wisdom and you *will* get it. You will discover that the Holy Spirit can give to you a word of wisdom which will guide you in the counsel of God.

When you've been challenged by an unbeliever, God will give you that word of wisdom—if you'll just look to Him. When you are faced with a difficult decision at home, seek His wisdom—and He has promised to guide you. Not in a showy, breathtaking way, perhaps, but He *will* guide you. The Bible tells us that in Christ Jesus are hidden all the treasures of wisdom and knowledge (Colossians 2:2,3).

And the most marvelous thing is that they are available to you for the asking. Right now!

9

How Did He Know That?

To one is given . . . the word of knowledge through the same Spirit.

—1 Corinthians 12:8

One weekend, many years ago when I was in Bible college, I returned home to go on a date with a girl whom I had known in high school. I started talking with her about a divorced person I knew, about how I believed the man had no scriptural basis for his divorce, and how wrong I thought he was in considering remarriage. "You know," I said, "God is no respecter of persons, and even though this man had been in the ministry, that doesn't give him carte blanche to do what he pleases. There is the Word of God to consider. Without a scriptural basis for divorce, I really question his position."

I went on talking like this for almost the whole evening—not knowing that this man had already proposed to my date! About two months later she married him. Without knowing it, I had exercised the gift of the word of knowledge.

What is the word of knowledge? It is information given to us supernaturally, knowledge of things that we could not know through natural acquisition or study. It's exciting to be used of God in this way. The Spirit will speak through you about a pertinent issue in someone's life, and when it's over you say, "Wow! Why did I say *that*?" It's a divine impartation of knowledge concerning a person or situation that could not come through natural thought processes. It's something that flashes into your mind which God prompts you to say.

In the previous incident the Lord was speaking to my date by the Spirit to warn her; but to her own sorrow, she refused to listen.

In the Old Testament

The word of knowledge was exercised by Elisha the prophet in a remarkable way. God gave to Elisha all kinds of knowledge—so much so that whenever Ben-Hadad, the king of Syria, was planning to invade Israel or ambush her troops, Elisha would issue a warning in advance. In this way Israel was able to escape every trap that Ben-Hadad set. Eventually the Syrian king began to get suspicious. He called in his generals and said, "Now, one of you fellows must be leaking information. We've got a security leak here, because it is impossible that Israel's king could know every move we make." He was asking for a confession.

But they replied, "No, king. It's not that. We are all loyal to you. But there is a prophet in Israel who knows even what you say to your wife when you go to bed at night." Such was the powerful way the word of knowledge was exercised in Elisha's life.

But because God is sovereign in imparting all His gifts, including the word of wisdom, there were other times when the Lord did not reveal to Elisha what was taking place. Once when Elisha saw a Shulamite woman approaching him in the distance—the same woman whom Elisha had prophesied the birth of a son—sent his servant Gehazi out to ask if everything was all right. Gehazi came back and said, "She said everything's OK," but Elisha replied, "There is something wrong, but the Lord hasn't showed it to me." He was surprised at this, demonstrating that the prophet didn't have a reservoir of knowledge he could tap at will. Every word of knowledge he received represented a new action of God.

In the New Testament

We often see the word of knowledge manifested in the life of Jesus In John 1:45-51, Philip goes to get Nathaniel and says to him, "Come and see this man. We think he's the Messiah." When Nathaniel arrives, Jesus says, "Behold, an Israelite in whom there is no guile." Nathaniel replies, "How did you know me?" Jesus answers, "Before Philip ever called you, I saw you sitting under that fig tree." Nathaniel is astonished and responds, "Oh! Truly, you are the Messiah!" "You believe this?" Jesus asks him. "Stick around, you're going to see a lot more than this."

Another time Jesus was with his disciples on the way to Galilee. Outside the village of Shechem sat the well of Jacob. While the disciples went into the city to buy some food for lunch, Jesus encountered a Samaritan woman at the well. In the course of conversation Jesus offers her what He calls "living water," and she gets pretty excited about it. "I'll take some of that water so I don't have to come out here every day and draw from this well," she says. Jesus responds, "First go call your husband." "Well, I'm not married," she replies. And Jesus says, "True enough. You've had five husbands, and the man you're now living with, you didn't bother to marry. So I'll buy that; you have no husband" (see John 4:6-18). He exercised a word of knowledge.

In the book of Acts, this gift is exercised through Peter and later through Paul. In Acts 5:3, Peter knew by a word of knowledge that Ananias and Sapphira had lied to the Holy Spirit when they claimed to have given the full sale price of a piece of property to the church. There was no way Peter could have known this except through a word of knowledge. And because of it, the church was cleansed.

Later, in chapter 8, Peter confronted Simon the sorcerer after he had attempted to buy the right to bestow the Holy Spirit on whomever he wished. "Your money perish with you because you think that the power of God can be bought," Peter said. "Therefore ask God to forgive you, for I perceive that in your heart there is a gall of bitterness" (see verses 14-23). Peter read what was in his heart through the word of knowledge.

In Acts 27, Paul was on his way to Rome. Against Paul's warnings his Roman jailers decided to sail from Crete. Soon a violent storm came up, shutting out the sun and battering the ship for several days. The people despaired of life and did everything they knew to save the ship—they threw out all the tackle, all the cargo, and nearly everything else, yet things only got worse.

In the night an angel of the Lord told Paul that, although the ship would be destroyed, everyone would be saved as long as they stayed together. So, in the morning, Paul stood up and said, "Men, be of good cheer. Last night an angel of the Lord stood by me and told me that though the ship was going to be wrecked, there won't be any loss of life." Sure enough, shortly thereafter, as they approached land, they got stuck on a sandbar and the ship was pounded to pieces by the wild surf. Yet not a life was lost. Paul had exercised the word of knowledge to encourage the whole crew.

In the Church Today

At Calvary Chapel, where I pastor, there is a Korean lady who was separated from her brother when her homeland was divided into north and south. He was in the north, she was in the south, and they had lost contact for some 40 years. One day the Lord started prompting her with a new concern for her brother, so she began praying that somehow God would help her find him if he were still alive.

She heard that he had been sent to Manchuria, so she prayed again that the Lord would help her contact her brother. While she was in prayer, the Lord gave her a phone number in Manchuria. She called that number and her brother answered! Just recently this woman returned from a trip to visit her brother. Before she left, the Lord had showed her a vision of her brother's house. When she arrived in town she quickly recognized the house she had been shown, and she was reunited with her brother! That's the word of knowledge—a marvelous gift of God.

At other times, this word of knowledge convicts and rebukes those who harbor "dirty little secrets." We've seen this aspect of the word of knowledge at work at Calvary Chapel. Every so often somebody brings their friends to church and later calls to tell us, "Our friends won't speak to us anymore. We brought them to church last Sunday and they are certain that we called you before the service and told you everything they were doing. You nailed them; what you said hit exactly where they were. We tried to convince them that we would never do such a thing, but they won't believe us. They're sure that we called you and ratted on them, and that now everybody in church knows their problems." They said their friends even imagined me looking at them during the whole sermon!

Beyond that, the Spirit often gives understanding of specific things occurring in someone's life. When this happens, you may be tempted to say, "Oh, what a horrible thought. That must be my wicked imagination. I shouldn't think that." Yet you'll often find that you're exactly right.

Years ago we were pastoring a community church. One Sunday my wife, Kay, pointed to a fellow in our church who enjoyed a very prominent position in the community. He was a great family man with a tremendous personality. Kay said to me, "When I looked at him this morning, I just knew by the Spirit that he was having an affair with his secretary. It came so strong. I first thought, *Oh, that's terrible to think such a thing; I should put that out of my mind.* But it keeps coming back. He's having an affair with his secretary." I replied, "Now, Kay, the Bible says we shouldn't have evil imaginations." She answered, "No! Every time I look at him, I see him with his secretary. He's carrying on!" I insisted, "Oh, come on. Not him!"

A few months later I received a phone call. This man and his wife were on the line together. They tried to speak, but all they got out was a feeble "Pastor Chuck." Then their voices broke, they started sobbing, and couldn't continue. So I said, "That's all right. I know what the call is all about."

"You do?" he asked incredulously.

"Yes. You've been in an affair with your secretary for the last six months. Come on over and let's talk and pray about it."

This man and his wife were shocked that I knew exactly what was happening. But the Lord had already shown it to Kay. (The Lord shows my wife lots of things; it's not easy living with a prophetess!)

In the Ministry of the Word

This gift of the word of knowledge often happens during the teaching of the Word of God. Frequently when I want to illustrate a particular point, I will make up a hypothetical case—and later discover that it hit someone right between the eyes. They say, "Why, that's me! *Who told him about me?*"

One Sunday night I was talking about how to identify a false prophet. "There are a lot of paper missionaries out there," I said. "They live in some of the most beautiful areas of the world, and take candy out to the villages and honk their car horn. When the little kids come running, they shoot pictures of them reaching out for the sweets. Then they'll send letters back home, along with pictures of a huge crowd of kids, and say, 'Recently we were at this village passing out Bible tracts. Look how eager the children are to receive. And God is blessing our ministry.' And their plea? 'Keep your support up.' Yet these 'missionaries' do nothing at all. They're retired but still use a mailing list to deceive the people back here in the States."

I continued, "Some right around here have these paper ministries. They have their mailing list which they use to bleed people every month. They live on Lido Island, drive white Cadillac convertibles and wear white wing tipped shoes. They live a high style life, but they don't have any real ministry at all."

The next morning I got an irate call. My secretary said, "This guy sounds awful mad. He wants to talk to you." So I replied, "Put him on." As soon as I picked up the phone, the man spat out, "I want you to know that I have a legitimate ministry."

"What are you talking about?" I asked.

"You know what I'm talking about!" he shouted. "Last night you were telling the people that my ministry wasn't legitimate. I live down on Lido Island. I drive that Cadillac convertible. But I have a ministry. It's a legitimate ministry. I want you to know that."

"Wait a minute!" I replied. "I've never heard of you. I don't know you. I was just making up a hypothetical case. But if I were you, I would ask the Lord just how legitimate your ministry really is."

At the time I gave that illustration, I thought I was drawing a word picture out of thin air. But not so. It was the exercise of the gift of the word of knowledge, and it nailed that guy to the wall. I even described him right down to his white wing tipped shoes!

Is the Word of Knowledge the Same as the Word of Wisdom?

Just as with the word of wisdom, the word of knowledge is not a vast reservoir that you can tap anytime you want. It is not a huge storage depot to which you have access at whim.

The Spirit is sovereign, not only in bestowing His gifts, but also in their exercise. The Spirit may move upon my heart and upon my mind and give me special knowledge, but He doesn't give me such knowledge in every situation. He does this only at special times and for special occasions. I can't tap it at will.

Again, just as in the case of the word of wisdom, the word of knowledge often is exercised without our knowledge—frequently without our even being aware of it.

I don't think Peter had any idea that he was speaking a word of wisdom when, in answer to Jesus' question, "Who do you say that I am," he replied, "You are the Christ, the Son of the living God." Jesus told him, "Blessed are you, Simon Bar-Jona, for flesh and blood has not revealed this to you, but My Father who is in Heaven" (Matthew 16:13-17).

Now, Peter didn't get any kind of a buzz or sensation or electric current running through his body accompanied, by the message, "He's the Messiah! He's the son of God!" His voice didn't get louder, neither did a tremor run through it, indicating some kind of supernatural activity was going on. He simply said in his normal voice, "You are the Christ, the Son of the living God." Yet it was not a "normal" statement; Jesus acknowledged that his words were a revelation from the Father.

Remember that the Spirit operates in a very natural way. Don't look to be somewhere out on cloud nine when the Spirit speaks through you. I always get a bit skeptical when someone comes up to me with a spacey look in his eyes and says, "The Lord has told me..." I have found that when the Spirit is working, He works in a beautiful, natural way.

What Purpose Do These Words Serve?

What is the purpose of this gift? Why would God show us such things? He doesn't give this gift just so we can be popular with the gossip circle, so we can reveal all the embarrassing things going on within the church. No, the Lord gives us these insights so that we might begin to pray, and intercede for hurting people and their needs.

Paul instructed Timothy to correct those who were in error, "that they may come to their senses and escape the snare of the devil, having been taken captive by him to do his will" (2 Timothy 2:26). So many times when people fall prey to the deception of the enemy, the Lord will show it to us. When you look at them you know something is not right. But the Spirit reveals to you their problems only so you might pray for them to be delivered from the power of Satan.

The same thing is true for the church body in general. The word of knowledge is given to us that we might see God's people delivered from the power of the enemy. We would take tremendous strides as a church if this gift of the word of knowledge were more broadly exercised.

A Word of Caution

I confess I am distressed by what we often see passed off as the word of knowledge. I'm sure you've seen or heard this bogus "gift" at work. Usually a large group of people has gathered and someone says, "I believe there is someone here tonight who has been very discouraged and very despondent, even considering suicide." Well, I daresay someone is discouraged and despondent every night of the week. Such a "revelation" isn't a word of knowledge, but a broad generalization. It's no word of knowledge to say, "someone has a knee that is bothering them." At my age, who doesn't have a knee that bothers them?

Don't get me wrong. I want to be as open minded as I can be—but not much so that I am gullible. I want to be open to all the Spirit is doing and wants to give. But when people pass off as spiritual gifts what is not of the Spirit, their actions belittle the genuine and prejudice others against the authentic work of the Spirit. I have seen many things passed off as spiritual manifestations or spiritual gifts that I am certain were not of the Holy Spirit. I am sure of this because God is not the author of confusion, but what was going on was clearly confusion.

Let God Use You

I thank God for the genuine experiences I have had with the Holy Spirit, and for the relationship I enjoy with Him. I am grateful for all that the Spirit has done and is doing in my life. But, I frankly confess that there is much more He would like to do in my life. It is my desire to be fully open to be led by the Spirit, to be used by the Spirit, that the Spirit of God might be manifested in my life however He may desire.

Our Heavenly Father longs to give us wisdom and understanding, and the word of knowledge is an important aspect of that wisdom and understanding. Oh, that we might be sensitive and obedient to the promptings of the Holy Spirit, thankful for His faithfulness and grateful that He speaks to our hearts even though at times we don't respond. May the Lord fill us with the fullness of His Spirit until He flows forth like a gusher of living water from our lives, healing and touching those around us with His unspeakable love.

10

How to Plant a Mulberry Tree in the Ocean

To one is given ... faith by the same Spirit.

—1 Corinthians 12:8,9

One of our problems is that we often try to generate faith from within using human methods. But Paul lists faith as one of the gifts of the Spirit.

The writer of Hebrews defines faith as "the substance of things hoped for, the evidence of things not seen" (Hebrews 11:1). My grandson helps me to see what the writer means. He is getting to the place where, by faith, he's got a mustache and beard. He's already started to shave by faith, confident that one day there's going to be something to shave. He is living by faith, confident of things hoped for but not yet seen.

Jesus was talking to his disciples one day concerning the importance of forgiveness. When they finally began to grasp how critical to God it is that we forgive those who wrong us, they said, "Lord, increase our faith." They recognized they could not forgive as Jesus was commanding them. It wasn't natural. The natural bent is to get even, to seek revenge. But the Lord insisted they were to forgive, so they prayed, "Lord, increase our faith" (see Luke 17:3-5). Only then could they be obedient and forgive as Jesus had commanded.

Their response opened the door for Jesus to talk about this special gift of faith. He responded, "If you have faith as a mustard seed, you can say to this mulberry tree, 'Be pulled up by the roots and be planted in the sea,' and it would obey you" (Luke 17:6). Now that's pretty awesome. Faith as a grain of mustard seed! I wonder what we could do if we had faith like an avocado seed?

Different Kinds of Faith

At the outset, let me make it clear that there are different kinds of faith.

First, we talk about *saving faith*. Paul said, "For I say, through the grace given to me, to everyone who is among you, not to think of himself more highly than he ought to think, but to think soberly, as God has dealt to each one a measure of faith" (Romans 12:3). I believe Paul's "measure of faith" is a reference to the saving faith God has dealt to everyone. If a person exercises that saving faith given to them by God, he or she will be rescued from sin, and will receive the gift of God, which is eternal life. Hebrews 12:2 declares that Jesus is the author and finisher of our faith. Therefore, this also seems to be related to saving faith.

How do you receive saving faith? Paul says it comes by hearing, and hearing by the word of God (Romans 10:17). You are saved "if you confess with your mouth the Lord Jesus and believe in your heart that God has raised Him from the dead" (10:9). Such faith accepts that, if we believe on Jesus Christ, we will be forgiven and cleansed of whatever sins we may have committed. This is faith that brings us salvation.

In Ephesians, Paul amplifies his teaching on saving faith when he writes, "For by grace you have been saved through faith, and that not of yourselves; it is a gift of God" (Ephesians 2:8).

Saving faith is trusting in Jesus Christ as our Savior, believing that He paid the price for our sins. It is believing that the blood of Christ was shed as a sacrifice and accepted by God. As our substitute, Jesus took our sins upon Himself and died in our place, that by our believing in Him we would not perish but have eternal life.

God has given to each one of us a measure of saving faith, which, when exercised, will save us from the guilt of our sins.

A second kind of faith is faith *that trusts in the promises of God*. This is the faith that causes us to commit ourselves to the Word of God, believing His promises, banking on His promises, and rejoicing in His promises. This kind of faith is often lacking in followers of Jesus.

Mark 16:9-14 tells us that after Jesus' resurrection, "He appeared to the eleven as they sat at the table; and He rebuked their unbelief and hardness of heart, because they did not believe those who had seen Him after He had risen." The disciples didn't believe the witness of the women, that they had seen the Lord and even held Him by His feet. Therefore Jesus rebuked them because they refused to believe He had done what He promised He would do (see also Luke 24:10; John 20:16,17).

Another time, when He was walking with the two disciples on the road to Emmaus, He said to them, "O foolish ones, and slow of heart to believe in all that the prophets have spoken!" (Luke 24:25). Here is God's Word, Jesus was saying, and yet you haven't believed or trusted it. How could you have doubted His promises?

This is the kind of childlike faith that increases and grows. Jude told us to build ourselves up in the most holy faith (Jude 20). Paul talked to the Thessalonians about increasing in faith (2 Thessalonians 1:3). This kind of faith grows as we experience the faithfulness of God. Through the years, we see the faithfulness of God to take care of us, to provide for us, and to guide us. And our faith expands. It increases to the extent that problems don't disturb us as much as they used to because we know that everything is in God's hands—He'll take care of it.

Abraham had this kind of faith. Romans 4:19 tells us that when God promised him a son, he did not consider his own age—almost 100 years old—nor the deadness of Sarah's womb. He put out of his mind the human factors which were totally against Sarah having a child. "It doesn't make any difference," he must have said. "God has given me the promise. So, if God's going to do the work, why should I consider how impossible it is? I'm not the one doing it; God's the One who's going to do it. Is anything too hard for God?"

Abraham did not waver at the promise of God, but began to give glory to God, for he was fully persuaded that what God had promised, God was able to perform. Abraham is a great model for us.

The third faith is what could be termed *healing faith*. Matthew 9 tells the story of a woman who had this kind of faith. Jesus was traveling with a great crowd, when suddenly He stopped and said, "Who touched me?" The disciples couldn't believe His question. The mob surrounding them was pushing, shoving, jostling, and trying any way they could to get close to Jesus. "Lord, you've got to be kidding," was Peter's response. "Everybody's pushing and shoving you, and you ask, 'Who touched me?' Everybody within 10 yards!" Jesus replied, "No, I felt power go forth out of me."

When she knew she could not hide what she'd done, the woman came forward and knelt before Him, trembling, and confessed that for twelve years she had been hemorrhaging. She had spent all her money on doctors but had gotten no better. She believed that if she could just touch the hem of His garment, she would be healed. So she made her way through the crowd until she got close enough to touch Him, and immediately her hemorrhaging ceased. She was healed. Jesus said to her, "Be of good cheer, daughter; your faith has made you well" (see Matthew 9:20-22; Mark 5:25-34). That could be classified as the faith to be healed.

I believe healing faith is related to and associated with what 1 Corinthians 12 calls the gift of faith. This gift of faith is related many times to healing and miracles. It cannot be mere coincidence that the gift of faith appears right next to the gifts of healing in Paul's list (verse 9). Many times there is a close relationship between the gift of faith and the gifts of healing.

Who Needs Faith?

Jesus spoke of the tremendous potential of faith in Mark 11. The Master was traveling to Jerusalem. He was hungry, He saw a fig tree, and He went over to it to get some fruit. But when He reached the tree He discovered it bore only leaves. So He cursed it.

The next day as He and His disciples passed by the tree, Peter noticed it had already withered and died. "Rabbi, look! The fig tree which You cursed," he said, "has withered away." Jesus answered, "Have faith in God. For assuredly, I say to you, that whoever says to this mountain, 'Be removed and be cast into the sea,' and does not doubt in his heart, but believes that those things he says will came to pass, he will have whatever he says. Therefore I say to you, whatever things you ask when you pray, believe that you receive them, and you will have them" (Mark 11:21-24).

What a tremendous promise! There are people who read Mark 11:21-24 and think it gives them carte blanche for anything they want. They get all excited over this potential of faith, and they begin to advocate that believers can have anything they desire—a new Mercedes, a new mansion, whatever! The sky's the limit; write your own ticket.

Yet it's important that we notice to whom the promise was made. Jesus was talking to His disciples. And what constitutes discipleship? He said, "If anyone desires to come after Me, let him deny himself, and take up his cross daily, and follow Me" (Luke 9:23).

God hasn't given us faith so that we can live a sumptuous, luxurious life. Faith is not a blank check to give us all that our flesh might desire. That is the furthest thing in the world that God wants for us; that would only destroy us. Jesus is talking in Mark 11 to His disciples who had denied themselves to take up their crosses in order to follow Him. To them alone is this promise made.

It therefore follows that you cannot use this faith for selfish enrichment. Faith has always been the key that opens the door for the work of God in the world. No one ever had greater faith than Jesus, or accomplished more than He did, yet He ended His earthly life on a cross and not in a Mercedes.

A Time for Special Faith

There are times in our lives when God gives us special faith for a unique circumstance. We become aware of the certainty that God will undertake for us, and we speak with assurance because we know it will be done. God gives us such faith so that we're not worried, we're not concerned, and we know there's no problem. We know God will take care of everything.

There are several things in my life at this very moment that concern others but are no great concern to me. God has given me faith to know that He's going to take care of them all. Yet there are other things that do concern me because, as yet, He hasn't given me such faith for them. Like the other spiritual gifts, faith is not a reservoir that I can tap at will; it is given by the sovereign will of God.

Many years ago after a Sunday morning service, some young people wheeled their grandfather up the aisle to where I was standing. They asked me to pray for him. Since he was in a wheelchair, I assumed they wanted him healed so he could walk. So I prayed, "Lord, you are a great God—you can do anything. It's nothing for you to help, whether we are weak or strong. Help us, Lord. We ask now that You would touch this man and that you would heal him. I pray in the name of our Lord Jesus Christ, the name above all names." While I was praying I had a very strong urge to lift the man up out of his wheelchair and to command him to walk.

Now, I admit that I had an argument with the Lord. I thought, *Lord, is that you telling me to do this? Is it really you?* And I hesitated; I was uncertain. I don't normally go around lifting people out of wheelchairs. Yet it was such a strong impression I finally did it. The Lord gave me the faith to ask that the man be healed and then command him to walk.

When I said, "Amen," I lifted the man to his feet and said, "Now, in the name of Jesus, walk." And the man began to walk (much to my great relief!). He walked up the aisle and then trotted back. His grandkids got so excited they were almost doing handstands. They exclaimed, "Oh! He had a cold and we wanted you to pray that God would heal his cold! He hasn't walked in over five years!" I was glad they hadn't told me that before and I thought, *Why weren't you more specific?*

Later that same week, on a Wednesday night, I was in Tucson, Arizona, speaking in a church that I pastored years ago. After the service a man came up to the front, pushing his wife in a wheelchair. She had suffered a stroke and he wanted me to pray that God would heal her so she could walk again. Of course, I immediately thought of the previous Sunday morning. I laid hands on her and prayed that God would heal her. I tried to pray the same prayer I had prayed on Sunday. I wracked my brain, thinking *Now, what did I say?* When I was through I patted her on the shoulder, encouraged her to continue to trust the Lord, and watched her husband wheel her out of the church. My son, Chuck, Jr., who had been with me the previous Sunday morning, asked, "Dad, why didn't you lift her out of the chair like you did the guy last Sunday morning?" And I replied, "Son, the Lord didn't give me the faith to do it."

If the Lord doesn't give you the faith to do it, I strongly recommend that you don't do it. The healing on Sunday was a gift of faith for that moment and for that situation. Such faith doesn't always come; it isn't there in every situation. And that is why you are able to recognize it as a gift of God.

Faith is a gift of the Spirit endowing you with the confidence that God is going to work in a specific instance. Such faith is planted there by God. It is a gift of the Spirit and it's glorious when it happens: I only wish it would happen more often. But the Holy Spirit is sovereign in the bestowing of these gifts, and so I am thankful when God gives to me the gift of faith for a certain situation.

Faith for a Specific Situation

This was just as true in Bible days as it is today. Even for the apostles, this faith wasn't there for every situation. It came on special occasions, according to God's sovereign grace and God's sovereign work. The apostles did not heal all the sick people whom they encountered.

Paul, the apostle, seemed to have the gift of faith as well as the gift of miracles. To the church in Jerusalem, he testified of the miracles that God had wrought among the gentiles through him. In Ephesus they even took Paul's sweat bands and laid them on sick people, who were then healed. Yet we read of Paul telling Timothy to drink a little wine for his stomach problems (1 Timothy 5:23); he speaks of his friend Epaphroditus who was sick almost unto death (Philippians 2:25-27); we read that he leaves Trophimus at Miletus because he was sick (2 Timothy 4:20). We even read of Paul's own thorn in the flesh. Three times he asked the Lord to remove it, but the Lord refused. Instead, Paul received God's abounding and all-sufficient grace (2 Corinthians 12:7-10; see also Galatians 4:13, 14).

This isn't faith that allows you to go out whenever you want and do whatever you want. These gifts remain the property of the Holy Spirit, who divides to each man severally as He will (1 Corinthians 12:11). I don't suddenly become a gifted man with the gift of healing so I can go around and cure anybody whenever I want. Rather, at special times and in circumstances that are in God's control, He manifests the power of the Holy Spirit through our lives.

Faith can't be worked up, though I have observed many people attempt to do so. It is isn't something that can be whipped into a frenzy until you achieve a higher state of believing. It comes as a gift; it's just there. Suddenly you have the faith to do it. Many times you wonder, *What am I doing?* But the Lord gives you the faith to go ahead and do what He's prompting you to do.

God, according to His sovereign purposes and sovereign will, can and does at various times manifest His power, His glory, and His ability. Those times of manifestation are always thrilling and exciting.

Suffering and Faith

Having great faith doesn't mean life will be a bed of roses. Remember that while Peter was delivered by angelic intervention, James was beheaded. It isn't that James had less faith; Peter ultimately was crucified upside down (according to church tradition).

Peter himself said, "Let those who suffer according to the will of God commit their souls to Him in doing good, as to a faithful Creator" (1 Peter 4:19). If you are suffering as a child of God, you are to believe that God is working out His purposes through it. You could pray, "I commit myself, Lord, to you. Work out your good purposes through these difficult experiences."

The author of Hebrews wrote of great men and women of faith who would not accept deliverance, "that they might obtain a better resurrection. Still others had trial of mockings and scourgings, yes, and of chains and imprisonment. They were stoned, they were sawn in two, were tempted, were slain with the sword. They wandered about in sheepskins and goatskins, being destitute, afflicted, tormented...." (Hebrews 11:35-37).

Now, wait a minute—*these* were men and women of great faith? Where are the Mercedes? Where are the jewels? Where are the Rolex watches? Something must be wrong here. But the writer isn't finished:

> ... of whom the world was not worthy. They wandered in deserts and mountains, in dens and caves of the earth. And all these, having obtained a good testimony through faith, did not receive the promise [the promise of the Messiah], God having provided something better for us, that they should not be made perfect apart from us (Hebrews 11:38-40).

The gift of faith will not keep you from all difficulties or sicknesses or problems. But it will provide something better for you: One day you will be made perfect. And that's worth waiting for.

Glory and Faith

Have you ever wondered why God chose faith to be the conduit through which we are saved? One reason is that it excludes boasting on our part. When we receive something by faith, it's clear that we haven't earned it. Faith shows that we are poor and needy and that God is rich and gracious.

God knows the tendency we have to desire glory, praise, and acknowledgement. It's a part of our nature—something that has been built in from early childhood. We want people to praise us.

When your child is standing on the table and says, "Watch me, Daddy, watch me!" and you turn and he jumps off the table, he wants you to say, "Wow! Big boy! My—that's great!" He wants you to admire his bravery, his courage in leaping off a high table. The problem is, this desire for praise is so strong that we also want to receive plaudits for things we don't do. We don't want to admit that we are needy, and one way of avoiding this is to pretend that we have no needs, and so we should be congratulated for our imaginary self-sufficiency.

God desires to receive the glory for the work only He can do. He does not want us receiving the glory that belongs to Him alone. Therefore, God does His works in such a way that man cannot take credit for them or receive glory from them.

This is why in Gideon's day, the Lord chose to rescue Israel from the Midianites with only a handful of soldiers. The Midianites had an army of more than 135,000 soldiers, and Israel raised an army of 32,000 to face them. But God said, "That's too many men." Gideon wasn't too sure about this, but God replied, "I know the hearts of these people, and if I deliver the Midianites into the hands of the 32,000, they will boast in what they have done. So go out and tell all of those men who are afraid to fight to go home." Gideon did so, and two-thirds of his army left, leaving him with 10,000 men. Then God said, "Gideon, you still have too many. I know the hearts of these people. If I deliver the Midianites into the hands of the 10,000, they will boast about what they have done. Get rid of some more of them." After a second reduction in his forces, Gideon was left with 300 men. This time God said, "Just the right number" (see Judges 7).

What was the Lord's purpose in using such a small force? That God might get the glory for what He did. Man is always trying to get glory for the work of God, and God doesn't appreciate that.

The same is true with faith, the gift of God. It isn't really *my* faith. If I have faith, it has been planted in my heart by God. "By grace you have been saved through faith, and *that not of yourselves. It is the gift of God*, not of works, lest anyone should boast" (Ephesians 2:8,9, emphasis added). God seeks to eliminate man's boasting.

To God be the glory, great things He has done! Let's give the glory to God and keep ourselves out of the picture.

Filling the Void

There is a tremendous need in our world for people to see the work and power of God. There's a great void in the hearts of men and women, and a great desire for the supernatural, planted there by God. Because so many churches deny the supernatural, people are turning to spiritism, satanism, eastern religions, and the New Age and channelers. They want to see some kind of evidence for the reality of the spirit world.

Through its faith, the early church demonstrated that Jesus had risen from the dead. I believe that the Lord once more wants to demonstrate that fact to the skeptical world around us. I pray that we might begin to walk in faith, that the world may see a fresh demonstration of the power of God and thereby be convinced of the reality of Jesus Christ, our risen Lord.

11

Hope for the Sick

To one is given . . gifts of healings by the same Spirit.
— 1 CORINTHIANS 12:8,9

My mother was a great woman of faith. From earliest childhood we were always taught that the Lord was the family physician. Whenever sicknesses of any kind struck us, the first treatment was always prayer. Of course, there were the practical things, too—the onion bags you wore on your chest to break up congestion, the flax poultices, etc. But whenever any of us began to get sick, we would go running home to mom and have her pray for us. We were taught to trust the Lord, and that God would heal.

My own children were raised in that same kind of environment. They were taught to trust the Lord for healing.

Now, I'm not opposed to doctors. That is one way God has provided for healing today. I have gone to doctors myself; I had my appendix removed after spending a week in fervent prayer and fasting, asking God to heal me. When He didn't, I had the doctor take it out.

I believe that God can and does use medical science today. God has given researchers much insight and knowledge of the human body, which has led to the design of useful drugs and operating procedures. If a person cannot be healed through prayer alone, then God has provided people with skills to diagnose and treat people.

Of course, when a doctor sews up a gash on your arm by putting in sutures, he's done all he can do. It's God who causes your flesh to repair itself. Doctors do what they can, but the actual healing comes from God.

That's the way it is with all healing.

Gifts, Not Gift

In 1 Corinthians 12:9 Paul tells us there are "gifts of healing." God seems to use certain people in helping others to believe that God will heal them. It is quite obvious that Peter had this gift—so much so that the sick would be set in the street so that his shadow would fall upon them and heal them. It is equally obvious that both Philip and Paul had this gift. We are told that people were cured even when they touched a handkerchief that had belonged to Paul.

It's important to see that these gifts are in the plural; the gifts of healing operate in different ways with different people.

My spiritual gift is that of teaching; I do not have the gift of healing. Yet for years I coveted the gifts of working miracles, faith, and healing. I would go out into the desert for prolonged periods of time, fasting and praying and waiting upon God for these gifts. In my earlier years, my ambition was to be a medical doctor, so I was interested in curing the ills of humanity. I had compassion for the sick.

When God called me into the ministry, I hoped that I could, through prayer, help a lot of people overcome their physical maladies. I knew that the gifts of the Spirit are divided to each person severally as He will, but I was hoping that it was His will that I might have these gifts. Yet it never happened, so I just committed it to the Lord.

Almost thirty years ago, however, I was conducting a Bible study in Laguna Beach at the home of some friends who had become quite interested in the subject of the Holy Spirit. I was living in Corona and commuting to Laguna Beach every Monday for these studies, which had become quite well-attended.

One evening a couple of ladies who had been deeply into the New Age movement came to the Bible study, brimming with excitement. The previous day they had driven to Los Angeles where Kathryn Kuhlman was conducting services in the Shrine Auditorium. They had seen several people healed miraculously through her ministry, and, as a result, they were genuinely converted to Christ. They were bubbling over in the joy of the Lord, and in the power of Jesus Christ that they had seen manifested in Los Angeles.

So dramatic were the changes in their lives that, as I drove home to Corona that night, I said, "Lord, if I only had the gift of healing, the gift of faith, I could see these kind of dramatic transformations." I hadn't spoken to the Lord about this for a long time and I was trying to convince Him that I ought to have these gifts. I told Him, "I understand why you didn't give this to me in the early years of my ministry. I realize that I would not have been able to handle it then. But I feel I've matured—what about *now*?"

Immediately I felt the Lord speak to my heart. "I've called you to teach My Word," He said. "Not all are teachers, not all have the gifts of healing." Once more, I was satisfied. I accepted His judgment and determined to do what God had enabled and gifted and called me to do. And for ten years I never talked to the Lord about it again.

But one night I was standing at the pulpit after an evening service in which there had been a beautiful move of the Spirit of God. Scores of people had streamed to the prayer room to be saved, while those who remained in the auditorium were swept up in a beautiful spirit of worship. As I stood at the pulpit, holding both sides and basking in what God had done for the people, enjoying the sweet flowing and moving of the Spirit as we worshiped and gave thanks, I said, "Lord, you've done so much here at Calvary Chapel. It's so exciting. There's probably only one aspect of the church in Acts that's missing: the gift of miracles and the gifts of healing. And although there are people who are being healed, and though we've seen a bunch of miracles, yet this is not quite what I read about in the book of Acts. And maybe, Lord . . . maybe, now I could handle it?" As I was standing there, the Lord again spoke to my heart. This time He said, "I have called you to the more excellent way."

He brought to mind what Paul had said in 1 Corinthians 12:31: "Earnestly desire the best gifts," which is what I thought I had been doing. But Paul goes on to say, "And yet I show you a more excellent way [than the gifts of healing or miracles]." And that is the gift of love. "Though I speak with the tongues of men and of angels, but have not love, it's meaningless. Though I have the gift of prophecy and I can understand all mysteries and have all knowledge and all faith—faith that could move mountains—if I don't have love, I'm nothing" (see 1 Corinthians 13:1-3).

You know what? I said, "Thank you, Lord. I'll walk and share your love." I haven't talked to the Lord about it since, and I don't expect to. Why should I settle for less when He has led me in the more excellent way?

Of course, I still pray for the sick. I believe in laying hands on them in the name of Jesus. I believe in anointing with oil—it's all scriptural. And some people are healed and some aren't. I leave that to God. I know I can't heal them; I know my own limitations. I might have great compassion and great empathy for the sick, but I can't heal them. All I can do is anoint the person, lay hands on them, and ask God to heal them. Then it's in God's court. I can't work up faith to heal. If God works and the faith is there, praise the Lord. But many times He doesn't work in this way.

I believe that any time you have been prayed for and have experienced healing, you have received a gift of healing. I do know I have been healed many, many times. So have my children. We have seen so many marvelous healings. But I, personally, don't have the gift. Nevertheless, God does heal.

Did the Gifts Cease?

There are those who say that the miraculous manifestations of God ceased with the apostles. They believe God gave the early church this supernatural power and these extraordinary manifestations to help get it started in a world that was antagonistic toward Jesus Christ. Because they did not have seminaries and great cathedrals, they needed a little boost to get started. These people say that now that we have great educational facilities and are well organized, we no longer need these divine manifestations of the Spirit. We can intellectually challenge unbelievers, and we can use our apologetics to convince the world of its need for Jesus Christ.

That might sound good in theory, but it hasn't worked out in practice. In a book called *The Ministry of Healing*, Dr. A.G. Gordon, the founder of the Christian Missionary and Alliance churches, reviews church history from earliest times. He shows that throughout church history there have been remarkable manifestations of healing among certain groups. Even John Wesley saw many people healed through believing prayer. Gordon concludes that to say healing ceased with the apostles is to deny what has been recorded by many reliable witnesses.

Beyond that, it doesn't seem consistent that God, who healed sicknesses in answer to believing prayer throughout biblical history—from Genesis to Revelation—would suddenly stop healing the sick. Surely no one can make a biblical case that God has ceased this ministry.

People *can* be healed today by the touch of God upon their lives. God is not limited, nor has He limited Himself. People who are sick can still be healed in response to believing prayer.

Old Testament Healings

Probably the first recorded healing is in Genesis 20, when Abraham went down to Philistia. There Abimelech desired his wife, and Abraham lied to protect himself, saying of Sarah, "She's my sister." When Abimelech took Sarah into his harem, God immediately plagued his wives and female servants so that none of them could conceive. One night the Lord spoke to Abimelech in a dream and said, "Abimelech, you're a dead man—you have the wife of another man in your harem." Abimelech replied, "Lord, I didn't know. How could I know? He said she was his sister."

Abimelech came to Abraham the next morning and said, "What have you done to me? She is not your sister, but your wife." Abraham replied, "I feared for my life because I knew she was beautiful. I thought you would see her and kill me so you could have her. That's why I said she was my sister." Abimelech answered, "Take your wife, and pray for me that God will heal me and my people." So Abraham prayed, "And God healed Abimelech, his wife, and his maidservants. Then they bore children" (Genesis 20:17).

In Exodus, God said to the children of Israel, "I am the Lord who heals you" (Exodus 15:26). He told them that if they would follow His laws and His statutes, He would put none of the diseases upon them that He had placed upon the Egyptians. As you study the biblical law, you will discover that it is really a health code. It deals with good hygiene and practical guidelines for health.

In Deuteronomy 32:39, God said, "Now see that I, even I, am He, and there is no God besides Me; I kill and I make alive; I wound and I heal; nor is there any who can deliver from My hand."

In Psalm 30:2 the psalmist declared, "O Lord my God, I cried out to You, and You have healed me." Later in Psalm 103 we are told to give thanks unto the Lord, "who forgives all your iniquities, and who heals all your diseases."

During the time of the kings, the Lord sent Isaiah to King Hezekiah with a message to set his house in order, for he was going to die. Hezekiah turned his face to the wall and began to plead with God. As Isaiah was leaving—before he even got out of the court—the Lord said, "Go back to Hezekiah and say to him that I have heard his prayer. I have seen his tears." Then the Lord promised that he was going to heal Hezekiah and give him another fifteen years of life (2 Kings 20:1-6).

Perhaps most significantly, when Isaiah was prophesying concerning the coming Savior, we read, "He was bruised for our iniquities; the chastisement for our peace was upon Him, and by His stripes we are healed" (Isaiah 53:5). I believe God was declaring prophetically that Jesus was going to suffer not only for our sins, but for our sicknesses; that He bore our sicknesses as well as our sins.

In the New Testament

The Gospel of Matthew describes how Jesus healed Peter's mother-in-law of a fever. That evening, from all around the area, many came to Peter's house, bringing with them the sick and those who were demon-possessed. Jesus cast out the spirits and healed all the sick, "that it might be fulfilled which was spoken by Isaiah the prophet, saying: *'He Himself took our infirmities and bore our sicknesses'*" (Matthew 8:16).

Without question, healing was a major part of the ministry of Christ. When He commissioned His disciples, He gave them power to cast out unclean spirits and to heal all kinds of sickness and disease. He told them, "Heal the sick, cleanse the lepers, raise the dead, cast out demons. Freely you have received, freely give" (Matthew 10:8). Two chapters later we are told that "great multitudes followed Him, and He healed them all" (Matthew 12:15). In chapter 14 we are told that when He saw the multitude, He was moved with compassion toward them and healed their sick. Matthew 15:30 declares that great multitudes came to Jesus, including the lame, blind, mute, maimed, and many others. The crowd "laid them down at Jesus' feet, and He healed them."

Jesus declared that His works of healing were signs of His relationship to the Father, that He and the Father were one. He said He was doing the work of the Father and that his healing ministry was, in fact, the work of the Father (see John 10:30-32).

Jesus commissioned His disciples to do the work He did, including the healing of the sick. That was a command, not a suggestion. And thus the healing of the sick was not only a great part of the ministry of Jesus, but of the ministry of the early church as well.

In Acts 4:30 the church asked the Lord to stretch forth His hand to heal. In Acts 5:16 we are told a multitude came to Jerusalem, and every one of the sick was healed. Acts 8 describes the remarkable healing ministry Philip had when he visited Samaria. Acts 28 describes the healing ministry of Paul on the island of Malta, how the Lord healed the island's governor through Paul, and then how the people began to bring their sick from all over the island for Paul to pray for their healing.

James asked, "Is anyone among you sick? Let him call for the elders of the church, and let them pray over him, anointing him with oil in the name of the Lord. And the prayer of faith will save the sick, and the Lord will raise him up" (James 5:14,15).

Throughout the New Testament—in many more passages than are cited here—there is both the promise and the experience of divine healing. It is a biblical given.

Why the Lack of Healing Today?

With such a biblical emphasis on physical healing, the question might well be asked, "If God healed in answer to prayer in the Old Testament; and the healing of the sick was such an integral part of the ministry of Jesus; and God continued to heal the sick throughout the recorded history of the church in the New Testament; then why do we not see more divine healing today?"

As I've stated, I don't believe God ever stopped healing the sick. I believe the lack of miraculous healing today lies more in the failure of man's faith than in the reluctance of a compassionate God to meet His children's needs. The reason we don't see much healing today is our general skepticism.

We are told that when Jesus came to Nazareth, His hometown, He could not do many marvelous works there. Why? Because of their unbelief. They were skeptical of Him because they knew Him only as a man. They said, "Is this not the carpenter's son?...Where then did this Man get all these things?" (Matthew 13:55,56). Because of their skepticism, He was hindered from doing the divine work of the Spirit in healing the sick.[1]

On another occasion the disciples were unable to cast out a demon from a boy. When they asked Jesus how this could be, He told them, "Because of your unbelief; for assuredly, I say to you, if you have faith as a mustard seed, you will say to this mountain, 'Move from here to there,' and it will move; and nothing will be impossible for you" (Matthew 17:20).

The reason why people aren't healed as often today as they seemed to be in the past can be traced to general unbelief. The fault is not God's, but ours.

A second, related question also could be asked: "Why do we not see more people in the church today with the gift of healing?"

I believe one of the reasons is that there have been far too many people trying to capitalize on this gift in order to enrich themselves. Certain celebrities have gained great personal wealth through their healing crusades. I don't claim they're frauds; their gifts may be real. My concern is that they use the gifts for their own monetary gain.

This is an extreme danger for anyone who has the gifts of healing. It is so easy to be lifted up in the flesh and to be encouraged to take advantage of the gift. But the gifts of healing were not given for our personal enrichment; they were given for the benefit of the church, and that people outside the church might be prompted to investigate for themselves the reality of Jesus Christ.

Why Isn't Everyone Healed?

Another question raised is: "Why isn't everybody healed? Why is it that some people are healed and some are not?" I'll give you my answer: I don't know. There are a lot of things that I don't understand about divine healing.

It's interesting to recall that Paul, an apostle who possessed the gifts of healing, was himself sick. He mentions his sicknesses to the Galatians, and reminds them how sick he was. He said, "You know that because of physical infirmity I preached the gospel to you at the first. . . . I bear you witness that, if possible, you would have plucked out your own eyes and given them to me" (Galatians 4:13,15).

In 2 Corinthians 12 Paul also mentions his "thorn in the flesh," and in 1 Timothy 5:23 he encouraged Timothy, his "son in the faith," to use a little wine for his stomach problems. Now, surely Paul had prayed for Timothy. I cannot believe that

Paul didn't lay hands on him several times and pray that God would heal this stomach disorder. But evidently God didn't see fit to heal him, so the apostle suggested a practical remedy— something along the lines of, "Don't drink the water in Mexico; you never know what's swimming around in that stuff. So drink wine instead."

Remember also that in Philippians 2:25-30, Paul tells how Epaphroditus almost died from an illness. In 2 Timothy 4:20 he says "Trophimus I have left in Miletus sick."

Why does God sometimes heal in response to believing prayer, and sometimes not? I don't know. I do know that many times people think they have developed a kind of formula about how to touch a person, where to touch them, and how to read body language. Some people have even developed seminars on healing. I find it interesting that some of those who have conducted such seminars get sick themselves. Just when you think you have all of the answers, God shows you that you don't. Healing doesn't come through a formula.

The only explanation I can give for lack of healing is that the Holy Spirit is sovereign not only in the bestowing of a gift, but also in its operation. If you have the gifts of healing, you can't pray for anyone you want whenever you want and always see them healed. As you pray for the sick, God will heal some, but there will be others who won't be healed. I do not believe we will ever know why some are healed and why others aren't; that is information God keeps to Himself.

The truth is, some of the most godly, holy, righteous people I know of suffer infirmities and die of cancer, while other horribly wicked people live in perfect health until the day they die of natural causes. We'll never understand the ways of God, and how He chooses to parcel out miracles of healing.

I think it can be a great witness to say, "I've prayed, I've asked the Lord for healing, and I know He can heal me, yet He has not seen fit to do so. I know He has a purpose and a plan for my sickness, and thus I've committed myself to His plan and to His will. He knows what's best, and I will rest in that. I'm not upset or frantic because I'm not healed. I'm just committed to Him." As Peter said, "let those who suffer according to the will of God commit their souls to Him in doing good, as to a faithful Creator" (1 Peter 4:19). It takes tremendous faith to say, "It's all in the Lord's hands, and He's doing what He knows to be best." Many times this is the greater miracle.

Hope for the Sick

It is my prayer that God would impart the gifts of healing to many people within the church. I believe it would help complete the ministry of the Spirit in and through the church, and that the church would profit and benefit through the exercise of this marvelous gift.

If you are sick, I encourage you to pray and to believe and trust God for your healing. I know that God can heal you, and I encourage you to trust in Him for that healing. Let medical science do what it can, but know that it has its limitations. God is not limited, however, and God is able to do exceedingly and abundantly above all that we ask or think. Trust in God and believe in God for your healing.

He does heal.

12

The Hardest Gift
to Possess

To one is given ... the workings of miracles.
—1 CORINTHIANS 12:8,10

Today we have a good understanding of certain basic laws of nature—of electromagnetism and gravity for example. By observing how these laws operate in our universe, we have harnessed great powers for our benefit. When a huge 747 jet rises into the air, it's not a miracle to us; it's simply the result of understanding the laws of aerodynamics.

But what if the apostle Paul saw a 747 taking off? Wouldn't he think it was a miracle? He'd say, "That can't happen! You can't get something that big into the air." But we have learned how air flowing over an air foil creates lift. Thus we seem able to defy the law of gravity by utilizing other natural laws.

Of course, we don't know all the natural laws. God, however, is master of natural laws that we can't even imagine. So when He does something we can't explain we say, "What a miracle! That's impossible—that can't be." But God is only using laws He invented. For Him, miracles are easy.

You might say a miracle is something that is humanly impossible but divinely simple. Difficulty must always be measured by the capacity of the agents doing the work. When God is the agent doing the work, talk of difficulty is absurd. Paul the apostle said to King Agrippa, "Why should it be thought incredible by you that God raises the dead?" (Acts 26:8). It's no problem for God to raise the dead. He was the One who breathed life into Adam when Adam was just inanimate matter, lifeless mud. It wasn't incredible at all; it was easy. God has been active performing such miracles for a long, long time.

The First Miracle

The Bible is full of miracles and probably the most awesome is found in the first verse. "In the beginning God created the heavens and the earth." If you believe that, you shouldn't have any trouble with the rest of the Bible. An omnipotent God, big enough to fashion the entire universe, is big enough to do anything.

Sadly, there are those who do not believe in miracles or in the supernatural. They believe that everything can be explained through natural phenomena.

They tell quite a story about gases in space that were compressed so tightly they finally exploded in a "Big Bang" some 15 billion years ago. Earth and the solar system were formed out of the blast, and, somehow, lightning striking the ammonia and hydrogen in earth's early atmosphere caused a chemical reaction in some primordial ooze, creating little cells complete with an internal code that enabled them to replicate themselves. Over millions of years, and through countless series of mutations, we arrived at us—with our ability to see and to think and to feel, and our body's wondrous capacity to create the exotic chemicals and hormones that make life possible. According to this story, we are the result of an impossibly long series of marvelous accidents and mutations. So here we are today—not a miracle at all. It's easily explained.

My granddaughter loves to hear about the beautiful princess who visited a pond where a friendly little frog liked to swim over, hop up, and croak to her. Every time she went to the pond, that kindly, sweet little frog would look so pitifully at her and croak. One day on impulse she thought, *Oh, you're a sweet little frog*, and kissed it—and it turned into a handsome prince! It seems that long ago the frog was a boy, but some wicked witch had put a spell upon him. The only way he could become a prince again would be for some beautiful princess to kiss him, but the witch had made him so ugly that she figured it would never happen. But it did! And in a flash he turned from a frog into a prince. Soon he married the princess and they lived happily ever after. Marvelous!

Of course, my granddaughter doesn't really believe the story; she likes it, but she doesn't really believe it. She likes it because it's a story, yet she's wise enough to know that frogs don't turn into handsome princes.

What a tragedy that this is exactly what many well-educated people do believe! Only they don't think it happened instantaneously; they believe it took millions upon millions of years. And after billions of fortuitous concurrences of accidental circumstances, that ugly primordial ooze turned into you and me. It's amazing what people will believe when they don't want to believe in God!

A faulty concept of God is the only reason for trying to explain away the miracles of the Bible. If your concept of God is narrow and limited—if you hold that God can operate only within the laws of nature that we presently know, and refuse to recognize that God is the One who created and formed the laws of nature—then you will have to explain away the Bible's miracles. Once you accept the God of the Bible, however, miracles are not a problem.

Old Testament Miracles

The life of Moses is dotted with miracles. It was Moses who brought the ten plagues upon Egypt and it was through him that God parted the Red Sea.[1] While the nation wandered in the wilderness, Moses struck the rock and water came gushing forth. All of these were supernatural happenings.

Joshua also had the gift of working miracles. We read of the Jordan River piling up in a heap and the children of Israel passing over on dry ground. We read of the walls of Jericho falling after they had been encircled by the Hebrew army thirteen times in seven days. And we read of the "long day" when Joshua had Israel's enemies on the run and God stopped the sun in its tracks so that it did not go down for almost a day.

Elijah also had the gift of working miracles. He prayed and it didn't rain for three years. He prayed again, and it poured. He was fed miraculously through this drought—first by the ravens, who twice a day brought him his food by the brook Cherith, and later by a widow whose nearly exhausted supplies of oil and flour were miraculously replenished day after day until the drought ended.

Then we think of Elisha, Elijah's successor, whose recorded miracles are twice those of his teacher. We remember how he parted the Jordan River with Elijah's mantle, how he healed the bitter waters of Jericho, how he raised to life the Shulamite's dead son, how he made the ax head float.

In Isaiah we learn how the sundial went backward as a testimony that God was going to heal Hezekiah. In Daniel we read of the three Hebrew boys who walked around in the middle of a blazing furnace, and we hear of Daniel spending the night in a den full of hungry lions whose mouths and claws were put out of action by angels. The Old Testament is full of miracles.

New Testament Miracles

The life of Jesus boasts scores of miracles, beginning with His virgin birth. We read how, at the feast in Cana, He began His ministry by turning water into wine. We learn how He healed the nobleman's son from a distance; how He raised from the dead at least three people, including the son of the widow from Nain, the daughter of Jairus, and His own friend Lazarus (who had been buried for four days). We hear how He fed the multitudes with five loaves of bread and two fish; and later we read how He walked on the water.

The book of Acts is crammed with miracles. In fact, if you take the miracles out of that book, there's not much left. We read of Peter being released from prison by an angel. We are told that signs and wonders were wrought through Stephen. We remember how Philip's missionary trip to Samaria was accompanied by amazing miracles.

Peter and Paul surely had the gift of the working of miracles. Peter raised Dorcas from the dead, and even his shadow falling upon the sick healed them. Paul's life seemed to be overflowing with miracles, from healing a pagan governor to raising Eutychus from the dead to suffering no ill effects from the bite of a venomous snake. Miracles were part and parcel of both their ministries.

Are Miracles for Today?

Does God work miracles today, or did all miracles cease with the last of the apostles? This is a question that has occupied theologians for many years. I counter with my own question: "Is God dead?" A miracle is a supernatural happening. If God is still alive and still working, then there will be supernatural happenings, and, thus, the days of miracles cannot be over.

Salvation is a miracle. When the rich young ruler, who came to Jesus seeking the way of salvation, finally went away sorrowful, Jesus turned to His disciples and said, "It is hard for a rich man to enter the kingdom of heaven.... It is easier for a camel to go through the eye of a needle than for a rich man to enter the kingdom of God." The astonished disciples replied, "Who then can be saved?" Jesus answered, "With men this is impossible, but with God all things are possible" (Matthew 19:23-26).

If a miracle is achieving something that is humanly impossible, then salvation is a miracle because it is humanly impossible for man to save himself. So to say that the days of miracles are over would be to deny that people can be saved today. Thank God that the days of miracles are not over; He is still in the business of working miracles.

I have seen countless miracles in the form of the transformed lives of men and women who were written off by society as hopeless, of no value. I have seen changes occur through the miracle of God's grace, changes the people could not bring about themselves, though they had tried so hard.

Most of us have experienced miracles of this sort. Think of an area in your life where you sought long and hard to have victory, yet found yourself defeated. Finally you gave up and determined that it couldn't be done, so you let God take over—and God did it. That's a supernatural happening. That's a miracle you've experienced in your life.

Does Anyone Have the Gift?

But are there people today who have the *gift* of the working of miracles? It is possible, although I don't personally know of any who have the real gift. I freely admit that we do not seem to be witnessing this gift today like they did in Bible times. The question then is, Whose fault is this? Is it God's fault or is it man's fault? Has God ceased bestowing this gift of the working of miracles?

I don't believe He has, but I also believe it would be extremely difficult for any person to possess the gift of working of miracles today. One reason is that the pressure to prostitute the gift would be tremendous. It would take a depth of commitment, of death to self, that I just don't observe in people today. I doubt there are many people in the world today whom God could entrust with this gift. Why not?

The first danger would be to use the gift for personal benefit. This is basically what Satan suggested to Jesus in the wilderness. After the Lord had fasted for 40 days, Satan came to Him and said, "If You are the Son of God, command this stone to become bread." In other words, "Use your miraculous powers to satisfy your own physical needs; use them in order to satisfy the flesh." But Jesus refused to do so. He said, "It is written, 'Man shall not live by bread alone, but by every word that proceeds from the mouth of God'" (Matthew 4:4).

Second, there is the danger of taking the glory yourself for what God has done. If you seem to be the instrument through which a miracle is accomplished, people are all too ready to put you on a pedestal. They look up to you in awe as some kind of mighty person of God. There is danger in accepting such adulation.

People often want to respond to the instrument more than they do to God. They are so grateful for what God has done, they want to reward the person God uses. In my own ministry, people have actually come up to me and said, "Can I touch you?" or "Please, pet my dog. He appreciates it so much."

When God used Peter to heal the lame man lying near the temple, Peter was quick to tell the adoring crowds, "Ye men of Israel, why marvel ye at this or why look ye so earnestly on us, as though by our own power or holiness we had made this man to walk?" (Acts 3:12 KJV). It was a mild rebuke, as if he had said, "You men of Israel, you worship the God of Israel who is the God of miracles. So why should you marvel at this? After all, He's the God who created the universe. Nothing is too hard for Him. Then why do you look on us as though we, through our own righteousness, have done this good deed? We're not the ones who should be capturing your attention." Immediately Peter pointed the people to Jesus Christ. The crowd was ready to exalt Peter for the miracle, but the apostle had enough wisdom not to take the glory from God. I think many modern-day evangelists would have passed the offering plate.

A similar thing happened to Paul. Through the apostle, God healed a 40-year-old lame man who had never walked. When the people of Lystra saw it, they said, "The gods have come down!" and they ran up the street to the temple of Jupiter, grabbed the priest and asked him, "Man, what are you doing here? Jupiter is down the street and he brought Mercury with him!" So the priest came dragging an ox to sacrifice to Paul and Barnabas.

It would have been easy for Paul and Barnabas to think, *All right! We've got them in the palm of our hands. Let's allow them* to think we're gods! Let's manipulate them—we'll ultimately get them around to the Lord, but in the meantime we can get a pretty good laugh. But they were unwilling to do that. They insisted they were only men, they tore their clothes in protest, and only with great difficulty were they able to restrain the crowd from sacrificing to them (see Acts 14:8-18).

Unless a person has come to the place where he does not have personal ambition or personal desires for glory, one of the worst things in the world would be for God to give him the gift of working miracles. It could absolutely destroy him. It's not an easy gift to have.

The Impediment of Skepticism

Other things also work against having this gift. First among them is our rationalistic world. All of us are affected by it; it's in our educational system, and has permeated our thinking, though we have tried to steel ourselves against it. It has infiltrated to such a degree that we just don't believe God will work miracles.

Let me give an example. I have a fairly good understanding of mechanics—good enough that I can't pray for my car to start when the battery is dead. I know enough that I can't pray, "Oh God, let it start this time." On the other hand, my wife knows nothing about mechanics, and she can pray that the car will start. So we sit there and she says, "Honey, just try it once more."

"It won't work," I insist. "It just can't start. I know it can't."

"Try it once more. Just try it."

"Why? There's no sense in trying it; I've tried it! The battery's dead. You don't understand."

"But try it!"

So I turn the key...and the thing starts up.

Our rationalistic minds work against believing in the supernatural. Jesus asked, "When the Son of Man comes, will He find faith on the earth?" (Luke 18:8). All of us would respond, "Oh, yes, Lord. Here we are! We believe, we believe." But I think there are definite limitations to our belief, expressed even in how we pray.

Some things are easy to pray for. You have a headache? No problem, I can pray for a headache. "Lord, please take that headache away. In the name of Jesus. Thank you, Father." And if the prayer doesn't work, take an aspirin. Easy. But then a parent comes into your office. "We just got the reports back," she says. "Our child has leukemia. Would you pray for her?" Leukemia—oh, my. Bone cancer—oh, no! You've *really* got to pray for leukemia; one of those little "Please, Lord, thank You in the name of Jesus" prayers doesn't work. This is serious. So you get on your knees and plead, "Oh, Lord, Lord God Almighty, Thou who rulest from Heaven..." And you offer your most heavy-duty prayer.

We have a tendency to carry over our limitations to God. We can't seem to escape it. What seems to be a simple thing for us, we figure is simple for God; what seems to be a difficult thing for us, must be a little tough for God; and what is impossible for us, we imagine is impossible for God.

Imagine that a Vietnam veteran who had his arm blown off asked you to pray that God would give him a new arm. What would you say to him? "Well, friend, I'll tell you what— God will probably give you greater dexterity in the arm that you've got. Some things we have to learn to live with. God just doesn't put new arms on people." Do you know that if you cut an earthworm in half, it will grow a new half? Cut a leg off an octopus and it will grow a new leg. So does God love octopuses and worms more than He does us? Would He do it for them, but not for us?

We do have our limitations, and I confess I'm in that group. I could not, in faith, believe that God would give a person a new arm. I just could not do that. It's not that I don't believe God *could* do it; I just don't believe God *would* do it. Don't misunderstand—that's a confession of my lack of faith. I'm not proud of it. I wish I did have the kind of faith that could pray, believing that God would give a person a new arm.

No doubt part of the reason for this lack of faith is the amount of fraud today concerning the working of miracles. There are those who would like you to think they have the genuine gift. They seek to deceive people into thinking they have the great power of God at work in their lives when they really don't. So often these people have a rationale. They say it helps increase people's faith. They use the old argument that the end justifies the means—but you'll never find any scriptural support for such stance.

One of our assistant pastors is also a newspaper columnist. Some time ago, he attended a healing meeting in Philadelphia. The first person in the healing line was an elderly man. Several tubes connected to an oxygen tank were close to the man's face, and the evangelist made quite a show over the tank and the tubes. The evangelist prayed for the man, who then took the tubes out and removed the tank. Then the evangelist told the man to run up the aisle. The old fellow scampered up the aisle and back again. The evangelist then asked, "How do you feel?" "Oh, I feel great!" the old man replied. The place went wild.

As this elderly man and his wife were going to their car after the meeting, my friend said to them, "Wait a minute. I need to talk to you about what happened tonight." The lady replied, "Oh, does the evangelist want us to rent the oxygen tank for tomorrow night, too?" My friend answered, "No, no. I just wanted to interview you about your husband." It turned out that the tank and the tubes were a one-time rental; the whole thing had been staged. They said the man really was healed earlier, but crusade officials wanted to stage it again to build the faith of the audience. But that's fraud. Unfortunately, there are a lot of fraudulent things done in the name of the Lord that are excused by the argument that they build people's faith. I can't buy it.

God doesn't need gimmicks. He doesn't need us to put on acts to convince people of His power. He is fully able to do the miraculous without our puny help.

Too Many Distractions

Another thing that hinders our possessing the gift of working miracles is our shallow relationship with God. Our modern age suffers from a great lack of depth in our walk with the Lord.

Many distractions work against a deep, substantial relationship. Jesus said that in the last days, the love of most would grow cold (Matthew 24:12). He warned about the traps that would hinder a deep relationship with Himself. He mentioned the cares of this life: the pressures of making a living, the deceitfulness of riches, and the desire for more and more things (see Matthew 13:3-23).

Our electronic age brings further distractions. Television, telephones, and radios constantly flood our minds with all kinds of stimuli and ideas, gobbling up time we might have spent in meditation upon God.

We are living in an age when man has become very, very broad, but not very deep. Through the mass media we can now broach many subjects. We know a little about everything, but not much about anything. We're shallow. And our relationship with God has suffered as a result.

In many ways, the days of the apostles were far superior to our own. More readily than today, they were able to have the kind of communion and fellowship with God that creates character God can use. Think about Paul, the apostle, when he walked from Jerusalem to Caesarea, about a three-day journey. He wasn't listening to music or keeping up on the local news. He was surrounded by nature—by the trees, the flowers, the animals. At night he would wrap himself in his blanket and look up at the stars. How could he not think about God and His creation and His works? Solitude is very conducive to communion with God, to meditation on God.

Today, if you go from Jerusalem to Caesarea, you don't walk, you drive. You're desperately trying to figure out what some Hebrew word says, and you're intently watching the traffic. They drive like crazy, so you've got to keep alert. You've got so much stimuli coming into your brain that you can't commune with God and have a time of real spiritual enrichment. In fact, the trip works against spirituality. You arrive tense because you've just had two close misses. *That crazy nut, I'd like to punch him out. He forced me off the road! He had no business trying to pass me with that other car coming. If I had not pulled off, there would have been a real smash-up. That idiot put my life in jeopardy and I'd like to really teach him a lesson or two*—all of these thoughts are in your mind, which means you can't be meditating on God and His love and His eternal plan.

Our whole society and manner of living has taken us away from simplicity. We are not as close to God as the saints of old, and that may be one reason why we do not see the gift of miracles as much in evidence today as it was back then.

A Possible Exception

If there is anyone I have ever met who may have possessed the gift of the working of miracles, it was a simple native woman from New Guinea. She lives in the jungle and leads a very simple life. As I sat on the grass and heard of the things God had done in and through her life, my heart burned. Quite an astounding testimony was given of how God had used her to do one miracle after another—marvelous things, such as the raising of the dead and the opening of blind eyes.

All were confirmed to us by the local missionary. God used her to start a school, which I visited. She herself had never attended school, but she started one because the Lord directed her to. I saw hundreds of students being trained there, all because of a simple woman who sat on the grass nursing her baby, and told me about the things God was doing through her life.

That woman has the advantage of not living in a society so filled with stimuli that her mind has no time to meditate deeply on God. I was amazed. I thought, *Oh God, I wish I could share this with the world.* I've earnestly wanted to return to the jungle and take with me a TV camera so I could film her whole story. If ever I have met anyone who had the gift of working miracles, it was this simple native.

Seek the Gift

God is working, and we can expect miracles whenever He does so. The Bible tells us to covet earnestly the best gifts, and surely this gift would qualify as one of the best—especially in the area of evangelism. That is where the gift was used primarily in the New Testament; it attracted people to the gospel and offered proof of the gospel's truth.

I encourage you to covet earnestly the gift of the working of miracles. It would take quite a bit of preparation to possess, but I don't believe it is out of reach or out of the question. I would love to see the hand of God at work among His children in a greater measure. And I believe that God desires to do it. So what hinders Him? I think we are the stumbling blocks; we are the ones who have clogged the flow of the Spirit in that realm.

Will we see this gift in operation before the Lord returns? Possibly. And if God should see fit, and the Holy Spirit should sovereignly will that this gift be manifested in the church, I for one would rejoice and be glad. We could use a few more miracles.

13

Speaking Forth
the Word of God

To one is given ... prophecy.

T he gift of prophecy is speaking forth the word of God through the anointing of the Holy Spirit. It is being a channel through which the Lord may speak.

We are told that God, in sundry times and in diverse manners, spoke to our fathers by the prophets (Hebrews 1:1). Peter tells us that prophecy came not in old times by the will of man, but holy men of God spoke as they were moved by the Holy Spirit (2 Peter 1:21).

Despite common belief, prophecy is not only foretelling the future. Most of prophecy is forthtelling, or speaking forth the word of God. In fact, the gift of prophecy as it was practiced in the early church was more often used for edification, for exhortation, and for comfort than it was for predicting future events (see 1 Corinthians 14:3).

Prophecy in the Old Testament

Prophecy was a common gift in the Old Testament. Moses was a prophet, and served as God's spokesman to the people. He gave God's guidance and instruction to his fellow Israelites. Most of what he said was God's direction for Israel's ongoing relationship with God, announcing those things that pleased God and that were required of them to live in fellowship with Him.

Of course, some of what Moses said was predictive. The psalm of Moses in Deuteronomy 32, for example, predicted that when the Israelites turned away from the Lord and followed other gods, they would be forsaken by God, be driven out of the land, scattered among the heathen, and become a curse and a byword.

Centuries after the song had been written, its truth suddenly hit the Israelites. As they sang "if we forsake the Lord, then we'll be scattered and be captive," they looked around at their Babylonian captors and finally realized their hardships had come upon them because they had forsaken God. That was the whole purpose of the song, so that one day, when its predictive aspects came to pass, they would get the message.

David is listed in Acts 2:30 as another prophet of God. Many of his psalms speak of the Messiah to come. The New Testament often quotes them, and says they were fulfilled in the life of Jesus. But, for the most part, his psalms were not predictive—they simply expressed praise to God.

Elijah and Elisha are other well-known prophets, yet most of what they said was not recorded in Scripture. They were God's spokesmen, warning the king and the people of God's coming judgment. At times, they were themselves the instrument of God's judgment upon the nation.

The Old Testament includes both the "major prophets" and the "minor prophets." Generally, all these prophets sought to call the nation back to its commitment to God. They warned of the consequences should the Israelites continue in their unrighteousness and apostasy, and often directed their prophecies against the surrounding nations—against Babylon, Edom, Tyre, Moab, and Egypt. While we can see historically how many of these prophecies came to pass, some remain to be fulfilled.

New Testament Prophecy

Even as there were pastors and evangelists and apostles in the New Testament church, so there was the office of prophet. Agabus was one of these prophets. Acts 11:27,28 says, "In these days came prophets from Jerusalem up to Antioch. And there stood up one of them named Agabus, and signified by the Spirit that there should be great death throughout all the world: which came to pass in the days of Claudius caesar" (KJV). In Acts 21:10,11 this same prophet came to Caesarea and predicted the bonds and imprisonment that awaited Paul in Jerusalem.

Acts 13:1,2 also says, "Now there were in the church that was at Antioch certain prophets and teachers" (KJV). Usually these men also served as pastors. Acts 15:32 says, "And Judas and Silas, being prophets also themselves, exhorted the brethren with many words, and confirmed them" (KJV). And Paul, in Ephesians 4:11, wrote, "And he gave some apostles and some prophets and some evangelists and some pastors and teachers."

Paul wrote to Timothy not to neglect the gifts which he had received through prophecy and the laying on of hands of the eldership (1 Timothy 4:14). It would seem that the early church would lay hands on people after a time of fasting and prayer, and those who exercised the office of a prophet would prophesy. Many times they would prophesy the gifts that God was bestowing upon the individual or speak of something pertaining to his life or to his ministry.

In today's church, we have pastors, teachers, and evangelists, and though I am not certain that we have apostles, it would seem that we should also have prophets: "And God hath set some in the church, first apostles, secondarily prophets [right under the apostles]..." (1 Corinthians 12:28 KJV).

In Scripture, women as well as men occupy the office of prophet. Miriam, the sister of Moses, was called a prophetess, as was Deborah and Huldah. Also belonging to the Old Testament period is Anna, the eighty-year-old woman who prophesied about Jesus when, as a baby, He was brought to the temple.

The New Testament also recognizes women prophets. The daughters of Philip were called prophetesses, and Paul, the apostle, gives rules to the women who were exercising the gift of prophecy in the church of Corinth.[1]

Now, if God placed both Old and New Testament women in the office of prophet, I see no reason why He wouldn't also call women to the office of prophet today. In fact, Joel prophesied that in the last days "your sons *and your daughters* shall prophesy" (Joel 2:28, see also Acts 2:17). Therefore, I see no reason why we should not allow women to hold various positions of leadership within the church.

Biblically, the only ministry from which women are barred is teaching men. In 1 Timothy 2:12 Paul says, "I do not permit a woman to teach or to have authority over a man, but to be in silence." This seems to be the only office within the church that is prohibited to women. The restriction is surely not to extend further. Paul himself instructs the church to let the older women teach the younger women (see Titus 2:3,4), and commended Timothy because his mother and grandmother taught him from the time he was a child concerning the things of the Lord.

The Purpose of Prophecy

Having the gift of prophecy does not necessarily give you the *office* of a prophet. The two are separate and distinct. Many people within the church can have the gift of prophecy. In fact, Paul encouraged all believers to covet the gift of prophecy: "Pursue love, and desire spiritual gifts, but especially that you may prophesy" (1 Corinthians 14:1). We are to desire all spiritual gifts, but especially this gift of prophecy. Why?

When Paul contrasts the gift of prophecy with the gift of tongues, he says it is far preferable to have the former in the church than the latter. He encourages prophecy in the public assembly, but not tongues, because "he who speaks in a tongue edifies himself, but he who prophesies edifies the church" (1 Corinthians 14:4). Prophecy is more valuable to the church because "he who prophesies speaks edification and exhortation and comfort to men" (14:3). Let's take a closer look at these three purposes of prophecy.

First, through prophecy God speaks to the church to edify us, to build us up, to encourage us to trust the Lord and lay hold of the promises of God, and to secure a position of strength in Christ Jesus. The Spirit speaks forth words that build us up, increase our faith, and fortify our relationships in Jesus Christ.

Second, through prophecy God exhorts us. Don't just mouth it—do it! Don't just hear it—practice it! We need those who will spur us to act upon what we know from the Scriptures. Through prophecy we are exhorted to praise, to prayer, and to Christian activity.

Third, prophecy has the ability to comfort us. We need to hear that God is on the throne, that He is watching over us, that He loves us, and that all things work together for good to those who love God. Sadly, we sometimes forget this. We are tempted to think that things are out of God's hand. We need to be reminded and comforted that God understands and knows, that God is in control, that God is on the throne, and that God rules from heaven.

Prophecy Today

Prophecy—both its predictive and forthtelling aspects—
has played a big part in my ministry over the years. It has
instructed me, guided me, and sometimes helped me to carry
on. Perhaps a little background will help you to see what I
mean.

The first 17 years of my ministry brought me little but
frustration. Ministry was no great joy because I saw very little
fruit. Yet I hung on because I knew God had called me to it.
One day the original Calvary Chapel group decided to call me
as pastor. I gratefully accepted their invitation, but soon afterward they called back and said, "Don't come. We're going to
disband." I replied, "Well, I've already resigned here. I'm coming anyhow."

The day after I arrived we were in a prayer group, hands
were laid on me, and a prophecy was given that seemed more
dream than reality. The Lord said he was going to make me a
shepherd of many flocks. At the time, it seemed preposterous.
Unknown to me, the church had also received a prophecy that
God was going to bless the church so greatly that the little
building it was meeting in would not be sufficient to hold all
the people who were going to come. The church was to remodel
its current building, then later move to a facility on the bluff
overlooking the bay. Eventually the church would have a
nationwide radio ministry, and would become known around
the world. To a group of twelve people who were so discouraged they were ready to quit, the message sounded impossible.
They were tempted to echo the words of 2 Kings 7:2: "Look, if
the Lord would make windows in heaven, could this thing
be?" It seemed totally absurd.

After our first Sunday service we all went out to lunch
together—we were that small—and as we sat in the restaurant
I drew out plans for remodeling the church. They all got
excited, but I didn't know why.

A year or so later, we outgrew our building and had to
look for a new facility. Before long we found some property on
Bay Street in Costa Mesa which we thought we could make
work. That was when they informed me of the prophecy.
"No," they said, "the church is to be on the bluff overlooking
the bay."

"But we're going to be overlooking Bay Street," I pro-
tested. I thought that would fit the prophecy.

"No," they insisted, "the prophecy said we would be overlooking the bay."

Nevertheless, we went ahead with our plans—and within a few days the city of Costa Mesa rejected our conditional use permit. This was a great blow to me, because we had sold our church already. I thought we were going to be able to build a new church and move to Bay Street, but now we had no building and nowhere to meet. I remember thinking, *Man, here we have a growing church and the pastor sells the building out from under the congregation. They're going to wonder what in the world they got hold of.*

When we dejectedly returned to the planning department to retrieve our plans, a lady who worked there said, "You know, maybe you could move to our church. We're going to be building a new facility and you could probably get our old one. It's the Newport Harbor Lutheran Church on the bluff overlooking the bay."

Even I could sense the Lord's leading on this one! For two years we met in the church on the bluff overlooking the bay while we built a little chapel. Then we went on the radio—and one-by-one the prophesies were fulfilled.

How Does It Operate?

How does the gift of prophecy operate? In my own experience, there comes into my mind a very strong impression or thought. Many times all I have is a first sentence. But as I speak forth that first sentence, the thoughts begin to flow, and I verbalize them. They can be revelatory, exhortive, or comforting.

When I begin to prophesy, I don't change my tone of voice. I don't suddenly get a vibrato so that everybody says, "Ooooh, this is prophecy. Now listen carefully." I continue in my normal tone, but I know it is prophecy because the things I am saying are new to me. I haven't studied them, they are not a part of my notes or something I have prepared to say. Rather, they are thoughts and inspirations coming to me at that very moment from the Spirit. As I say them, I judge what I am saying…and it's good. I think, *Wow! That's tremendous. What a powerful point. Man, that's great.* I get excited about it because it comes as a revelation to me even as I am speaking it.

A lady in one of the churches I used to pastor often came up after a Sunday morning when a third of the sermon had been the exercise of prophecy. She'd smile and say, "I have a suspicion that you enjoyed that sermon this morning more than I did." I'd say, "You're right!" I knew it was coming as a revelation of God under the anointing of the Spirit. I'm amazed at the thoughts the Spirit brings forth and the truths He unfolds. Few things are more glorious or exciting!

Rules for Prophecy

First, 1 Corinthians 14 lays out certain rules in regard to the exercise of prophecy. The overarching principle is that church services are to be conducted decently and in order (14:40). God is not the author of confusion (14:33), and church services ought to be conducted with a mind toward the response of unbelieving guests. When this rule is obeyed, then the secrets of people's hearts are revealed through the exercise of prophecy, and they will go away saying, "God is in you of a truth" (14:24,25 KJV).

Second, Paul tells us, "Let two or three prophets speak, and let the others judge" (14:29). Often those in Pentecostal circles have a tendency to attach a "Thus saith the Lord" to their prophecies. But did the Lord really say it? Is it in keeping with what God already has spoken? We're to judge prophecy. If I say to you, "Brother, the Lord told me He wants you to go to Africa as a missionary," you'd better seek the Lord for yourself rather than taking off for Africa on my word alone. Judge it to see if it bears witness with your heart.

People have often said to me, "Chuck, it seems to me that the Lord has been saying you should do this or that," and I find it is the very thing I have been mulling over in my own mind, wondering, *Is this something the Lord wants me to do?* Their words come as a confirmation. At other times people have said to me, "Thus saith the Lord . . ." and come up with all kinds of condemning words. I reply, "I don't accept that. The Scripture asks, 'Who is he that condemneth? It is Christ that died, yea rather, that is risen again who is even at the right hand of God, who also maketh intercession.' And yet you're coming to me with condemnation in the name of the Lord Jesus who said, 'I didn't come to condemn. I came to save.' " If someone comes to me with terrible condemnation, I shrug it off. Jesus didn't come to condemn me; He came to save me.

All prophecies are to be judged. There are at least three scriptural bases for judging prophecy.

1. *Does the prophecy line up with the already revealed Word of God?*

The Word of God is forever established and God is not going to give any revelation that conflicts with His written Word. If what is being proclaimed conflicts with the written Word, it is no problem to judge it as false. It is not of the Lord, for the Lord will not contradict himself. The Word of God is the filter through which we can judge whether a prophecy be of God.

The prophet Jeremiah said, "'The prophet who has a dream, let him tell a dream; and he who has My word, let him speak My word faithfully. What is the chaff to the wheat?' says the Lord" (Jeremiah 23:28). I believe that God can and does speak to man through these means. But I know He speaks to us through His Word, and visions and dreams are but as chaff compared to the wheat of the Word of God. It is the Word of God that nourishes and strengthens. Chaff can choke you, but the Word of God will sustain and feed you.

2. *Does it line up with the facts?*

I sometimes receive "Thus saith the Lord" letters that do not line up with the facts. Sometimes they accuse me of motives that I do not have. Because they don't line up with the facts, I reject them as false prophecy.

If the prophecy is a prediction, then I observe to see whether the things come to pass. If the things do happen and the message honors the Lord, then you can judge that it must have been of God. The prophecies of Agabus in the book of Acts, for example, came true and proved he was a genuine prophet of God. He said there was going to be a worldwide drought and there was; he said Paul was going to be arrested in Jerusalem and he was. It is therefore easy to declare that Agabus was a true prophet of God.

3. *Does it honor Jesus Christ?*

Deuteronomy 13 tells us that a prophet may be false even if his prophecies come true. If a man urges you to go after other gods which you have not known and serve them, Moses warns he is a false prophet; the Lord is using him to prove what is in your heart, to see whether you love the Lord with all your heart and with all your soul.

If anyone tells you to do something contrary to the Word—though he may show signs or seems to read your mind or tells you what your name or address is or tells you what happened to you this past week—or if he should say, "Jesus Christ is not the only way to God; there are many roads to heaven," then God is testing you to see if you will hold true to His Word. Will you let the Word be the final authority of your faith and practice?

The final rule for exercising the gift of prophecy is found in 1 Corinthians 14:30: "If anything is revealed to another who sits by, let the first keep silent." In other words, make room for others. Many times as a person is speaking, the Spirit will begin to amplify things for me that are said, giving me illustrations or clarifying some point. Often I'll get up afterward and expand on what the Spirit had been instructing me. But I hold my peace until the first speaker is finished. "For you can all prophesy one by one" (14:31), Paul says. Speak in an orderly fashion. Don't all get up and start prophesying at once—that would be mass confusion. But prophesy one by one, that all may learn and all may be encouraged.

Paul tells us that the spirits of the prophets are subject to the prophets (1 Corinthians 14:32). That is, you have control over the exercise of this gift. This is true with all the gifts. I do not believe the Holy Spirit ever takes away control of your faculties. Demonic spirits can take control of a person's motor functions, but I do not believe God ever does so.

I have heard people say, "The Holy Spirit just made me do it," or "It came upon me and I didn't know what I was doing." I can't accept that. The spirit of the prophet is subject to the prophet. You are in control.

Dealing with False Prophets

The Scriptures warn repeatedly about those who would speak in the name of the Lord yet proclaim only their own ideas. It's a prevalent practice. I get probably three or four letters a week of the "Thus saith the Lord" variety which merely expresses the person's own ideas.

Sometimes people try to manipulate you by fear. "Brother, you'd better be careful. I prophesied to a man last week, and he laughed at it and he fell dead when he walked away." You don't need to be afraid of them. In the early years of my ministry, some fellows were convinced of some false doctrine and were insistent that I espouse their beliefs to my congregation. They called me out on a Saturday night and began to prophesy over me. They said they saw a black coffin...and I was in it. God was going to smite me dead if I didn't accept their doctrine.

I wasn't afraid. I didn't go home and say, "Oh my! Am I going to die?" I had the Word of God and I stood on it.

The early church had to deal with false prophets. Itinerant preachers would travel around to the newly formed churches, and some of them were false prophets. Both the Old and New Testaments warn about these phonies.

Jesus repeatedly spoke about false prophets. In the Sermon on the Mount He said, "Beware of false prophets, who come to you in sheep's clothing, but inwardly they are ravenous wolves" (Matthew 7:15). In Matthew 24:11, He predicted that "many false prophets shall rise and shall deceive many" (KJV), while in Matthew 24:24, He warned, "For there shall arise false Christs, and false prophets, and shall shew great signs and wonders; insomuch that, if it were possible, they shall deceive the very elect" (KJV).

The apostle Peter wrote, "But there were also false prophets among the people, even as there will be false teachers among you, who will secretly bring in destructive heresies, even denying the Lord who bought them, and bring on themselves swift destruction. And many will follow their destructive ways, because of whom the way of truth will be blasphemed. By covetousness they will exploit you with deceptive words" (2 Peter 2:1-3). That's the mark of a false prophet—he'll try to defraud you. When someone does that, you don't need the gift of discernment to know he is a false prophet.

In the years after the apostles had passed from the scene, the church developed what came to be known as the *Didache* ("teaching"). It was a little rule book sent around to the early churches that taught local congregations how to discern whether a man was a true or false prophet. For example, it said that if a man sought to take an offering for himself, then he was to be classified as a false prophet. If he ordered them to prepare a meal for the poor but then ate of it himself, he was a false prophet. The *Didache* said false prophets were trying to live off of the churches and enrich themselves.

They still do this today.

If you get a computerized letter that says,

Dear Brother Smith, last night as I was in prayer I saw your face, and God placed a heavy burden upon my heart for you. I could hardly sleep through the whole night thinking about you and praying for you, and I know that there must be something seriously wrong or the Lord wouldn't have laid such a heavy burden upon my heart for you. You know how much my wife and I love you, and we talk about you all the time.

Really? They don't even know me! But that's the bottom line of a false prophet: greed.

Please write to me today and let me know what's going on so that I can get rid of this heavy burden. And when you write, could you please enclose a check for $100? Our ministry is going through severe trials at this time...

It's so sad. Another example of deceitfulness was brought to my attention. One lady in our church came up to me one day and said, "Oh, Brother Smith, it's so wonderful. This famous evangelist would love for me to come to dinner at his house." And I said, "Ohhh. Let me see the letter." It had been sent to 500,000 people in the United States. Bring the chicken.

Desire the Gift

Paul tells us in 1 Corinthians 14:39: "Therefore, brethren, desire earnestly to prophesy." We are to covet this gift of prophecy.

I want to encourage you to earnestly desire and seek this marvelous gift of God. You may not hold the office of prophet, but God can use you to prophesy. Prophecy is indeed a real blessing to the church for edification, exhortation, comfort, and learning. And all those blessings are in far too short a supply.

14

Unmasking
the Evil One

To one is given ... the discerning of spirits.
—1 CORINTHIANS 12:8,10

Scientists tell us there is much more space in an atom than solid matter—in fact, some 30,000 times more space than mass. In a hydrogen atom, made up of one proton and a single orbiting electron, there is so much space that if you could enlarge the proton to the size of a baseball, the electron would be about the size of a BB, rotating around the proton ten miles away at the speed of 10,000 miles a second.

If the earth were a proton and the moon an electron and the space between them had the same ratio as exists in a hydrogen atom, the moon would be 1,000 times further away than it is now. Or think of it this way—If all the atoms in your body should suddenly collapse, leaving no space between the solid matter, we would have to get a powerful microscope to find you—you would be a microscopic speck of dust (but you'd weigh exactly what you do now).

We know there are dwarf stars whose density is much greater than that of atoms on earth. There is a star of the first magnitude called Sirius (also called the dog star). In 1888, they discovered it was actually a double star. The smaller of the two, Sirius B, is called a "pup." It is a dwarf star that rotates around the major star. The density of this pup is thought to be so great that one cubic inch of Sirius B would weigh 1,750 pounds.

Neutron stars are even more dense than this—by about a million times! One cubic inch of a neutron star would weigh 1.75 *billion* pounds. And still there is space in that cubic inch!

Because there is so much space in an atom, experts say it is theoretically possible for two worlds to coexist at the same time and in the same place, both passing through each other, unconscious of the other's existence. All it would take is for them to be made up of different molecular structures.

Two Coexisting Worlds

Now, in a sense, that is what the Bible teaches. It tells us there are two worlds coexisting, each passing through the other. For the most part, we are not conscious of that other world—but it is very conscious of us. The Bible calls it the world of spirits. This spiritual world is very real, and has a tremendous influence on all of our lives, either for good or for evil.

The Bible says of angels, "Are they not all ministering spirits sent forth to minister for those who will inherit salvation?" (Hebrews 1:14). We are grateful for the Holy Spirit, and for His influence upon our lives for good, convincing us of sin, drawing us to Jesus Christ, and molding and shaping us into the image of Jesus.

But there is another realm of spirit beings that is hostile to us and our walk with Christ. These spirit beings try to exert an extremely negative influence upon us. As Paul wrote, "We do not wrestle against flesh and blood, but against principalities, against powers, against the rulers of the darkness of this age, against spiritual hosts of wickedness in the heavenly places" (Ephesians 6:12). A battle goes on and all of us are engaged in it.

Unfortunately, evil spirits are able to appear as angels of light, and thus it is possible for a person to be deceived by them. The Bible says Satan himself is able to transform himself into an angel of light (2 Corinthians 11:14).

Beyond that, even as we try to analyze our own thoughts, questions arise: Does that thought come from God, from my flesh, or from Satan? Who planted that thought in my mind?

The inability to discern got Peter into trouble before he was filled with the Holy Spirit. Peter and the other disciples were in the area of Caesarea Philippi when Jesus asked them, "Who do men say that I am?"

The disciples answered, "Some say John the Baptist, some Elijah, and others Jeremiah, or one of the prophets." Jesus repeated, "But who do you say that I am?" Peter replied, "You are the Christ, the Son of the living God." Jesus answered him, "Blessed are you, Simon Bar-Jonah, for flesh and blood has not revealed this to you, but My Father who is in Heaven" (Matthew 16:13-17).

Jesus then began to predict that He would be betrayed, turned over to the Gentiles, crucified, and slain, then rise again the third day. Peter began to rebuke Him: "Far be it from You, Lord," or "Spare yourself, Lord." Jesus replied, "Get behind Me, Satan! You are an offense to Me, for you are not mindful of the things of God, but the things of men" (Matthew 16:22,23). In other words, "You can't discern the difference between divine values and human ones."

We all have that problem. When a thought comes to us, is God warning us of something? Or did the thought come out of our own mind? Or, worse yet, was the thought planted by Satan?

That is why we need to have the gift of discerning of spirits.

How Does This Gift Function?

Many times you get an uneasy feeling about a person or a situation and you don't know why; you can't quite put your finger on it. I'm not talking about the "gift of suspicion" that some people seem to have. But there are times when you sense a definite uneasiness within you, an unrest. That could very well be the gift of discerning of spirits. You may be picking up on something that's not obvious to everybody. But if you're walking in the Spirit and are spiritually attuned, you'll sense that power of darkness strongly and clearly.

I have discovered that having the discerning of spirits can sometimes present a problem. You sense a deceiver's true character so clearly and definitely that you assume everybody must be able to see he's a total phony—and you are amazed when someone believes or follows him. You can't understand how anyone could be so gullible—it's so plain, so obvious, why can't they see?

Consider David "Moses" Berg, for instance. In the '70s he won a tremendous following of young people who called themselves the Children of God. He produced pornographic materials that were used to entice people into the fellowship as well as sending the girls out as prostitutes to snag new recruits.

When you read his material, you say to yourself, "Any fool can see that this man is a false prophet." You can't understand how anybody could possibly be deceived by the things he says. And yet they were.

Telling True Prophets from False Prophets

It is enormously significant that Paul mentions the gift of discerning of spirits right after the gift of prophecy. I see a divine order in this. Throughout history, prophets of God have spoken God's word to His people. But just as there have been true prophets, there also have been false prophets who led people astray. It is critically important to discern whether someone is giving a true prophecy of God.

Remember, Satan is an extremely clever counterfeiter. He has been able to imitate almost every work of God. We read that when the Antichrist comes he will be able to produce all kinds of supernatural signs and wonders, working miracles so that many people will be deceived (see 2 Thessalonians 2:9,10).

As we draw ever nearer to that day, we need the discerning of spirits. We need that revelation of God that comes to our heart by the Holy Spirit, whereby we know whether something is truly of God.

First John 4:1 says, "Beloved, do not believe every spirit, but test the spirits, whether they are of God; because many false prophets have gone out into the world." Paul, in 2 Corinthians 11:13-15, said, "For such are false apostles, deceitful workers, transforming themselves into apostles of Christ. And no wonder! For Satan himself transforms himself into an angel of light. Therefore it is no great thing if his ministers also transform themselves into ministers of righteousness."

Today many false prophets are gaining great fame. As a shepherd over the flock of God, I feel a certain responsibility to warn the church against some of these false prophets. The problem is: The minute I begin to give names and incidences and proofs that a person is a false prophet, there are always those souls who are offended. "Oh, how can you say that about brother so and so?" they ask. "I was blessed by his ministry; I was healed when I reached out and touched the television set. And I've been supporting him." It's difficult to warn people of false prophets who want to take advantage of them when they're already involved with them.

Jesus predicted that false Christs and false prophets would one day appear who, if possible, would deceive even the elect through the great signs and wonders they would perform. That is why it's so crucial to have the gift of the discernment of spirits.

You can't always tell false prophets by what they say. Many times what they say is 99 percent correct—that's what makes them so dangerous. You can't always tell them by their actions, either—Jesus said they would perform great signs and wonders.

Both Peter and Paul warned that a certain sign of a false prophet was his intention to defraud you, to take your money and make it his. Through feigned words they will take advantage of you financially. Through flattery and fine speeches they aim to rip you off. Peter wrote, "By covetousness they will exploit you with deceptive words" (2 Peter 2:3). And Paul said these men were "destitute of the truth, who suppose that godliness is a means of gain" (1 Timothy 6:5).

There is a key: If anyone teaches you that godliness is a path to riches, Paul says you can consider him or her a false prophet. "From such withdraw yourself," he commands (1 Timothy 6:5).

Just before warning us against false prophets, Jesus declared that "wide is the gate and broad is the way that leads to destruction, and there are many who go in by it. Because narrow is the gate and difficult is the way which leads to life, and there are few who find it" (Matthew 7:13,14). Yet false prophets stand at the broad gate on the broad path and say, "All roads lead to God. Take this one!"

We need this gift of the discerning of spirits so that we might know whether a man is speaking to us for God, out of his own flesh, or for Satan.

Discernment in the New Testament

We read that Jesus did not need anyone to tell Him about man because He knew man and what was in man (John 2:25). The Gospel of John says that "Jesus knew from the beginning who they were who did not believe, and who would betray Him" (John 6:64). Many people who followed Jesus appeared to be disciples, but later turned away. From the outset He knew who these people were—He had the gift of discerning of spirits.

Perhaps the most classic use of the gift of discerning of spirits is found in Acts 8. Philip had gone to Samaria, where a man named Simon dabbled in magic. This man was able to mystify the people with his magical feats and made many of them think he had some kind of supernatural powers. When Philip arrived to preach Christ, the evangelist began performing marvelous miracles through the power of the Holy Spirit. Devils were being cast out, people were being healed of all kinds of illnesses, lame people were walking, blind people were seeing. When the people saw this power of God in Philip, many of them believed on Jesus Christ and were baptized. Among those who were baptized was Simon, the magician.

When the church in Jerusalem heard that the Samaritans had received the gospel and that a great move of the Spirit was sweeping Samaria, they sent Peter and John to investigate. When they arrived, they discovered that the Holy Spirit had not yet come upon these believers, so they began to lay hands upon them, and the people received the gift of the Spirit. When Simon saw what was happening, he approached Peter and John with a proposition. "Say," he said, "how much will it cost me to buy this trick, that whoever I lay my hands on will receive the Spirit?"

Simon was attempting to do something common among magicians. My father was an amateur magician, and if he saw someone do some especially good trick, he would approach the magician afterward and say, "I would like to buy that trick." It's a common practice to buy the secret of how the trick was done. The same was true in ancient times. And so this Simon, a magician, wanted to buy what he thought was a trick.

What he received from Peter was a stinging rebuke. "Your money perish with you," Peter scolded, "because you thought that the gift of God could be purchased with money! You have neither part nor portion in this matter, for your heart is not right in the sight of God. Repent therefore of this your wickedness, and pray God if perhaps the thought of your heart may be forgiven you. For I see that you are poisoned by bitterness and bound by iniquity" (Acts 8:20-23).

Peter, through the discerning of spirits, was able to see what was in this man's heart. Although Simon had made an outward profession of faith, had been baptized, and was following Philip, his spirit was wrong. No doubt a lot of people were rejoicing that Simon the sorcerer had accepted the Lord— "Isn't it wonderful?"—yet Peter perceived bitterness and probably jealousy in Simon's heart. It's not hard to understand why. Philip was the new kid on the block, and he had attracted the attention of the crowds. The people used to think Simon had some great power of God at work in him, but when they saw the genuine article, they turned away from him and followed Philip.

We also see the discerning of spirits in the life of Paul the apostle. In Acts 13, Paul and Barnabas arrive at the isle of Cyprus, where they encounter a Jew named Bar-Jesus ("the son of Jesus"), who was a sorcerer and a false prophet. The governor of the country, a prudent man named Sergius Paulus, called for Barnabas and Saul to hear from them the word of God. But Elymas the sorcerer (Bar-Jesus) withstood them and sought to turn away the governor from the faith.

> Then Saul, who also is called Paul, filled with the Holy Spirit, looked intently at him and said, "O full of all deceit and all fraud, you son of the devil, you enemy of all righteousness, will you not cease perverting the straight ways of the Lord? And now, indeed, the hand of the Lord is upon you, and you shall be blind, not seeing the sun for a time" (Acts 13:9-11).

From that moment on, this man went around seeking someone to lead him by the hand. When the governor saw what had happened, he believed and was astonished at the doctrine of the Lord. I'll bet! Through the gift of the discerning of spirits, Paul had determined that this Elymas was an instrument of Satan seeking to pervert the ways of truth.

Some time later Paul and Silas traveled to the city of Thyatira where a young woman with a spirit of divination began following them and crying out, "These men are the servants of the Most High God, who proclaim to us the way of salvation" (Acts 16:17). Notice that what the girl was saying was absolutely true. Paul and Silas were, indeed, the servants of the Most High God, and they had come to proclaim the way of salvation. What the girl was saying was true—but her spirit was wrong. Paul knew it through the gift of discerning of spirits, so when he had had enough, he turned around and cast the evil spirit out of the girl.

Using the Truth to Lie

That last story illustrates an important principle: False prophets oftentimes speak truth. As Jesus said, "They are as wolves in sheep's clothing." You can't tell a false prophet by the way he looks—he looks like a sheep. You cannot always tell him by what he says—much of what he says is true.

Although these wolves often speak partial truths, you have to realize that they change the lexicon. What they mean when they use familiar terms is not what you understand when you hear those terms. They change the definitions in order to deceive.

Ask a Jehovah's Witness if he believes that Jesus Christ is the Son of God and he'll say, "Oh, most certainly." Next ask, Do you believe that He died for our sins? "Most certainly." Then, do you believe that you are saved by faith in the work of Jesus Christ and His blood that was shed for us? "Most definitely."

Talk to a Mormon and he will affirm the same things. When you question him he will say, "But we *do* believe in Jesus Christ." The question is, who is the Jesus Christ that he believes in? Mormons teach He's the brother of Lucifer. Long ago Elohim was seeking to redeem man and asked His sons for advice. After both Lucifer and Jesus gave their respective schemes of redemption, the Father rejected Lucifer's plan and endorsed the plan of Jesus. That made Lucifer furious and he determined to upset Jesus' strategy. Is this the Jesus of the Bible? Hardly.

And who is the Jesus that the Jehovah Witnesses believe in? He was Michael, the archangel, a created being of God. Although these cultists say they believe in Jesus as the Son of God, when you start defining terms, you discover that what they teach conflicts radically with the Bible.

We would be deceived less often if we remembered that we cannot tell what a person really believes by merely noting the terms he uses. He may be saying the right words but meaning something diametrically opposed to what we think he's saying.

The real danger of a false prophet is that you can be drawn into his net unaware. He will throw out a few hooks, get you to distrust what the church has taught, then say, "You can't really trust the Bible, either. You need our books to help you interpret the Scriptures. If you just read the Bible alone you will be in darkness. But you can set the Bible aside and read our books, for they explain the Bible to you and then you will be in light." And so, with a few hooks they draw people into their net—all because people do not have the discernment of spirits.

A Case of Mistaken Identity

The discernment of spirits is an important gift, and I am certain it has operated many times in your life, even without your knowledge. You get an uneasy feeling when someone comes along and seems to say and do the right things, but you sense something isn't quite right. There is something you can't put your finger on, something intangible, and it makes you uncomfortable. When I get that kind of a check in my spirit, I always walk very carefully. But I have not always been correct in my evaluation of a person.

We were young and green in the ministry I pastored a church in Tucson. I was a part of a denomination at the time, and received a letter from our denominational headquarters warning of a couple who were fleecing area churches. The letter described the couple as name-droppers and smooth operators who had taken many churches for tidy sums of money on the pretense of borrowing funds and bringing them right back. As I sat reading this letter, there came a knock at the door. I got up to answer it and found a man and a woman who fit the description perfectly. They wore dark glasses and immediately began dropping the names of all the leaders of the denomination. I thought, *Man, I've got them.*

I acted very cool toward them, even cold. They said, "You know, we started the church here in Tucson."

"Yeah? Tell me about it," I replied.

A few moment later they asked, "May we see your new sanctuary?"

"I suppose, if you want to."

As they looked at the facility, they quickly got very dramatic. "Honey, look—it was worth it all," he said. Under my breath I sneered, "Give me a break, man. You're not fooling me."

Then he started his spiel. "We were just passing through town and our car broke down."

Man, I've heard that one so many times, I thought.

"We don't have the money to get the repairs. We need X amount to get the thing fixed."

Yeah, yeah. I know all about it. I was certain this was the dirty couple.

"When do you have church services?" they asked.

"Well, today is Wednesday; we have church tonight," I replied.

"Oh, we're going to come," they promised.

Yeah, I've heard that one before, I thought.

Much to my surprise, they really did show up. And to my utter astonishment—and deep shame—one of the long-time members of the church saw them, let out a scream, hugged them both and exclaimed, "Oh, how are you?"

But...but...it couldn't be! Could it? It was. *They were legitimate!*

And I had been so bitterly, icy cold to them. Oh, did I feel horrible. I had shown an utter lack of discernment. I should have shown them compassion and love, but instead I displayed only suspicion and hostility. The couple stayed around town for a few days, painting a few houses to earn enough money to get their car fixed. They never did put the bite on me or say, "We need some money." Finally, I showed them the letter. "See how you two fit the description?" I asked sheepishly. Then I asked for forgiveness.

Save Yourself Some Trouble

The Lord wants us to be wise. Yet there are limitations to our wisdom, and that's where the Spirit comes in. He is able and eager to help us discern the good from the bad, the right from the wrong, the truth from the lies.

I admit I've been taken in by deceivers more than once. But every time I've been hoodwinked there was a check, there was a warning...and I ignored it. "No, they're fine," I'd say. "I can tell—see the look in his eye?" How important it is that we learn to follow the leading of the Spirit! It saves us from a lot of trouble.

Through the gift of the discerning of spirits we can be protected from those who profess to be something they are not. Through this gift we can detect and reject those who try to foist their pernicious doctrines upon the church.

I pray that the Lord will give us the kind of spirit that will enable us to discern between the Spirit of truth and the spirit of error. Because without it, we simply won't survive in this world.

15

An Affront to the Intellect; a Blessing to the Soul

To one is given...different kinds of tongues.
—1 CORINTHIANS 12:8,10

My son Jeff has a natural talent for languages. He can be in France for just a few days and by the end of that time he'll be talking to people on the street. Then he can pack up and go to Sweden and a few days later he'll be conversing with them.

I'm not like that at all. I took three years of Greek and three years of Latin, and I can't communicate with anybody who doesn't speak English.

I'm glad there are many people like my son who have a natural ability to pick up foreign languages—but that's not what the gift of tongues is about. The gift of speaking in tongues is the ability to speak fluently in an unknown language through the agency of the Holy Spirit. It is the ability to worship God through praise in a language you have not naturally learned.

What Are Tongues?

Paul lists speaking in tongues as one of the gifts of the Spirit. In 1 Corinthians 12:28 he says "And God has appointed these in the church: first apostles, second prophets, third teachers, after that miracles, then gifts of healings, helps, administrations, varieties of tongues." Notice that tongues is last on the list. This appears to reflect an order of priorities: First apostles, last speaking in tongues. While tongues is a desirable and valued gift, we shouldn't exalt it out of measure. On the other hand, just because it's listed last doesn't mean it's unimportant. All of God's gifts are good and to be desired.

After Paul lists the various gifts, he asks a series of rhetorical questions. Does everyone have the gifts of healing? Do all speak with tongues? And the answer, of course, is no; not all have the gift of healing, and not all speak with tongues. But all the gifts he lists are legitimate.

First Corinthians 14 (KJV several times mentions speaking in an unknown tongue. The Greek word we translate "tongue" is *glossa*. The word "unknown" is added by the translators of the King James Bible, but it fits the concept. Tongues is speaking in a language that the speaker himself does not understand. It could be a known language (as Paul said in 1 Corinthians 13:1, "Though I speak with the tongues of men") or it could be the dialect of heaven ("Though I speak with the tongues of...angels").

It is fascinating that Paul suggests there is an angelic language ("Though I speak with the tongues of...angels"). The question is, what is it? What is the language of heaven? While we don't know what the language of heaven may be, we can be sure there is one. Therefore when you speak in tongues, you may well be communicating in a real dialect, even if it isn't used by some tribal group of man.

The Covenant of Language

Let's pause for a moment and ask a key question. What is language? Have you ever thought about it? Language is fascinating. It's a covenant that we make with each other, an agreement that certain sounds express certain ideas. As long as you and I agree that these sounds express particular concepts, we can communicate.

Many kids have their own secret clubs with their own secret languages. It's fun to be able to speak in a code your non-club friends can't understand. Maybe "ugh" means, "let's go to Dairy Queen later and get a hot fudge sundae." And "nug" means, "Great idea. Who's buying?" "Tug" means, "I'll treat." And "lug" means, "you're on." So one day you turn to your friend and say, "Ugh," and he says, "Nug." You reply, "Tug," and he answers "Lug," and immediately you head out to get ice cream. Those outside your club say, "What in the world just happened?" But as long as you have agreed that certain sounds express particular ideas, you can communicate.

Now, speaking in tongues is a covenant that you establish with God. I say to God, "by faith I'm going to trust the Holy Spirit to communicate to You my love, my devotion, my thanksgiving, my gratitude for those glorious things You have done for me—feelings my English language can't adequately express." Tongues express the overflowing worship of my spirit and the praise from my heart that I feel toward God.

Savonarola, the fifteenth-century Italian reformer, said, "When prayer reaches its ultimate, words are impossible." That's where tongues comes in. The miracle is not that I'm speaking peculiar sounds; the miracle is that God understands them as the expression of my spirit. Through unknown tongues I pour out my love to Him in deep appreciation and thanksgiving for all that He's done for me.

Are They Real Languages?

Often the unknown words I speak are indeed a known dialect of man. For years, as I would pray and worship the Lord in tongues, I would frequently notice the word *kurios*. It was probably one of the most common words I spoke. Years later, as I studied Greek, I discovered that *kurios* is the Greek word for "Lord." How appropriate that I would be saying "Lord" over and over again in my worship and praise to Jesus!

Or consider another example. Lynn Hinojosa is a lady in our church, who when she speaks in tongues often speaks in French. Not just the common street French, but an aristocratic variety. And she's never studied the language!

In the early years of Calvary Chapel our family often attended a summer camp in Arizona. The kids all got to go to camp for free. I conducted the camp, and in this way we got a week or two of vacation in the mountains. One year as we prepared to leave for camp, Lynn laid hands on our daughter, Jan, and began to pray in French. Now, Jan's college major was French and she understood everything the woman said. She was praying that God would use Jan's life as an inspiration to the young girls to whom she would be ministering, and offered a beautiful prayer of intercession for God's help and assistance.

Jan said that as Lynn was praying, "I was trembling all over, because I realized this was a prayer of the Holy Spirit for me. What a thrill to realize that the Spirit was interceding for me! It was so glorious to know that this prayer was the Lord's desire for me."

Tongues in the Old Testament

Of all the gifts of the Spirit, this seems to be the only one not manifested in the Old Testament. There is one possible exception. When King Hezekiah was told by the prophet Isaiah to set his house in order for he was going to die, the king turned his face to the wall and began to pray desperately to God for healing. His experience is described in Isaiah 38: "Like a crane or swallow, so did I chatter. I did mourn as a dove. Mine eyes fail from looking upward. Oh, Lord, I am oppressed; undertake for me!" It may be that Hezekiah made inarticulate sounds—speaking in tongues—as he pled for his life.

Whatever the truth in Hezekiah's case, it is certain that speaking in tongues was promised in the Old Testament. Isaiah prophesied, "For with stammering lips and another tongue He will speak to this people, to whom He said, 'This is the rest with which you may cause the weary to rest,' and 'This is the refreshing'; yet they would not hear" (Isaiah 28:11). This prophecy probably would not be allowed in theological circles as an argument for the gift of tongues, except that in 1 Corinthians 14:21 Paul quotes this very text to prove that God had predicted His people would one day speak in tongues.

Tongues in the New Testament

Some like to point out that Jesus Himself did not practice the gift of tongues. That's true. But it would have been impossible for Jesus to speak in an unknown tongue, for He knows every tongue. Since He is God and knows all things, it would be impossible for Him to speak in an unknown tongue. Nevertheless, Jesus did predict that this gift would be given to those who believed on Him. He said, "And these signs shall follow them that believe. In my name they shall cast out devils. They shall speak with new tongues" (Mark 16:17).[1]

The practice of speaking in tongues first took place on the day of Pentecost (see Acts 2). The disciples were gathered in an upper room when suddenly there came a sound from heaven like a mighty, rushing wind, which filled the house where they were seated. Cloven tongues as of fire rested upon their heads and all 120 disciples began to speak in other tongues as the Spirit enabled them (or as the Catholic Douay version says, "as the Spirit prompted their speech").

They were all speaking foreign languages (in Greek, *glossos*) which they did not learn naturally. We are told that devout Jews from all over the world were gathered at the feast. When word got out, crowds gathered to see what had happened. They all marveled: "Look, are not all these who speak Galileans? And how is it that we hear, each in our own language in which we were born? . . . we hear them speaking in our own tongues the wonderful works of God" (Acts 2:7,8,11).

They were amazed because they heard the apostles speaking in various dialects (in Greek, *dialecto*). These untaught Galileans were speaking the languages of the Medes, the Parthians, the Persians, the Mesopotamians—at least 17 dialects from around the globe. So, although to each apostle the language he was speaking was an unknown tongue (a *glossos*), listeners in the crowd recognized it as a familiar dialect (a *dialecto*).

The next incident of speaking in tongues occurs in Acts 10, when Peter went to the house of Cornelius, a centurion from Caesarea. As Peter was speaking to those gathered in Cornelius' home, "the Holy Spirit fell upon all those who heard the word. And those of the circumcision who believed were astonished, as many as came with Peter [from Joppa], because the gift of the Holy Spirit had been poured out on the Gentiles also. For they heard them speak with tongues and magnify God" (10:44-46).

Acts 19 describes how Paul noticed something missing in the church at Ephesus. He asked them, "Did you receive the Holy Spirit when you believed?" They replied, "We have not so much as heard whether there is a Holy Spirit." So Paul probed, "Into what then were you baptized?" "Into John's baptism," they answered. Then Paul explained that John baptized unto repentance, but spoke of One who was coming after him, Jesus Christ. Then they all were baptized, Paul laid hands on them, and "the Holy Spirit came upon them and they spoke with tongues and prophesied" (19:1-6).

Two Kinds of Tongues?

By comparing these accounts in Acts with 1 Corinthians 12-14, some people have concluded that the Scriptures describe two distinct kinds of tongues.

In Acts 2, foreigners heard in their own dialects the apostles' declaration of the wonderful works of God. Yet in 1 Corinthians 14:2, Paul said, "For he who speaks in a tongue does not speak to men but to God, for no one understands him; however, in the spirit he speaks mysteries [or divine secrets]." This is why some deduce that there are two types of tongues. One they call the "sign gift" of tongues: the manifestation that a person has received the gift of the Holy Spirit. The other they call a "prayer language": a tongue God gives to assist people in their prayer life.

To be honest, this can't be established as a doctrine. We simply don't have enough evidence to decide which view is correct. Those who espouse two types of tongues could be right, but their argument must be made by reading into the text rather than by letting the text speak for itself. I for one am willing to leave it an open question.

How Is the Gift to Be Used?

A better question is, How is this gift to be used in the life of the believer? Tongues is exciting! It builds you up in your walk with God, and invigorates your relationship with Him. It does this in several ways.

1. *Tongues assist your prayer life.*

Tongues is a gift to assist your prayer life. Paul says, "If I pray in a tongue, my spirit prays, but my understanding is unfruitful. What is the result then? I will pray with the spirit, and I will also pray with the understanding. I will sing with the spirit, and I will also sing with the understanding" (1 Corinthians 14:14,15). Paul, by his own admission, prayed in tongues and even sang in tongues.

In the next two verses, the apostle tells us that when we pray in an unknown tongue, our spirit is praying, even though others may not understand. Nevertheless, he says, "you indeed give thanks well" (14:17). Paul says the gift of tongues is a good way to praise the Lord privately.

In Romans 8:26 the apostle tells us that the Spirit helps us pray when we don't know what to pray for. It's comforting to know that I can continue to pray for my friends through the help of the Holy Spirit even when I'm unsure what I should ask. In many cases I will pray in an unknown tongue, allowing the Spirit to intercede for me. Even as He makes intercession for me through groanings too deep for words, so will He also make intercession through the unknown tongues I speak. If the Spirit is praying, we can have the confidence that we are praying according to the will of God, though we may continue to be unsure of what the will of God is in a particular situation.

And what is the result of being aided by the Spirit in worship, in praise, and in prayer according to the will of God? It brings a wonderful rest. Speaking in tongues refreshes us and gives us rest—just as Isaiah prophesied: "This is the rest with which you may cause the weary to rest...this is the refreshing" (Isaiah 28:12).

I can rest knowing that I am adequately praising God, that He receives my worship and understands it as the expression of the deepest core of my being—deeper than my intellect, deeper than my consciousness. From that deep area of the spirit, God can receive and appreciate the love and praise that I offer to Him. He understands that I want to see His work and His will triumph in all the situations that prompt my prayers. How very peaceful, satisfying, and fulfilling it is to rest in the knowledge that God understands and interprets these unknown tongues.

2. *Tongues assists your devotional life.*

Speaking in tongues is designed to help your own private devotional life. It's a great way to praise the Lord. "You indeed give thanks well," Paul said. The gift of tongues finds its greatest benefit in the personal devotions of the believer.

One of my inadequacies is expressing the full measure of my love, appreciation, and thankfulness to God for all He has done for me. Words are inadequate. They can't express the depth of feeling I have for my Lord. I know I'm not alone in this deficiency. Doesn't the Bible speak about "the peace of God, which surpasses [human] understanding" (Philippians 4:7)? Doesn't it refer to "joy unspeakable and full of glory" (1 Peter 1:8 KJV)? And doesn't Paul pray that his friends might be able to comprehend the width and length and depth and height of the love of Christ, which passes knowledge (Ephesians 3:18,19)?

We're dealing here in realms that are beyond us. God's love surpasses knowledge and outstrips human understanding. His joy is indescribable and full of glory. Quite simply, you have to experience it. That's why the psalmist said, "O, taste and see that the Lord is good" (Psalm 34:8).

Whenever we try to express to God our thankfulness and gratitude for the wonderful things He has done for us, we immediately encounter the limitations of language. This is exactly where the gift of tongues can assist us.

3. *The gift of tongues assists in edifying the believer.*

The third purpose of speaking in tongues is to edify the believer. The word "edify" means to build up or to be strengthened. We are exhorted in the Scripture to edify one another in love. In 1 Corinthians 14:4, Paul declares that speaking in tongues edifies the one who speaks: "He who speaks in a tongue edifies himself."

This aspect of tongues is unique. Tongues is the only gift of God that edifies you personally and individually. All of the other gifts serve to edify the church and to build up the body. But this one gift was given to build *you* up, to strengthen *you*. Speaking in tongues strengthens your walk, your relationships, and gives you the power to commune with God on a deep, spiritual level.[2]

Limited Use in Church

Tongues was a popular gift in the Corinthian church and many people liked to exercise it to excess. That is why Paul wrote, "I thank my God I speak with tongues more than you all; yet in the church I would rather speak five words with my understanding, that I may teach others also, than ten thousand words in a tongue" (1 Corinthians 14:18,19).

In several ways Paul restricted the use of tongues in church services. First, he restricted it to services in which an interpreter was present. In 1 Corinthians 14:28, he wrote, "If there is no interpreter, let him keep silent in church, and let him speak to himself and to God." In other words, don't speak out in tongues during church if no interpreter is present.

This brings up a very important point. Some believers contend that they have no control over their speaking in tongues. It is thought that somehow the Spirit takes over and they lose control—the Spirit overrides their will and they speak out in tongues. I remember the testimony of a good saint of God who described how she received the gift of tongues. The gas meter reader had come by her house and she went out to ask him a question, when she suddenly started to speak in tongues. The man got so frightened he ran off. Her point was,

"I had no control over it." But Paul definitely teaches that the Spirit of the prophet is subject to the prophet. You *do* have control; you don't have to speak out. "If there is no interpreter present, let him speak to himself and to God."

Second, Paul limited the number of persons who could speak in tongues during a service: "Let there be two or at the most three, each in turn, and let one interpret" (1 Corinthians 14:27).

Third, everything should always be done "decently and in order" (1 Corinthians 14:40). Utterances in tongues should never disrupt church services. They should never be given when the pastor or speaker is ministering the word of God. In some circles a sermon will often be interrupted by utterances in tongues—so much so that they were sometimes referred to as "tongues and interruptions." Paul said, "God is not the author of confusion" (1 Corinthians 14:33)—and it gets very confusing indeed when such interruptions frequently take place.

Let everything be done decently and in order.

Tongues Will Cease

In 1 Corinthians 13:8 we are told that tongues will one day cease. Why? Because when we are in our glorified bodies and we know, even as we are known, it will be *impossible* to speak in an unknown tongue. I imagine we will have a universal language that everyone will use; perhaps it will be the language of heaven or the language of angels.

But while tongues will cease, Paul tells us "Love never fails. But whether there are prophesies, they will fail; whether there are tongues, they will cease; whether there is knowledge, it will vanish away" (1 Corinthians 13:8).

We don't know everything (even if we think we do at times!). We only prophesy in part, "but when that which is perfect has come, then that which is in part will be done away" (13:10).[3]

Tongues won't last forever. And what a glorious day that will be when they are no longer necessary, for we will be in the very presence of the King Himself! I am certain that the language of heaven will have an adequate vocabulary to express our love and praise.

An Old Rumor

Of all of the gifts and manifestations of the Holy Spirit, speaking in tongues is by far the most controversial. Theological debates really heat up when you discuss the gift of tongues. There are some churches that forbid the use of tongues—even to the point of claiming it is of the devil.

Probably one of the oldest rumors in the church (and it continues to circulate) is that someone was speaking in tongues and another person in the audience understood the language. This second person happened to be a missionary or a student of that language, and he recognized all kinds of horrible, blasphemous things being said about Jesus. That rumor has been around since the days of the Corinthian church. Paul wrote, in 1 Corinthians 12:3, to refute it: "No one speaking by the Spirit of God calls Jesus accursed, and no one can say that Jesus is Lord except by the Holy Spirit." Paul was saying, "No, no. It doesn't happen. No man by the Spirit calls Jesus accursed."

But Paul realized that certain controls were necessary, so after describing tongues, he gave rules for their use and concluded with, "do not forbid to speak with tongues" (1 Corinthians 14:39). He makes it clear that we are not to forbid speaking in tongues *as long as it is done within scriptural parameters.*

Why do some people so vigorously oppose tongues? For one thing, speaking in tongues is extremely hard on human pride. Our minds rebel against uttering sounds that we do not understand; it's an affront to our intellect. "Why should I speak to God in a language that I do not understand?" they ask.

But if God has given a gift, there must be something worthwhile in it. We want to be open to whatever God might desire to do for us to enhance our walk with Him. So what if our intellect is insulted whenever we speak in tongues? Our spirit is edified through it. So we make a choice to let our intellect be insulted while our spirit is being edified.

Speaking in tongues is a powerful, God-given tool. It brings an intimacy and communion and fellowship with God that can be achieved in no other way. And that is why Satan fights so hard against it.

Let Love Be Paramount

With tongues, as with all else in the Christian life, we must never forget the supremacy of love. Whatever you believe about tongues, love must be paramount. We must remember that the gift of speaking in tongues has no real worth unless the believer also manifests love. As Paul said, "Though I speak with the tongues of men and of angels, but have not love, I have become as sounding brass or a clanging cymbal" (1 Corinthians 13:1). Such loveless folk make noise, but it is meaningless. It makes no sense and says nothing. Paul insists that the gift of speaking in tongues, unaccompanied by this divine, *agape* kind of love, is a meaningless sound.

Many people seek to use tongues as a sign of spiritual superiority. They consider tongues a sign of being filled or baptized with the Spirit. But if you do not have love, tongues are a sign of nothing. They are meaningless noises lacking any significance without the love of God at work in your life.

On the other end of the spectrum, some people condemn all of those who speak in tongues—even saying tongues are of the devil. But if you have no love for those who speak in tongues, your religion is nothing but a meaningless diatribe.

The answer in all cases is to walk in love. "And now abide faith, hope, love, these three," the apostle wrote, "but the greatest of these is love" (1 Corinthians 13:13).

So, if you speak in tongues, enjoy. But do not despise those who misunderstand the gift, or think of yourself as spiritually superior to them. You're not.

If you do not speak in tongues, do not despise or forbid those who do, nor attribute this gift of God to Satan. Speakers in tongues love our Lord with great emotional fervency, and they're as much of the body of Christ as you are.

Let's all walk in love. If a person speaks in tongues, fine, as long as he does it within the scriptural context. If a person doesn't speak in tongues, fine. He can still have a very close, intimate, marvelous, spiritual relationship with God.

Tongues is not the issue. The issue is how much love is manifested in your life by the presence of the Holy Spirit. That's the real test of the Holy Spirit in your life. Can you accept someone who is different from you? Can you love someone who may believe differently than you, but yet acknowledge that Jesus loves you both?

Let's face it: Jesus has brought us all into His family so that we might learn to love one another even as the Lord loves us.

And that's a whole lot.

16

What Did He Say?

To one is given...the interpretation of tongues.
—1 CORINTHIANS 12:8,10

The interpretation of tongues is a companion gift to the speaking with tongues. It is the only gift for which a person is told specifically to pray. Paul said, "Let him who speaks in a tongue pray that he may interpret" (1 Corinthians 14:13).

Without the gift of interpretation of tongues, an utterance of tongues has no place and no value in a public church service. In fact, Paul says, "If you bless with the spirit [that is, in tongues], how will he who occupies the place of the uninformed say 'Amen' at your giving of thanks, since he does not understand what you say?...If the whole church comes together in one place, and all speak with tongues, and there come in those who are uninformed or unbelievers, will they not say that you are out of your mind?" (1 Corinthians 14:16,23).

I can answer Paul's last question: Yes, they will think you're crazy.

I remember inviting a close friend to visit my church. Ed Hanke was a big kid who later played defensive end for the San Francisco 49ers. We went everywhere together after school. I was witnessing to him and coaxed him to come with me to church one Sunday morning.

As we sat in the pew, a lady in front of us started breathing heavily. I panicked, because I knew that her heavy breathing always preceded an utterance in tongues. I quickly bowed my head and started pleading, "O God, please don't speak to us in tongues today!" I knew Ed would never understand it, and I knew there would be embarrassing questions afterward that I couldn't answer.

But, God, I guess, didn't hear my prayer, because in a moment the tongues were loosed. And so were Ed's questions. Unfortunately, my answers weren't. Had I known then what I know now, I might at least have been able to help Ed understand what was happening. I would have told him that tongues and the interpretation of tongues are marvelous gifts of God— sometimes the Lord even uses them to bring an unbeliever to faith in him (more about that later).

Translation or Interpretation?

I grew up in a Pentecostal church that practiced speaking in tongues and the interpretation of tongues in its public services. As a young man I was very confused at how these gifts were exercised. I would often hear short utterances in tongues, followed by a long interpretation. At other times I would hear a long utterance in tongues followed by a short interpretation. This made no sense to me.

Occasionally I would count how many times a phrase was uttered in tongues and then count to see if a corresponding phrase was repeated that many times in the interpretation. Often it wasn't. Not only did I question the interpretations given, but eventually I began to question the validity of the experience itself.

Now, I had a great respect and reverence for these gifts. I always bowed my head and prayed during these manifestations. That is probably why I sometimes feared I might be bordering on the unpardonable sin in trying to analyze these things.

I now realize that part of my problem occurred because I had confused tongues and *translation* with tongues and *interpretation*.

Translation and interpretation are not identical. A translation is a word-for-word transfer of significance from one language to another. Interpretation goes a little further than translation. It tries to explain the meaning of an expression regardless of the words used in the original language. The words are not as central in an interpretation as are the concepts.

I have had translators who sought to be interpreters. I would make a short remark and they would take a couple of minutes to interpret my remark. They weren't just translating for me; they were interpreting, and I always wondered what they were saying. Quite often I discovered that they didn't understand me.

Several years ago I was speaking in a large Presbyterian church in Korea. I opened with one of the best jokes I have, to warm up the people and let them know I was human. When my punch line was translated, they all sat there looking dumbfounded. I thought, *This is going to be tough. These people don't respond.* After the service I asked one of my hosts, "What do you think I said?" I discovered the translator didn't get the joke at all and totally botched the punch line. I made a practice from then on that if I were going to tell any jokes, I'd tell them to the translator first. If he laughed, then I would use them. If he didn't laugh, I'd shelve them. Without a good translation, jokes just don't work.

In the interpretation of tongues, an interpretation does not have to match the length of the utterance in tongues. The utterance in tongues could be short yet have a prolonged interpretation (or vice versa). An interpretation gives the sense or meaning of an utterance in tongues, not just a word-for-word transfer from language to language.

The Purpose of Interpretation

The Greek word translated "interpret" is *hermeneia*, from which we get our word "hermeneutics," which refers to the science of scriptural interpretation. Normally this word is rendered "translation," but it would seem that the gift can refer to an interpretation as well.

The gift of the interpretation of tongues is designed to edify the whole body of Christ. If the gift of tongues were operating in a church service without the companion gift of the interpreting of tongues, then only the person speaking in tongues would be edified. Therefore, Paul said, if a person feels an urge to give an utterance in tongues in a place where no one is present to interpret, he should speak only to himself and to God (1 Corinthians 14:28).

I disagree with those who say the gift of interpretation is to be desired every time you speak in tongues, even in your own private devotional life. Tongues need to be interpreted only when they are spoken in a public service. Paul said he thanked God that he spoke with tongues more than all the

Corinthians, but also said, "If I pray in a tongue, my spirit prays, but my understanding is unfruitful" (14:14).

This obviously implies that when Paul prayed in an unknown tongue in his devotional life, he didn't understand what he was praying about. He didn't understand the praises or the petitions he was offering. And that means that those who say, "You should have the gift of interpretation so that every time you speak with tongues—even in your devotional life—you can understand what you are saying" do not have a scriptural basis for their position.

The Old Testament and the Gift of Interpretation

Is there any corollary to this gift of interpretation in the Old Testament? I can think of only one incident that might be considered a case of tongues and interpretation. When King Belshazzar hosted a wild banquet, the form of a hand suddenly appeared and started writing on the wall. The king began to quake in fear and called for his wisemen and his counselors to interpret these words. But they were unable to do so. Finally, the queen mother suggested, "During your grandfather's reign there was a man who had the Spirit of God dwelling in him; call him and he will be able to interpret these words." So Daniel was called and interpreted for Belshazzar the handwriting on the wall.

The writing was in Aramaic, the official language of the day, so surely the king's wise men and counselors could read the words themselves. Yet the words needed interpretation. The words were *mene, mene, tekel, upharsin*. The words literally meant, "numbered, numbered, weighed, divided." When Daniel was brought in, he rebuked Belshazzar for his gross sin as well as for his failure to heed the lessons his grandfather learned. Then he interpreted for the king the writing on the wall. This was his interpretation, found in Daniel 5:

- *Mene* (numbered): "God has numbered your kingdom, and finished it."

- *Tekel* (weighed): "You have been weighed in the balances, and found wanting."

- *Uhparsin* (Peres; divided): "Your kingdom has been divided, and given to the Medes and Persians."

Notice that Daniel's interpretation is longer than the words themselves. Had Daniel merely translated, he would have said "Numbered, numbered, weighed, divided," and the king wouldn't have known any more than he already did. But Daniel gave him the chilling interpretation, the divine significance of the words. Had I been a young man with Daniel and Belshazzar in Babylon, I probably would have wondered how so few words could prompt such a long interpretation. But that's the difference between translation and interpretation.

The New Testament and the Gift of Interpretation

It is interesting that we have no recorded cases of the exercise of this gift in the New Testament.[1] All we have is Paul's teaching on the subject in 1 Corinthians, and that is very limited. We have no documented incidents where the combined gifts of tongues and interpretation were used. That leaves us with little to go on.

In his commentary on the book of Acts, G. Campbell Morgan suggests that when the disciples began to speak with tongues on the day of Pentecost, the miracle was that the people from the various linguistic groups heard them speaking in their own languages—not that the disciples were actually speaking their dialects. Morgan implies that the disciples were all speaking Greek; but that the members of the audience all *heard* in their own languages the disciples speaking of the marvelous works of God. It's an interesting idea, although I personally don't agree with it.

A Personal Pentecost

Several years ago, when Calvary Chapel was in a transitional form, we gathered each Sunday night in the East Bluff Community Center. One evening, on Pentecost Sunday, 55 or 60 of us had assembled to remember the descent of the Holy Spirit upon the church.

At the end of our Bible study, I suggested that we all worship and praise the Lord and wait upon Him as they did when the Spirit descended on Pentecost. As we did so, Lynn— the woman I mentioned in the previous chapter—began to speak in French. With my three years of Latin I was able to pick up a portion of what she was saying, and I could tell that she was giving lovely praise to God.

Lynn was thanking the Lord for the beautiful new song He had put in her heart. It was her love song to him, a song of joy and blessing. It was especially moving because, prior to her conversion, she had been singing in nightclubs. When she accepted the Lord she left that lifestyle and began to use her beautiful voice to sing for Jesus. This night, in French, she was thanking the Lord and praising Him for the joyous new song He had put in her heart. I could understand just enough to enjoy her celebration, but not enough to give an interpretation.

My wife, however, who doesn't understand any French at all, began to interpret. And I began to rejoice. It was exactly what I had understood! I knew that neither Lynn nor my wife knew or had studied French, so to hear such a perfect interpretation of Lynn's expressions of praise and thanksgiving to the Lord—so close to a literal translation—I had my own Pentecost that night.

A Jewish visitor from Palm Springs who was going through some marital problems had joined us that night. A friend had brought her so I could counsel her after the meeting. When the people left and we were getting ready to talk, she said, "Before we get into my problems, I would like you to explain to me why the one lady spoke to the group in French and why the other lady translated what she said."

"Would you believe it if I told you that neither of those ladies know French?" I asked.

"No, I wouldn't" she replied.

"Well, I've known the one lady for years and I know she doesn't know any French—I'm married to her," I said. "I also know the other lady and I'm sure she doesn't know French."

Then I took her to the Scriptures, and showed her the gift of speaking in tongues and the gift of interpretation of tongues. "What you witnessed was an example of what Paul was talking about here, where one speaks in an unknown tongue and another interprets," I explained.

"Well," she said, "that was the most beautiful French I have ever heard. It was spoken with a perfect aristocratic accent. I lived in Paris for five years and it isn't street French; it was the aristocratic form of the language. And the other lady gave a perfect translation."

"Well, what do you expect from the Lord?" I asked.

She paused, and then said, "Before we get to my problems, I think I had better accept the Lord."

She did so, and then her problems were gone, too.

What happened that night was a true manifestation of speaking in tongues with an interpretation. The interpretation was addressed to God in praises and thanksgiving for Lynn's marvelous new song and the work of God's Spirit that had transformed her life. When this Jewish lady heard it and understood it—both in French and from the interpretation—she was convinced of the reality and the truth of Jesus Christ, and she received Him that night as her Lord.

How Does this Gift Operate?

How does the gift of interpretation operate? The Bible says there are diversities of gifts and diversities of operation. That means that the gift of interpretation may operate one way in my life but a different way in your life.

I love the fact that God is so diverse. He doesn't do things in a patterned way so that we begin to pigeonhole Him and say, "This is the only way He does things." I think He works in diverse ways so that we will be open to however God chooses to work.

Although I can tell you how the gift operates in my life, that doesn't mean it will operate in your life the same way. When I exercise this gift, I understand what is being said as if it were being spoken in English. The thought or the praise or the thanksgiving just comes into my mind. Quite often, the person speaking in tongues goes on for a few minutes and I can't immediately remember what was said. But when I begin repeating the thoughts that first came to me, the rest returns to my mind as I continue to speak. The interpretation begins to flow.

Of course, I do not get an interpretation every time I hear someone speaking in tongues. I appreciate that fact, because it helps me to realize this is a gift from God; that it's not my personal property. *The interpretation of tongues is a gift of the Holy Spirit*. The Holy Spirit anoints you to give an interpretation, and you know it when you have it (and you *sure* know it when you don't).

If someone is giving an utterance in tongues and I don't receive an interpretation, I don't immediately doubt the validity of his or her gift. It just means that God didn't choose to give me an interpretation of what they said. And that's fine with me.

Interpretation or Prophecy?

Just as there is a difference between interpretation and translation, so is there a difference between interpretation and prophecy. Oftentimes, as a young man, I was told a service had featured tongues and interpretation, when in fact I now believe it had been tongues and prophecy.

The Bible says that if I speak in an unknown tongue I'm not speaking to man, but to God. "He who speaks in a tongue does not speak to men but to God, for no one understands him; however, in the spirit he speaks mysteries" (1 Corinthians 14:2). I do not find any place in the New Testament where tongues are addressed to man.

In fact, Paul asks how a person who hears an unknown tongue is going to say "amen" to the giving of thanks, since he can't understand what is said. Paul recognized that God never addressed the church through the exercise of tongues; rather, tongues addressed God with praises or thanksgiving.

Therefore, if speaking in tongues is addressed to God, then a true interpretation of those tongues must also be addressed to God. If an utterance in tongues magnifies God, then the interpretation should also magnify God. If the utterance in tongues gives thanks and praise to God, then the interpretation will also give thanks and praise to God. God doesn't speak to the church in tongues, even when the utterance is interpreted.

On the other hand, God does address the church through prophecy. Through prophecy—not through tongues and their interpretation—He exhorts, teaches, comforts, and edifies His church.

Thus, I think it's unscriptural to talk about "a message in tongues with interpretation" as if it were a message from God to the church. So many times such interpretations begin with something like, "Thus saith the Lord: My children, if you will hearken to Me and lift up your voices and praise Me, then I will bless you and I will pour out My Spirit upon you." Such an exhortation to the church is said to be the interpretation of an utterance in tongues, but it is not; it is actually the exercise of the gift of tongues, followed by prophecy.

As I have sought to analyze this, I realize that the people are sincere and they love the Lord. I'm certain they have a genuine experience with God and I don't discount that. But, I think what I was observing was an utterance in tongues, followed by the gift of prophecy. "He that prophesieth speaketh unto men to edification, and exhortation, and comfort" (1 Corinthians 14:3 KJV). And if you'll notice the content of the supposed interpretation, which I believe to be a prophecy, the content is generally edification, exhortation, or comfort. And, thus, I think that the people actually believe they are experiencing the gift of tongues with interpretation, when in reality it is tongues and prophecy.

What I think happens is this: When the utterance in tongues is given, a person with the gift of prophecy sitting nearby is emboldened to stand up and give a prophecy which edifies and exhorts the congregation. His utterance was not an interpretation of tongues; it was a prophecy addressed to the church by God.

Barbarians in Church!

Our word "barbarian" comes from the Greeks. They called anyone who spoke in a language they did not understand "barbars." To them, foreign tongues sounded like someone saying "bar-bar-bar-bar." People who spoke these odd tongues were unintelligible, and therefore called bar-barians.

Through the wonderful gift of the interpretation of tongues, tongues speakers do not have to be barbarians in the assembly of the church. When someone gives an utterance of tongues to praise, honor, and give thanks to God, another sitting by who is gifted with the interpretation of tongues can edify the church by clearly proclaiming the beautiful words that have been spoken.

Sometimes, God may choose to use the exercise of these gifts to bring an unbeliever from the kingdom of darkness into the glorious light of the kingdom of God. But more frequently, He simply blesses the church by proclaiming in an understandable tongue the glorious things that have been declared in an unknown language.

Either way, it's a treat for anybody. Even barbarians.

17

Helps—
the Quiet Ministry

God hath set some in the church ... [with] gifts of ... helps.
—1 CORINTHIANS 12:28 KJV

[Whether] ministry, let us wait on our ministering.
—ROMANS 12:7 KJV

Because there are so many things that need to be done if a church is to sustain a full ministry, I think the gift of helps is one of the most important in the body of Christ.

We are prone not to place much honor upon this gift. Oftentimes it goes unnoticed and unrecognized because we tend to notice those who are up front, and we magnify the gift of teacher or evangelist. But I believe God places the more abundant glory and honor upon gift of helps (see 1 Corinthians 12:23,24).

No Need to Ask

What a glorious and wonderful thing it is when God brings alongside you those who have the ministry of helps. They don't have to be asked to do things; they see what needs to be done and quietly go about doing it. They exercise their ministry quietly, without a lot of fanfare. They don't draw attention to themselves. It's a beautiful, quiet ministry, and I am tremendously grateful for those who have it.

Every Monday morning from my office window I see an example of this ministry at work. The husband of one of the women in our church regularly brings his wife to an intercessory prayer group. While she is praying, he walks through the parking lot picking up the paper cups and other refuse left from Sunday. I thank God for that man. No one asked him to do it; he simply saw on Monday that trash had been left in the parking lot from Sunday, so he thought, *Here's something I can do.* That's a ministry of help, and our parking lot would look a lot worse if it weren't for his ministry.

A few years ago, two retired men in the church realized that our air conditioners have filters which need to be changed regularly. They developed a schedule for replacing the filters in our air conditioners—all 100 or so. They drew up a chart that told them when to order the filters and when to install them. Unfortunately for us, one of these men is already receiving his heavenly reward and the other has moved from the area! But I was always blessed when I saw them come over to the church.

I also think of all these ladies who are involved in various ministries at Calvary Chapel. It would be impossible for us to have successful programs if it weren't for these ladies who are involved in the ministry of helps. They get lessons together, organize groups, and see that there is room for everybody. It's glorious to watch how God has gifted these women, and how they offer themselves in service to the Lord. They don't exercise the gift for public recognition, and would be very embarrassed if someone called public attention to their work.

Not for Recognition

Of course, there are many people who don't fit such a description. They do things for recognition even though Jesus said, "Take heed that ye do not your alms before men, to be seen of them: otherwise ye have no reward of your Father which is in heaven" (Matthew 6:1 KJV).

Years ago I accepted a pastorate in a community church. My first Sunday there a beautiful floral piece had been placed on the table in front of the platform. After the service the head of the Board of Elders came up to me and said, "Pastor Smith, I know this is your first Sunday—you're new here and all—but if you want to continue to see those flowers in front, you'd better make mention of them." I replied, "You probably didn't know what you were getting into when you voted to take me as your pastor. I don't believe in giving public recognition to people, because I feel I would be robbing them of their heavenly reward." "Even so, pastor," he insisted, "if you want to see flowers there, you'd better mention them." The following Sunday a beautiful arrangement of flowers once again graced the table, but I made no mention of them. Sure enough, that was the last week they made an appearance.

That's not the gift of helps. Those graced with this gift do their service for the Lord and look to Him for the recognition and reward of what they've done. They exercise their gift with joy, as a service to the Lord. They know the Lord loves a cheerful giver.

Serve with Joy

The gift of helps should never be exercised out of duty or obligation because then you will feel resentful toward your "ministry." I know something about this, because the Lord has taught me some interesting lessons in this regard.

I want the grounds around our church to look clean and neat; I don't want our property to appear as though we don't care. Therefore, as I walk around the campus, I usually pick up any litter that might be lying around.

Now, with a school of almost two thousand students operating here, there can be a lot of litter. Students aren't the most tidy creatures in the world; they let their papers go and leave their empty pop cans everywhere.

Not long ago, as I was walking to my office, I found myself picking up these papers and cans and depositing them in the trash can—and resenting it. "Trashy kids!" I began to complain. I was getting angry about it. The job felt like washing dirty clothes—it never ends.

I began scooping up the pop cans and crushing them in my hands, resentment rising in my spirit. Then the Lord spoke to my heart. "Who are you doing this for?" He asked. "Well, for You, Lord," I replied. "Then forget it," He said. "If you're going to do it with that attitude, I'd rather you didn't do it."

It was a good reminder. Whatever we do for the Lord we should do cheerfully, for the sheer joy of knowing that we're doing it for Him. "Whatever you do in word or deed, do all in the name of the Lord Jesus, giving thanks to God the Father through Him" (Colossians 3:17). The same is true with the gift of helps. Exercise it for the glory of God and as to the Lord, realizing that He wants us to exercise our ministry joyfully.

If you find yourself resenting the work you are doing, then it would be best to stop doing it. Rather than being a positive experience for you, it will be a negative one. If you're growing bitter or resentful, upset that you've been asked to do some job, then you should know that your "service" goes against you rather than for you. God doesn't want clenched-teeth service.

I've observed that those with the gift of helps are always excited and thrilled that they can do something for the Lord. They bubble over with gratitude to think they have a service they can offer to God, and appreciate that He's delighted to let them serve Him this way.

Helps in the Scripture

Joshua had the gift of helps. Moses gave him orders and Joshua stood by to carry them out. Joshua was there to be a right-hand man for Moses, to help him in whatever way he could. He was a faithful servant, exercising his gift of helps—so much so, that when Moses died, God chose and ordained Joshua to take over the leadership of the nation.

In the New Testament, Timothy was a servant of Paul. He often accompanied Paul on missionary trips, helping him in many capacities. When Paul needed to move on, he'd say, "Timothy, you stay here for awhile." Later Paul would write and say, "Come and meet me, Timothy. And when you do, would you bring some parchments and some of the other things I need?" Timothy was a tremendous help to Paul, as were Priscilla and Aquilla, whom Paul called "my helpers in Christ Jesus: Who have for my life laid down their own necks" (Romans 16:3 KJV).

The book of Acts tells us that when the early church ran into a problem with its welfare program, the apostles chose seven men filled with the Holy Spirit who enjoyed a good reputation, and put them in charge of the program (see Acts 6). These men were appointed to the ministry of helps, to run the church's welfare plan.

One Ministry Leads to Another

As we are faithful in the place where God has called us, the Lord often expands our circle of ministry. If God has called me to stoke the furnace, then I need to be faithful in stoking. Whatever God has called me to do, I should do it to the best of my ability, with a willing and ready and joyful heart. I should do it as unto the Lord, not as unto man. And very often God will expand my ministry.

In the parable of the talents in Matthew 25, Jesus told the story of a man who traveled to a distant country, leaving his estate in the care of his servants. To one servant he gave five talents, to another two, and to another one. Upon his return, the man discovered that the servant who had been given the five talents had doubled his money. When the servant presented ten talents to his master, his lord replied, "Well done, good and faithful servant; you were faithful over a few things, I will make you ruler over many [or larger] things" (Matthew 25:21).

We see this principle in action in Acts 6 also. As the seven men appointed as deacons were faithful to their ministry, they were given greater responsibilities and circles of ministry. Philip, one of the seven and a gifted evangelist, was granted the gift of the working of miracles and of healing. It was he who went up to Samaria to bring Christ to the people there, and a tremendous revival broke out under his leadership.

Another of the seven was Stephen. As he was faithful in his ministry, God used him to challenge the Jewish high council. I am convinced that the apostle Paul eventually came to Christ as a direct result of Stephen's witness and martyrdom. When the Lord apprehended Paul on the road to Damascus, in effect Jesus said, "It's been hard for you to kick against the pricks of your conscience which has been goading you because of what you heard from Stephen. You heard the truth and it struck, but you've been fighting against it" (see Acts 26:14). Had Stephen not been faithful in the place of ministry that God gave him, we might never have heard of Paul. He might have remained Saul, and the church would have been the poorer for it.

Ministry as a Help

In Romans 12:6,7 Paul wrote, "Having then gifts differing according to the grace that is given to us, whether . . . ministry, let us wait on our ministering" (KJV). I believe he was referring to the gifts of helps. Ministry is an outgrowth of the gift of helps.

What is a minister? I am afraid people have many false ideas about what a minister is—and probably the portion of the church most confused are the ministers themselves.

Three Greek words are translated "minister." The word *diakonos* literally means "servant." From this Greek word we get our English word "deacon." Jesus used this word when He said, "If any man desire to be first, the same shall be last of all, and servant [*diakonos*] of all" (Mark 9:35 KJV). This is the same term used in Romans 12:7. If your gift is that of a *diakonos*, then wait upon your serving, your ministry. Most of the time when the word "minister" is used in the New Testament, it is this Greek word *diakonos*.

The ministry is not a profession to be chosen by idealistic young men; the ministry is a calling of God. To be a minister does not mean that you exercise rule or authority or control over people, but that you are their servant in the things of God. A lot of damage has been done in people's lives and to the church because of the attitude that ministry is some kind of spiritual dictatorship. It isn't. A minister is a servant.

Another Greek word, *leitourgos*, is also translated "minister" or "servant." In ancient times, this term usually referred to a wealthy person who gave himself for free public service. He was an unpaid public administrator, a volunteer who served the community at his own expense.

The Septuagint (the Greek translation of the Old Testament) uses this word, *leitourgos*, to translate the Hebrew term for "priest." We get our English word "liturgy" from this word.

The last Greek word translated "minister" is *hyperetes*, from the two Greek words *hyper* and *etes*. The word *hyper* means "under" and the word *etes* means "rower." If you're a *hyperetes*, you're not even on deck! The *hyperetes* were the guys down in the galley doing the work, while the *nautis*, the seamen, got all the credit. You've heard the term "galley slave"— that's what these *hyperetes* were, the "under rowers."

When Paul stood before King Agrippa in Caesarea, making his defense, he used this word to describe himself. He told how he was on the road to Damascus to imprison those who called upon the name of the Lord when suddenly, about noon, a light brighter than the sun shone upon him and knocked him to the ground. As he was lying there he heard a voice saying, "Saul, Saul, why do you persecute me?" He tells Agrippa that Jesus told him He had appeared to make Paul a "minister" and a witness. The word "minister" here is *hyperetein* (Acts 26:16). Jesus said, "Paul, I want you to be an under-rower."

I think we could use a few more "under rowers," don't you?

A Gift and a Calling

There are a lot of people who see some aspect of the ministry and are attracted to it. They think, *Oh, I would like to do that. That looks like it would be interesting.* So often the person sees the more glamorous aspects of the ministry. He sees that ministers have the opportunity to stand before thousands to teach the ways of God, and he thinks, *My, I would like to stand before thousands of people. I would like to receive that satisfying feedback from people who are grateful for the truths they have learned of God through the ministry of the Word.*

Maybe they're tired of their job. Maybe they are in a midlife crises and desire a career change. Whatever the reason, on their own and without the gift or the anointing of the Spirit, they seek to enter the ministry. Pulpits across the United States are filled with men like this, to whom the ministry is a profession and not a calling. Such men don't understand that ministry is a gift of God. It is a calling.

Paul, writing to the church of Ephesus, said, "Whereof I was made a minister, according to the gift of the grace of God given unto me by the effectual working of his power" (Ephesians 3:7 KJV). In other words, Paul didn't just one day decide he was going to be a minister; he was *made* a minister. He saw his position as a gift of the grace of God and he exercised that gift through the power of the Holy Spirit. Paul often spoke about being made a minister. In 1 Timothy 1:12, for example, he said, "I thank Christ Jesus our Lord who has enabled me, because He counted me faithful, putting me into the ministry."

True ministry can be fulfilled only as you are anointed by the Holy Spirit. When Paul's friends were trying to dissuade him from going to Jerusalem in Acts 20 (they knew hardships and imprisonment lay ahead for him) he replied, "I consider my life worth nothing to me, if only I may finish the race and complete the task the Lord Jesus has given me—the task of testifying to the gospel of God's grace" (verse 24 NIV). Paul had received his ministry from the Lord Jesus and he was determined to see it through to the end. You don't do that unless you know you've been called to it.

The ministry isn't something you put yourself in or that you do on your own. You must be called by the Lord. First Peter 4:11 says, "If any man minister, let him do it as if the ability which God giveth, that God in all things may be glorified" (KJV).

Jesus, the True Model

Jesus is the true example of what the minister and the ministry are all about. Jesus said, "For even the Son of man came not to be ministered unto, but to minister, and to give his life a ransom for many" (Mark 10:45 KJV). Jesus set the formula for the ministry. We are not here to be ministered to, but to minister. We are not here to be served, but to serve. Perhaps we'd be better off if we got rid of the term "minister" and returned to the original idea: servant.

Jesus not only talked about serving, He lived it. On the night He was betrayed, He gathered with the disciples in the upper room. He took a towel, girded himself, grabbed a basin, and went around the room washing the disciples' feet. Then He said, "Do you see what I've done? Do you get the picture? I have set an example for you. This is what the ministry is all about; this is what a minister does. He serves people even in the lowest of tasks."

In that day, it was only the flunkie servants who washed feet. Others got to wait on tables or serve in nicer capacities, but the flunkies washed feet. And Jesus said, "Do you see what I've done? The ministry is about serving others."

Earlier the Master had said, "I do not seek My own will but the will of the Father who sent Me" (John 5:30). That's how you identify a true servant. Service isn't doing your own will; it's doing the will of the One who sent you—even when His will leads to places far from comfort or safety. That was Jesus' commitment even in the garden, when He prayed, "Father, if it is Your will, remove this cup from Me; nevertheless not my will, but Yours, be done" (Luke 22:42). Jesus submitted Himself to His Father as a servant, and was willing to drink the cup if that is what His Father chose.

Philippians 2 tells us that Jesus took on the form of a servant and was obedient even to death on the cross. Throughout His life, Jesus gave Himself to serve the needs of the people. Though He was physically tired, He continued to minister. He chose to serve people who constantly made inordinate demands upon Him. He couldn't go anywhere without crowds surrounding Him, grabbing at His garments, and jostling for position. At times He was so pressured and pressed by the people that He was forced to get in a boat and speak to the crowds while floating a few dozen yards from the shore. People simply were not fair to Him. That drains a person.

Yet, time after time, Jesus was moved with compassion for the men and women whom He saw as sheep without a shepherd. He saw the hunger of their hearts, and so He gave that extra attention and love. And that's where the Spirit comes in for us. He gives us the strength and the power we need. If you're trying to serve out of the energy of your flesh, you'll end up wiped out and destroyed. But if you depend upon God's Spirit, God will give you the grace and the strength and the power to serve joyfully. That's what it means to serve—and that's what we're called to do.

Men and Women Both Minister

In the New Testament the ministry was not confined to men. Jesus was often ministered to by women. When the Savior left the synagogue in Capernaum He went to the house of Peter, where Peter's mother-in-law was sick with a high fever. Jesus laid His hand upon her and healed her, and immediately she rose up and ministered—*diakonei* in Greek—unto them (Matthew 8:15). She probably fixed him a pita sandwich or a falafel. Ministry takes many forms!

The names of Joanna and Susanna went down in the Scriptures because of their service. Luke 8:3 says these women ministered of their substance to Jesus. We are also told about other women from Galilee who ministered to him.

A Place to Serve

It is a blessed privilege to serve God. Though not all of us have the gift of helps or of ministry, we've all been called to serve Him. It is not our place to tell Him how or where we will serve; rather, we are to be available to serve wherever, whenever, however He might ordain. God has a place of service for every one of us in the body of Christ. All of us have been called to ministry, not just the "minister" who stands behind the pulpit. We have all been called to serve God. Ultimately, that's what all ministry is about.

The true gift of helps is an important and necessary gift within the body. There is so much to be done and no one man, woman, or ministerial staff can do it alone. There's a place of ministry for everybody. Do you know your place in the body? Are you fulfilling your place in the body? Are you using your gift?

There are many opportunities to exercise the gift of helps. If you hear of someone who has gone to the hospital, why not prepare a meal for the family, take it to them, and consider going over to clean their house? If the person is hospitalized for a prolonged period of time, you can be sure the house will become a mess. Go over and help, showing the love of Christ in a very practical way. We have men who volunteer to do tune-ups and brake work on the cars of the ladies in the church who have no husband and cannot afford to have the work done. Others prepare food for the homeless.

What a joy and blessing it is to be able to serve God. I pray that each of us will discover the place that the Lord has for us in the body of Christ, and that we might see the body of Christ functioning as one, as we sensitively minister to each other's needs, loving and caring for each another. Only in that way will we find the satisfaction and fulfillment of knowing that we are doing that which pleases our Lord. That is ministry, and there's nothing better.

18

Enough Milk, Already!

And God has appointed these in the church ... teachers.
—1 Corinthians 12:28

When I was in seminary, the most brilliant professor there did not have the gift of teaching—and his class was the most boring on campus. Other less brilliant professors did have the gift of teaching, and they made us want to learn. They made it exciting.

I hate to admit it, but I can't remember a thing I learned in the brilliant professor's class. But my other professors—the ones who had the gift of teaching—shared truths that are still part of my life and understanding today.

The truth is, it's not your brilliance that counts. It's whether you have the gift of teaching.

It's More than a Skill

Paul tells us that God has set in the church, first of all apostles, and then prophets, and then teachers. All three have been ordained by God to instruct the people in the Word of God.

There is a gift of teaching, just as there are other spiritual gifts. I recognize that God has given me this gift for the building up of the body of Christ.

As I prepare to teach, I wait upon the Lord in my study, seeking the mind of the Lord and enlightenment from the Holy

Spirit on the Word of God. God ministers His love and truth to my heart. Only then am I prepared to share that which I have received from the Spirit, ministering God's truth to God's people.

To the Corinthian church Paul wrote, "For I received from the Lord that which I also delivered to you" (1 Corinthians 11:23). Whenever I stand before a congregation to teach God's Word, it is always my prayer that I can preface my remarks with these words of Paul: "That which I have received from the Lord, I also deliver to you."

Yet it's interesting that the gift of teaching doesn't always work. There are times when I get up to teach and the anointing of the Spirit just isn't on me. That puts pressure on me, and I hate it. I push and push; there is no natural flow. I know the message is falling flat, and the reason is that the anointing is simply not there.

There are other times, however, when I get up and the message just flows. The thoughts, the ideas, the inspiration, the anointing—it all comes out like a river going downhill. Then it's easy. There are few things more joyful and exciting than when God is flowing through you to communicate His Word and His truth to others.

The fact that sometimes the gift is there and sometimes it isn't indicates that teaching is not a natural ability; you can't do it anytime you choose. It is a gift of God, and you must depend upon God for its exercise. Just when you think you have it, God takes it away and lets you enjoy one of those evenings in which you push and shove but get nowhere. Then you say, "Oh, Lord, never again. Don't do that to me again! I need You. I depend upon You. I can't teach without You." Teaching is a gift that depends upon the anointing of the Spirit to make it flow.

Teaching or Preaching?

The apostle Paul enjoyed a three-fold ministry. He says he was "appointed a preacher, an apostle, and a teacher of the Gentiles" (2 Timothy 1:11). His distinctions tell us there is a difference between the gift of preaching and the gift of teaching. The church has suffered tremendously because we have failed to recognize this difference.

Preaching is declaring or heralding the truth of God to bring people to a saving knowledge of Jesus Christ. It is evangelistic, proclaiming God's Good News that He has provided for the forgiveness of sins through His crucified Son, who took our guilt and died in our place. Preaching persuades people to receive Jesus Christ as their lord.

Teaching, on the other hand, is not for the unconverted, but for the converted. Teaching enables those who have accepted Jesus Christ as their Lord to grow in the grace and the knowledge of God. Preaching is for the sinner; teaching is for the saint.

There has been far too much preaching in the church, and far too little teaching. In fact, the church has almost been preached to death. The church needs teaching so that more believers will grow and become mature in their relationship with Jesus Christ.

The author of Hebrews lamented over his readers: "For though by this time you ought to be teachers, you need someone to teach you again the first principles of the oracles of God; and you have come to need milk and not solid food. For everyone who partakes only of milk is unskilled in the word of righteousness, for he is a babe" (Hebrews 5:12,13). It's as if he said, "Look, you've been around long enough. At this point, you ought to be able to teach the Word of God, but you're still in need of being taught." Why? Because their diet consisted only of evangelism. They had been preached to, but they had not been taught so that they might mature.

A couple of verses later the writer says, in effect, "Let's go on to maturity. Let's not go back and keep laying the foundations over and over. Foundations are important, but you have to build on them. Once the foundation is laid, you must construct the building—that's the whole point. So let's develop, let's grow in our relationship and walk with the Lord. Let's not stay in this infant state. Let's mature."

The Corinthian believers had a similar problem. Paul wanted to teach them the deeper things of the Spirit, but found himself restricted because they hadn't grown. "And I, brethren, could not speak to you as to spiritual people but as to carnal, as to babes in Christ. I fed you with milk and not with solid food; for until now you were not able to receive it, and even now you are still not able" (1 Corinthians 3:1,2). In other words, "There are a lot of things I'd like to tell you, but you're not ready for them. So I've given you milk. It seems as if it's still necessary that you be bottle-fed because you haven't grown."

The purpose of the gift of teaching is to enable a believer's spiritual growth and development. Many people make a great mistake in thinking that spiritual growth comes from experience alone; it doesn't. It is only as the Word of God feeds our spirits that real spiritual growth comes. That is why this gift of teaching is so vital and necessary in the church.

If ever there were a time when the gift of teaching needed to be exercised, it is today. Carnality in the church is as rampant today as it was in Corinth, and as a result the church stagnates in a state of arrested spiritual development. At a time when we should be mature, having grown and developed, we are still babes in Christ. That's a tragedy, indeed.

Once a person has come to faith in Jesus Christ, his or her greatest need is to be taught the Scriptures. The purpose of the pastor-teacher is "for the equipping of the saints for the work of ministry, for the edifying of the body of Christ, till we all come to the unity of the faith and the knowledge of the Son of God, to a perfect man, to the measure of the stature of the fullness of Christ; that we should no longer be children, tossed to and fro and carried about with every wind of doctrine, by the trickery of men, in the cunning craftiness by which they lie in wait to deceive, but, speaking the truth in love, may grow up in all things into Him who is the head—Christ" (Ephesians 4:12-15).

Without the solid teaching of the Word of God, believers remain in a state of arrested spiritual development. Through the prophet Hosea the Lord cried, "My people are destroyed for lack of knowledge. Because you have rejected knowledge, I also will reject you from being priest for Me; because you have forgotten the law of your God, I also will forget your children" (Hosea 4:6).

When all the church hears is preaching—when all we hear is that we should repent and forsake our sins and believe in Jesus Christ who died for us—we remain babes in Christ. The gospel message is glorious—and the sinner needs to know it—but Christians already know. We have accepted the truth that Jesus gave Himself for us, dying in our place. Now, let's go on in our walk with the Lord. Let's grow up and reach full maturity in the things of Christ. That only happens through the teaching of the Word of God.

Teaching in the Old Testament

The gift of teaching is first mentioned in Exodus 4:12, when God says to Moses, "Now therefore, go, and I will be with your mouth and teach you what you shall say." The Lord promised Moses that He would be his Teacher, enabling him in turn to teach the Israelites. Just three verses later God says about Aaron, "Now you shall speak to him and put the words in his mouth. And I will be with your mouth and with his mouth, and I will teach you what you shall do." In the first reference the Lord promised He would teach Moses what to say; now He tells him that He will instruct him in what to do. Both things are necessary.

Centuries later, the nation of Israel found itself in dire circumstances. The reason for their calamity was that "for a long time Israel has been without the true God, without a teaching priest" (2 Chronicles 15:3). Their terrible situation was caused by a lack of teaching, which in turn caused God to be absent from their midst.

Teaching always has been crucial for the people of God. That is why the promise of Nehemiah 9:20 is so precious: "You also gave Your good Spirit to instruct them." How we need this gift at all times and all places!

Teaching in the New Testament

The ministry of Jesus Christ was largely a ministry of teaching. Throughout the Gospels we find Him teaching the people about His Father. Fifty-eight times in the Gospels Jesus is addressed as "master," which means "teacher." He was known and recognized as a teacher.

It is no surprise, therefore, that at the end of the first Gospel Jesus tells His disciples, "Go therefore and make disciples of all the nations, baptizing them in the name of the Father and of the Son and of the Holy Spirit, teaching them to observe all things that I have commanded you; and lo, I am with you always, even to the end of the age" (Matthew 28:19,20).

The apostle Paul took this command seriously. After his conversion and sojourn in the Arabian desert, he visited Jerusalem. The church there found him a little too hot to handle—he was too eager to go after the religious leaders, especially the Pharisees—so they sent him into forced retirement at Tarsus.

But he was too good a man to just sit around in Tarsus. Barnabas knew Paul had a Grecian cultural background, as well as fine Hebrew training, so he concluded that this former enemy of the church would make an excellent minister to the growing Gentile church in Antioch. Acts 11:26 tells us, "And when he had found him, he brought him to Antioch. So it was that for a whole year they assembled with the church and taught a great many people."

Paul (Saul) is named in Acts 13:1 as a teacher in the church in Antioch, while Acts 15:35 tells us, "Paul and Barnabas also remained in Antioch, teaching and preaching the word of the Lord, with many others also." Paul not only taught but preached, exercising a combined gifting that we still see today. These combined gifts accent and complement each other.

Paul spent a year teaching the Word of God in Antioch, a year and a half teaching in Corinth (Acts 18:11), and two or three years teaching in Ephesus. In Acts 20:20, he declares to the Ephesian elders how he kept back nothing that was profitable to them: "Therefore," he said, "I testify to you this day that I am innocent of the blood of all men. For I have not shunned to declare to you the whole counsel of God" (Acts 20:26,27).

What a a marvelous declaration for any minister to be able to make to his people: "I have declared to you all the counsel of God!" I know of only one way that a person can make that declaration, and that is to take a congregation through the entire Bible, from Genesis to Revelation. Only when you have gone through the Bible from cover to cover can you safely say, "I have declared to you all the counsel of God." God has been pleased to allow me to take the people of Calvary Chapel through the Bible seven times during my ministry, and it has been tremendous each time. Nothing can compare to digging into the Word of God, verse by verse and book by book.

It was this kind of expositional preaching that Ezra the scribe gave to the Israelites who, with Nehemiah, were rebuilding Jerusalem at the end of the Babylonian exile. The people gathered and the words of the law were read to them and then explained. Nehemiah 8:8 says, "So they read distinctly from the book, in the Law of God; and they gave the sense, and helped them to understand the reading." This is the expositional teaching of the Word of God, and it feeds the flock as nothing else can.

Anointed to Teach

It is all-important that the Holy Spirit anoint us for the gift of teaching. Without the Holy Spirit we cannot even know spiritual truth, much less teach it. "The natural man does not receive the things of the Spirit of God, for they are foolishness to him; nor can he know them, because they are spiritually discerned" (1 Corinthians 2:14).

Recently there has been another classic example of why the Holy Spirit is so necessary if we are to accurately understand the Word of God. A group of scholars, calling themselves "The Jesus Seminar," meets regularly to bless the church by telling us which of the Scriptures contain the genuine sayings of Jesus and which ones are fabrications. These men give the impression that if we don't accept their conclusions, it's only a sign of our ignorance. After all, they are the scholars.

In their latest meeting, these men determined that Jesus never did promise to come again to establish a kingdom on the earth. That idea, they said, was conjured up afterward by the disciples who were disappointed by the crucifixion. To cover their embarrassment that Jesus died without bringing in His kingdom, they fabricated this whole concept.

They say Matthew got a little heavy-handed when he reported that Jesus said, "Then the sign of the Son of Man will appear in heaven, and then all the tribes of the earth will mourn, and they will see the Son of Man coming on the clouds of heaven with power and great glory" (Matthew 24:30).

A similar explanation is given of John 14:1-3, where Jesus is recorded to have said to His disciples, "Let not your heart be troubled; you believe in God, believe also in Me. In My Father's house are many mansions; if it were not so, I would have told you. I go to prepare a place for you. And if I go and prepare a place for you, I will come again and receive you to Myself; that where I am, there you may be also." They say this was John's idea, not Jesus'—that John put those words in the mouth of Christ.

The same is true when the thief was hanging on the cross and saw the inscription, "Jesus of Nazareth, King of the Jews." Luke records that he turned to Jesus and said, "Lord, remember me when You come into your kingdom." Jesus "supposedly" said, "Today you will be with Me in Paradise." But of course, they say that's only what Luke recorded. That in fact, Jesus had expected the kingdom to be set up in His lifetime and was as disappointed as everybody else when it didn't happen. So say the scholars of "The Jesus Seminar."

We have a decision to make. Are we going to believe the writers of the Bible who were inspired of the Holy Spirit, or are we to believe these modern-day scholars who have applied their scholarly training in a futile endeavor to understand the Word of God through human reasoning alone?

The Bible declares that when Jesus ascended into heaven, a cloud received Him out of the disciples' sight. As they were looking up into the sky, watching Him until He disappeared, suddenly two men in white clothes appeared and said, "Men of Galilee, why do you stand gazing up into heaven? This same Jesus, who was taken up from you into heaven, will so come in like manner as you saw Him go into heaven" (Acts 1:11). That's what the Bible declares and there is no reason to doubt it.

If you really want to understand God and His Word, unaided human scholarship, devoid of the Spirit, will be of no value. No man can understand the things of the Spirit unless the Lord teaches him. There is a realm of understanding beyond our human reason and intellect. The Spirit teaches us the things of God through His power and His anointing.

That's the lesson we learn from no less an authority than the apostle Paul. Now remember, Paul was a brilliant man. You cannot read his writings without recognizing his brilliance. He declared that he had been schooled at the feet of Gamaliel, one of the leading rabbis of the day. Yet Paul had no interest in trying to persuade men intellectually. Rather, he desired that his preaching would be a demonstration of the Spirit's power. That is why he wrote to the Corinthians, "My speech and my preaching were not with persuasive words of human wisdom, but in demonstration of the Spirit and of power, that your faith should not be in the wisdom of men but in the power of God" (1 Corinthians 2:4,5).

There's a difference between intellectual conversion and heart conversion, between believing in your mind and believing in your heart. Paul was interested in reaching the heart. He knew it is the Spirit that reaches the heart of man, not mere human intellect.

How desperately we need to remember this today. Trust in the Holy Spirit to give you wisdom, to give you guidance, to give you the understanding you need. John wrote, "You do not need that anyone teach you; but as the same anointing teaches you concerning all things, and is true" (1 John 2:27). The Holy Spirit will teach us and anoint us with His understanding.

Without Him, there is no true teaching of the Word of God.

I have said it more than once: An uneducated, Spirit-filled man of God is a more reliable source to the truth of God than an unconverted scholar who understands Greek, Hebrew, and Aramaic. Only the Spirit can help us truly understand and walk in the way of God. And He has repeatedly said that is exactly what He longs to do.

The Result of Good Teaching

It is generally not hard to see the results of good teaching in a believer's life. Isaiah 54:13,14 paints a tremendous picture that I have seen lived out over and over in the lives of well-taught saints of God: "All your children shall be taught by the Lord, and great shall be the peace of your children. In righteousness you shall be established; you shall be far from oppression, for you shall not fear; and from terror, for it shall not come near you."

Great peace is the result of good teaching; fear and terror will be gone. Why? Because through the teaching of the Word, you come to understand the greatness of God, the love of God, and the concern of God for you. When you catch a glimmer of how much God loves you and how much He works for your welfare, you don't have to fear the uncertainty of the future. You're not terrorized by the events bombarding your life. Instead, you have great peace, great confidence. You think, *God loves me. God's on the throne. God's watching over me. God's going to see me through.*

What a blessing this gift of teaching is to the church. For you who teach Sunday school, please recognize what a vital and important ministry God has given to you. You have the opportunity to bring into those pliable young minds many of their primary and first impressions of God. Encourage them to memorize the Scriptures. Let them know how much God loves them, and plant in their hearts the foundational truths of the God we worship in spirit and in truth.

If you have the gift of teaching, use it. Seek the help and guidance of the Holy Spirit to make you a better teacher. Pray that through the Spirit of God you will plant into young minds and hearts the lasting truths of the eternal God. So many of us can go back in our memories to the Sunday school room and remember the lessons we were taught concerning the Lord. We recall those beautiful illustrations that enabled our young minds to grasp the truth. Those lessons last a lifetime.

Exercise your gift of teaching. Invite the children from the neighborhood into your home and teach them about God. Use the gift that God has given you. As Paul said to Timothy, "Stir up the gift of God which is in you" (2 Timothy 1:6). Stir it up! And then stand back and see God do marvelous things through you.

19

Just Do It!

*Having then gifts differing according to the grace that is
given to us, let us use them. . . . He who exhorts in exhortation.*

—ROMANS 12:6,8

It had been a rough few days for Martin Luther,
the embattled father of the Protestant Reformation. Luther had
a tendency toward depression, and he was slipping into one of
his not-uncommon foul moods. For days he rarely talked to
anyone, and he snapped at those who tried to speak with him.
Finally his wife had had enough. Dressing all in black, former
nun Katherine von Bora knocked at the door of her husband's
study and roused him from his desk. Her dark appearance
startled the reformer and he demanded, "Why are you dressed
like that? What has happened?"

"You have been acting as though God were dead, so I
thought I would dress for His funeral," replied Katherine, who
then calmly spun on her heels and left the room. A chastised
Martin got the point and his humor quickly improved.

It's amazing what an apt word from an exhorter can
accomplish.

What Is Exhortation?

People with the gift of exhortation encourage and urge us
to put into action the things we know we should be doing.

With most people, the problem isn't knowing what they should do; it's doing it. We humans seem to need someone else to urge and compel us to appropriate action.

When you're discouraged and tempted to give in to a defeatist attitude—like Martin Luther did—the exhorter comes along and says, "Now, come on, the Lord is not dead. God knows what's going on. He knows exactly what you're going through. Now just commit it to the Lord and trust in Him."

Unfortunately, many believers do not live up to what they know to be right. They are hearers of the Word, but not doers. They know the truth, they even consent to the truth, but they do not practice it. Thus, they need encouragement. They need a push.

Exhortation encourages the person to go ahead and do what he really needs to be doing. For example, some of us need to be exhorted to pray. We already know we should be praying more than we do. We know that prayer should be our first resort and not the last. Yet so often we get caught up in the pressures of life. We work ourselves silly trying to find the answers on our own. Finally, we pour out our heart to our exhorter friends and they ask, "Have you prayed about it?"

"Um, well, I intend to."

"Friend, let's pray. Let's pray right now. Let's agree together this moment. Come on, let's ask God about this matter."

Many of us are natural procrastinators. "I hope to get to that next week," we say. "I don't have time for it today, but maybe tomorrow." Not long ago an excellent article appeared in the *Reader's Digest* on the subject of procrastination. One of our daughters is a classic procrastinator and my wife suggested that she read the article. "Oh, yes, I saw that article," replied our daughter. "I'm going to read it one of these days."

Not a few of us suffer from this tendency to put off what we know we should be doing. We let things slide, and we need someone to come along and say, "Now, look! Get in and do it! Do it *now!*"

That's the gift of exhortation—urging us to do what we know we should. The exhorter comes alongside us and says, "You've heard it, now let's do it. You know it, now let's practice it. Let's go."

Some Are Gifted, Some Aren't

There is an actual gift of exhortation. Certain people are gifted in this area, strengthening and reminding us of what we should be doing. When these people talk about prayer, for example, you are left with a strong desire to pray. Every time I read a book on prayer by E.M. Bounds, I end up on my knees and commit myself to pray more. He is an exhorter in the area of prayer.

Of course, some people who attempt to exhort don't have the gift. Their words don't comfort, they rile. You want to say, "Look, why don't you just do it yourself!" They're irritating, not inspiring. Thank God that there are people with the genuine gift of exhortation to show God's will. People who make you want to do what you know you should do.

Through exhortation we are enabled to abound more and more in the things of God. As Paul said, "Furthermore then we beseech you, brethren, and exhort you by the Lord Jesus, that as ye have received of us how ye ought to walk and to please God, so ye would abound more and more" (1 Thessalonians 4:1 KJV). Paul is exhorting us to conduct ourselves in a way that increasingly pleases God.

Exhortation in the Old Testament

In the Old Testament practically every prophet was an exhorter; for examples of exhortation, just read through the prophets. They exhorted the people to turn from their idols and return to the living God—to get back into a right relationship with the Lord. In times of battle, the prophets encouraged the people to trust in God and allow the Lord to be their defense. They encouraged the nation to believe that God would be with them and would bless them and give them victory.

David not only exhorted others to pray and give thanks, he also exhorted himself in times of discouragement. At least three times he wrote, "Why are you cast down, O my soul? And why are you disquieted within me? Hope in God" (Psalm 42:5,11; 43:5). When he found himself dejected, discouraged, and upset, he asked himself, "Hey, what's wrong? Why are you so upset? Trust in the Lord." There are times when we can actually exhort ourselves. We must learn to speak to ourselves to do that which we know we should be doing.

David's son, Solomon, exhorted the people to trust in the Lord with everything within them. "Trust in the Lord with all your heart, and lean not on your own understanding; in all your ways acknowledge Him, and He shall direct your paths"

(Proverbs 3:5,6). Much of the Proverbs is exhortation to do what Moses had taught the people to do in the first five books of the Bible. Exhortation is prevalent in the Old Testament.

Exhortation in the New Testament

The classic exhorter of the New Testament is James. If you want to understand what the gift of exhortation is all about, read his book. You can almost hear him today: "Now, look. You say you have faith? Great. Show me your works and I'll see your faith. Don't just say that you believe; prove it. Show me your faith by your actions. Let us see the reality of what you believe through the works that you do. Otherwise, you're only deceiving yourself. Real faith isn't just saying something. It isn't just repeating an apostle's creed. It isn't just standing up at the right time and sitting down at the right time. It's doing the things that the Scriptures tell us to do. Put your faith into action, put it to work. But don't just talk about it."

Peter also exercised the gift of exhortation. In 1 Peter 5:1-9 he wrote:

> The elders who are among you I exhort, I who am a fellow elder and a witness of the sufferings of Christ, and also a partaker of the glory that will be revealed: Shepherd the flock of God which is among you, serving as overseers, not by constraint but willingly, not for dishonest gain but eagerly; nor as being lords over those entrusted to you, but being examples to the flock; and when the Chief Shepherd appears, you will receive the crown of glory that does not fade away.

> Likewise you younger people, submit yourselves to your elders. Yes, all of you be submissive to one another, and be clothed with humility, for "God resists the proud, but gives grace to the humble." Therefore humble yourselves under the mighty hand of God, that He may exalt you in due time, casting all your care upon Him, for He cares for you.

> Be sober, be vigilant; because your adversary the devil walks about like a roaring lion, seeking whom he may devour. Resist him, steadfast in the faith, knowing that the same sufferings are experienced by your brotherhood in the world.

Notice how many exhortations are here. Peter exhorts the elders of the church, the younger people in the church, and everyone else. He gives so many exhortations: feed the flock of God; take oversight of the church; don't lord it over God's heritage but be examples; submit to each other; humble themselves under the mighty hand of God; cast their cares upon Him; be sober and vigilant; resist the enemy, Satan; and be encouraged that we are not alone in the struggle.

Paul was another exhorter. Writing to the Romans he said, "I beseech you therefore, brethren, by the mercies of God, that you present your bodies a living sacrifice, holy, acceptable to God, which is your reasonable service" (Romans 12:1). This was an exhortation to action, to activity, to let our faith be seen by what we do.

Paul really got rolling as he closed his first epistle to the Thessalonians:

> Now we exhort you, brethren, warn those who are unruly, comfort the fainthearted, uphold the weak, be patient with all. See that no one renders evil for evil to anyone, but always pursue what is good both for yourselves and for all. Rejoice always, pray without ceasing, in everything give thanks; for this is the will of God in Christ Jesus for you. Do not quench the Spirit. Do not despise prophecies. Test all things; hold fast what is good. Abstain from every form of evil" (1 Thessalonians 5:14-22).

In his second letter he says, "We command and exhort through our Lord Jesus Christ that they work in quietness and eat their own bread. But as for you, brethren, do not grow weary in doing good" (2 Thessalonians 3:12).

To Timothy, the apostle wrote, "Therefore I exhort first of all that supplications, prayers, intercessions, and giving of thanks be made for all men, for kings and all who are in authority" (1 Timothy 2:1,2).

Jude was yet another exhorter. He wrote, "Beloved, while I was very diligent to write to you concerning our common salvation, I found it necessary to write to you exhorting you to contend earnestly for the faith which was once for all delivered to the saints" (Jude 3). Even from these few examples we can see the important place exhortation holds in the New Testament.

Exhortation Today

One of the most beautiful gifts of exhortation I have ever had the privilege of observing belonged to a little old lady in her nineties. Mother Berg used to travel across the United States in a big, old Cadillac, stopping at churches across the country to exhort the people. Although she lived in Huntington Beach, she had a radio ministry based in Florida, which was beamed throughout the Caribbean. She was a real sweetheart.

Whenever I would get discouraged or anxious about my ministry, I would go over and knock on Mother Berg's door and let her exercise her gift of exhortation. I'd always come away encouraged, strengthened, helped, and with a new perspective.

When she attended our church, I always asked her to say a few words to the people. Her favorite theme was, "God is still on the throne." She would say, "You're acting as though He abdicated His throne. You're acting as though God is not in control. The way you're acting, you'd think that God wasn't in charge any more, that He no longer rules. But God *is* on the throne."

Mother Berg had a way of making the truth so real that you could suddenly see the whole situation in a new perspective. God really was in control, on the throne, and ruling. Of course you can cast your cares upon the Lord! Of course you can commit your situation to the Father! You can walk away free from any nagging fear or torment within because you regained your true perspective. Your mind was now reassuring you, *God's in control of my life. He's in control of everything in my life. God is on the throne, and God will take care of it.*

How often we need this kind of exhortation that builds us up in Christ and brings comfort to our troubled souls! Yet this isn't the only kind of exhortation we need.

At Calvary Chapel, one of our pastors, Romaine, has the gift of exhortation. It's not uncommon to hear him say something like, "Okay, get off your duff and get out of here and trust the Lord. Don't come crying to me about your problems. Trust the Lord! Don't look to me for help, look to the Lord. I can't help you, but the Lord will." He has a tremendous gift of exhortation, and it's a good balance for our church. I have the gift of teaching; Romaine has the gift of exhortation. He exhorts the people to put into practice the things they've learned from the Scriptures.

My wife, Kay, also has the gift of exhortation. But the way the gift operates in her life is different from the way it operates in Romaine's life. Kay talks to you about trusting in the Lord and spending more time in prayer, she has a way of making you eager to get closer to the Lord and be more intimate with Him, to experience more of His love, and to more frequently express your love to Him.

The gift is the same in both cases, but its operation is quite different.

A Companion Gift to Prophecy

The gift of exhortation is often a companion gift to the gift of prophecy. Paul writes in 1 Corinthians 14:3, "He who prophesies speaks edification and exhortation and comfort to men," while Acts 15:32 says, "Now Judas and Silas, themselves being prophets also, exhorted the brethren with many words and strengthened them." So we see that the gift of exhortation is often tied to and related to the gift of prophecy.

Exhortation is also quite naturally linked to preaching. Luke tells us among his many exhortations, that John the Baptist "preached to the people" (Luke 3:18). The purpose of the preacher is to move people to action: to trust their lives to God, to believe on the Lord Jesus Christ and repent of their sin, and change their lives.

In several places exhortation is related to sound doctrine. In 1 Timothy 4:13, Paul said, "Till I come, give attention to reading, to exhortation, to doctrine." In 2 Timothy 4:2, he said, "Preach the word! Be ready in season and out of season. Convince, rebuke, exhort, with all longsuffering and teaching." And in Titus 1:9, Paul wrote, "holding fast the faithful word as he has been taught, that he may be able, by sound doctrine, both to exhort and convict those who contradict." So we see that sound doctrine is often related to this gift of exhortation.

Notice Paul exhorted Titus to remain in "sound doctrine." What makes it "sound?" Both its commitment to the truth and its practicality. It must be practical, because if doctrine isn't workable, it is of no value.

A lot of people are consumed with their orthodoxy, with being absolutely right—almost to the point of legalism. They get into the bondage of having to be absolutely right on every little point, and often reach the stage of dead orthodoxy where they become dead right. There's no life, no joy, no excitement in their relationship with Jesus. They're too concerned about chapter and verse and right doctrine to notice that their relationship with God has dried up.

Unless doctrine can be put into practical use in my life, it isn't helpful. To know that God is omnipotent is not enough; I must also trust in the omnipotent God. That's what exhortation urges us to do.

To What Are We Exhorted?

The Scripture exhorts us to many things. In Acts 11:23, for example, the apostles exhorted the people to cleave to the Lord. In Hebrews 12:5 we are exhorted not to despise the chastening of the Lord. First Thessalonians 2:12 exhorts us to "walk worthy of God." This is such an important exhortation because people who won't read the Word of God will read your life. If your walk is inconsistent with your talk—if you're out witnessing to everybody but your walk falls short of what you're saying—your witness will be effectively nullified.

In Hebrews, we are warned against a human tendency to drift away: "Therefore we must give the more earnest heed to the things we have heard, lest we drift away" (Hebrews 2:1).

How easily we drift away! We tend to forget the things of God, to get so involved in ourselves, and so overwhelmed with our problems that we fail to see the power of the omnipotent God, who has adopted us as His sons and daughters. We forget that He is willing and eager to show His love to us by showering us day by day with His attention and His blessing. So easily we move away from that place of blessing.

That is why we must be encouraged and urged to get the focus of our life on the Lord and not on the problem, not on ourselves, not on the miseries or the discomfort or the pain or the hardships that we may be suffering. Exhortation focuses our eyes on the Lord. It corrects our vision.

Jesus warned us that there would be innumerable temptations to take our eyes off Him. He spoke of things that can impede the fruitfulness of the Spirit in our lives: the deceitfulness of riches, the desire for other things, hardships, difficulties, and tribulations. If we are not wary, any one of those usurpers can choke out our fruitfulness so that our lives becomes dry, unproductive, and barren.

This is why exhortation is so critical; it helps us to cling and cleave to the Lord. Many times that's about the only thing left to us. The world around us is crumbling, friends have let us down, and we have nothing left but to wrap our hands tightly around the Lord.

When we lose sight of the Lord, discouragement, anxiety, and fear begin to grip our hearts. We begin to wonder how we are ever going to get through some problem, and we slide toward despair because we can't see any way out. We lose sight of the Lord and of His greatness and His power.

The exhorter gets you back on track, gets your eyes focused on the Lord, once more helping you see things in the right perspective. As you lay out your problem, pour out your heart, and speak of the overwhelming challenges facing you, the exhorter is able to direct your attention away from your difficulties and toward the Lord and His greatness and His power and His love and His care and His concern for you. He reminds you that God is on the throne.

There are so many appropriate exhortations. You can see why exhortation is a gift that needs to be practiced perennially.

A Powerful Witness to the World

If there were more people with the gift of exhortation today, the church would be walking straighter than it is, and we'd have a more powerful witness to the world.

We need exhortation. We need to be reminded. That is why Peter said in his second epistle, "Friends, I'm writing to you about these things, not because you don't already know them, but because you do. I want to jog your memory about them; I think that's the safe thing to do. I especially want to do this because I know that before long I'm going to be checking out and leaving this old tent. I'm writing to you so that after I am gone you may still be reminded of these crucial truths of God" (see 2 Peter 1:12-15).

If you have the gift of exhortation, I exhort you to use it. Maybe you're the kind of exhorter who has a way of getting the flock all charged up and ready to go to battle against the forces of darkness. Perhaps you can stir the people into action.

Or maybe you're the kind of exhorter who has a knack for helping people to trust God, to believe Him for great things. I was thinking recently about how many of our songs actually are exhortations of this sort. "Trust and obey, for there is no other way to be happy in Jesus, but to trust and obey." How much we need such exhortation. We talk about it more than enough; now it's time to do it.

Just Do It!

Exhortation is a glorious and wonderful gift. And surely it is necessary if the body of Christ is to be well-rounded, putting into practice the things that we know and have been taught. I think there's little doubt all exhorters were pleased with an advertising campaign a few years ago that enjoyed huge success in the athletic footwear business. They may not have cared much for the product, but I'm sure they enjoyed the message. It was right down their alley, and it's always an appropriate exhortation:

Just do it!

20

Keep It Simple

He that giveth, let him do it with simplicity.

—ROMANS 12:8 KJV

Whenever I meet someone who says, "Everything I have belongs to God," I confess I get a little skeptical. I'm always leery of such folks. I have found they usually say things like this as an excuse for not giving *anything* to God. It may all belong to God, but God never sees any of it.

But I also know people who, beyond all doubt, have a giving nature. They have the proper attitude toward material things; possessions are not terribly important to them. God has blessed them with many talents and resources and they are eager to use them for the Lord. They view themselves as stewards of God's possessions, and, therefore, they are free and gracious in their giving.

We probably all know people of whom the phrase is true, "He would give you the shirt off his back." When you are in their homes, no more do you express admiration for something they have than you find it at your doorway, gift wrapped, and addressed to you. They have the gift of giving.

I knew a fellow from Laguna Beach who definitely had the gift of giving. One night as he was walking home, a stranger walked up beside him and stuck a gun in his ribs. "Give me everything you've got," he demanded. My friend apologized and said, "I'm sorry. I have only five dollars—will you take a check?" Now, that's the gift of giving.

The Law of Giving

Our universe operates under both physical and spiritual laws. As gravity is a physical law, so is the law of giving a spiritual law. Jesus said, "Give, and it will be given to you: good measure, pressed down, shaken together, and running over will be put into your bosom. For with the same measure that you use, it will be measured back to you" (Luke 6:38). Paul said it this way: "He who sows sparingly will also reap sparingly, and he who sows bountifully will also reap bountifully" (2 Corinthians 9:6).

This law of giving is demonstrated in agriculture. If you plant a field of corn and are frugal in the planting of seed—perhaps you plant each seed two feet apart instead of six inches—you'll reap a sparse crop. If you sow sparingly, you're going to reap sparingly. But if you sow bountifully, you'll also reap bountifully.

That is exactly God's law of giving. A lot of times it is diffucult to understand how these spiritual laws operate. And because we don't see how they could possibly function, we say, "Since I can't understand how that works, I'm keeping my money."

But do you understand how electricity works? Probably not, but I'll bet you don't mind using it. We don't understand the law of gravity, either. We also know that mass attracts, but we don't know why it attracts. We can measure the force of the attraction and we know that the larger the mass, the greater the attraction—but we don't know why. Yet we recognize gravity as a law of nature, and so we are very careful to obey it. We're don't jump off of twelve-story buildings just because we don't understand how the law works. We respect the law, and conduct ourselves accordingly.

It's the same way with the spiritual laws of God. They work in ways that we can't really understand, but we'd be wise to respect them. That's certainly true with the law of giving.

Jesus says, "Give, and it will be given to you: good measure, pressed down, shaken together, and running over. . . . For with the same measure that you use, it will be measured back to you." If you give by the teaspoon, you'll receive by the teaspoon. Give with a shovel, and you'll receive with a shovel. Give generously, and you'll receive generously. Whatever measure you use to give, that same measure will be given back to you.

In Romans 11:35, Paul asks, "Who has first given to Him and it shall be repaid to him?" In other words, "Show me a case where man has given to God and God didn't give back several times over."

People have told me, "Chuck, we just can't afford to tithe." Well, I can't afford not to tithe. I wouldn't dream of withholding from God what He tells me is His.

Through the prophet Malachi, God asks, "Will a man rob God?" The people respond, "In what way have we robbed You?" And God replies, "In tithes and offerings." God then encourages the nation to "bring all the tithes into the store-house, that there may be food in My house, and prove Me now in this . . . if I will not open for you the windows of heaven and pour out for you such blessing that there will not be room enough to receive it" (Malachi 3:8-10).

If we give to God what is God's and what God requires, then the Lord has promised He will pour out blessings to numerous to contain. As Malachi tells us, this is a spiritual law you can test. Give it a try. And when you do so, you'll discover that it works. The more you give, the more God brings back to you. Try it, you'll like it.

How Are We to Give?

The Bible gives us several guidelines about how we are to give. Let's consider just seven of them.

1. *Give with simplicity.*

Paul said, "He that giveth, let him do it with simplicity" (Romans 12:8, KJV). Some people make their giving so compli-cated that it's hard to receive it. A fellow from Houston, Texas, recently sent me a letter containing two checks, one signed and the other (larger) one, unsigned. He took issue with an article I had written for a Christian magazine, and listed about ten questions for me. He said if I answered those ten questions to his satisfaction, he would sign the larger check. I returned both of his checks, and included answers to the ten questions—along with a little note: "I'm sure I didn't answer your ques-tions to your satisfaction because I'm not telling you what you want to hear. So keep your checks." This man didn't want to give with simplicity; his gifts came with strings attached.

About 30 years ago a church in Huntington Beach was really beginning to grow. It met in a very old building right downtown, across from the police department. The church had a young, aggressive, excellent pastor, and was growing along with the town's population.

The church had no parking lot—only street parking was available—because an added educational unit consumed just about every inch of space on the little downtown lot. But the church had an option on about 15 prime acres, and the plan was to sell the building downtown, buy this acreage, and build a new facility in the heart of the new growth area. The pastor came over to my house to show me the plans and the details. It was all very exciting.

Then, one of the elders in the church spoke up. "When my family gave this property to the church, we had a clause put in the deed stipulating that if ever this property was sold, it would revert back to the family," he declared. "Thus, if you sell this property, it becomes the family's and you can't use the money to buy a new church. This church has to stay where it is." Now, that's not giving with simplicity. That's giving with strings attached.

As a result, my pastor friend got so discouraged he resigned from the church. As far as I know, that church is still on a little lot with no parking in downtown Huntington Beach, and it's struggling. What a tragedy. Giving with strings attached eventually caused major problems for the church.

If you give, give. Don't put strings on your giving. Do it with simplicity. Keep it simple. Don't make giving complicated.

2. *Give without calling attention to yourself.*

When we give, we're not to do so ostentatiously. Jesus said that you need to be careful how you give, to make sure you don't draw attention to yourself. If you give to be seen by others, you will already have received your reward in full; that's all you'll ever get. If your motive is to have people say, "Oh my, isn't he wonderful? Isn't he generous? Isn't that marvelous what he's doing?" then that's your reward. You already have everything you're going to get. Jesus said, "When you give, don't be like the Pharisees who like to sound a trumpet before them so that everybody knows what they're giving" (see Matthew 6:1,2). I don't know if the Pharisees actually hired trumpeters to precede them as they dropped their money into the treasury, but we do know they made a big to-do. They gave with a lot of show in order to impress people.

Jesus commanded us to steer clear of their example. He said, "When you do a charitable deed, do not let your left hand know what your right hand is doing, that your charitable deed may be in secret; and your Father who sees in secret will Himself reward you openly" (Matthew 6:3,4).

3. *Give willingly, from the heart.*

When the children of Israel were preparing to make the tabernacle, God gave to Moses the design of all the fixtures that were to be created—furnishings made with silver, gold, precious stones, and special types of cloth. This was not a poor man's tabernacle; it called for the best the people had. The Lord said to Moses, "Speak to the children of Israel, that they bring Me an offering. From everyone who gives it willingly with his heart you shall take My offering" (Exodus 25:2).

God didn't want anybody to give who wasn't giving from their heart. God *never* wants a person to feel pressured to give to Him. Whatever you give to God, you should give only that which you can give willingly, from your heart.

The beautiful thing about this story in Exodus is that the people had a heart to give, and began to bring in their gold and their silver and their jewelry to make the tabernacle. The women even gave their mirrors of highly polished brass for use in making the brazen altar! That's really a sacrifice.

Finally, those who were counting and weighing all the gifts spoke to Moses. "The people bring much more than enough for the service of the work which the Lord commanded us to do," they said (Exodus 36:5). So Moses had a commandment proclaimed throughout the camp: "Let neither man nor woman do any more work for the offering of the sanctuary" (Exodus 36:6). Incredible as it may seem, they had to restrain the people from bringing more. Not only was the amount collected enough to construct the tabernacle, it was actually too much! That's what happens when God moves upon the hearts of His people to give.

4. *Give cheerfully.*

Paul instructed the Corinthians that they should not give grudgingly (2 Corinthians 9:7). I can surely understand that. I know how I would feel if I came over to your house to borrow a cup of sugar, and afterwards, I heard from all my friends about how angry you were over giving it to me. Although you told me I didn't need to replace it, you're complaining to everyone you meet that I didn't return it. I'd be tempted to take you a five-pound pack, dump it on your front porch, and say, "Take your lousy sugar."

If we don't like it when people give grudgingly to us, think how God must feel. If you're griping about what you're going to give to God, then keep your money. I'm sure God is saying, "Keep the lousy stuff. I don't need it." God doesn't want it if it's given grudgingly or out of sheer duty. Paul said, "Not grudgingly, or of necessity; for God loves a cheerful giver." I like the Greek word he uses for "cheerful." It's the term *hilaros*, which eventually dropped into English as the word "hilarious." That's the kind of giving God wants from us.

In the Old Testament they called this kind of giving a "free will offering" to the Lord. Every man gave freely. In the same way, Jesus said to His disciples, "Freely you have received, freely give" (Matthew 10:8). Paul said, "Let each one give as he purposes in his heart" (2 Corinthians 9:7). Give of your own free will an amount that you've decided upon. Never give out of pressure or constraint, because then you will be prone to begrudge what you're giving.

Jesus indicated it isn't the amount that's important. One day He was watching the people putting their money into the temple treasury. He saw the wealthy parading by in all their pomp and circumstance, dropping in their large gifts. But when one little widow shuffled by and dropped in two mites—a quarter of a cent—Jesus turned to His disciples and said, "Did you see that? She gave more than all the rest, because they merely gave from their surplus. This woman gave of her very livelihood; that's all she has" (see Mark 12:41-44).

In the Lord's eyes, it wasn't the amount given that was important, but the heart behind the giving, and what it cost to give. The Lord seems to love sacrificial giving. Yet if a person has the gift of giving, he doesn't look at it as a sacrifice. He thinks, *I'll give this to the Lord. I wish I had more to give.*

As you purpose in your own heart, the Bible says, so give. That's something between you and God, for God loves a cheerful giver.

5. *Give honestly.*

Don't make a pretense about giving more than you really are, because the Lord doesn't appreciate that. Remember the story of Ananias and Sapphira in Acts 5? They violated this principle and paid for it with their very lives. God doesn't like it when we pretend to give more than we really are. You don't have to give everything; God doesn't require that. But He hates hypocrisy—just ask Ananias and Sapphira.

6. *Give freely.*

Jesus said, "Freely you have received, freely give." The psalmist said, "I will freely sacrifice to You; I will praise Your name, O Lord, for it is good" (Psalm 54:6).

Did you know that the word "give" and its related forms are used in the Bible 1,981 times? We might infer from this that God has a lot to say about our giving, and that would be true. But did you know that the vast majority of these references speak not of what we give to God, but of what God has given to us? It's true, probably on a ratio of five to one.

Our primary example for giving should be Jesus Himself. As Paul said, "For you know the grace of our Lord Jesus Christ, that though He was rich, yet for your sakes He became poor, that you through His poverty might become rich" (2 Corinthians 8:9).

R.G. LaTourneau certainly followed his Lord's example. Back in the '40s and '50s, this sharp, innovative fellow made a fortune inventing and manufacturing heavy-duty earth-moving equipment. When he started his business he made a covenant with God to give ten percent of all his profits to the Lord. As time went on and he began to be blessed more and more, LaTourneau made a new covenant to give God twenty percent. As the business continued to increase he raised it to thirty, then forty, then fifty, then sixty, and by the time he went home to be with the Lord, he was giving ninety percent to the Lord's work all over the world. *Ninety percent.* God had so blessed him that the ten percent he kept for himself was more than enough to live on. He learned that God simply won't be outgiven.

We give to God of our resources, but in reality we're only giving back to God what is His already. What do I have except what I've been given by God? So if God has given it to me, then it really belongs to Him. So if I give it back to Him, I'm only giving back what is His already.

My own attitude on giving has changed through the years. It used to be, *How much of my money can I afford to give to God this month?* Now my attitude is, *How much of God's money dare I spend on myself this month?* All "my" money is God's; I'm only giving back to Him what is His. He has made me a steward over His goods for a short while. I want to give a good accounting of my responsibility in spending that which He has placed in my hands.

7. *Give because of love.*

Whether we are giving to God or giving to someone in need, our giving must be motivated by love. Paul said, "Though I bestow all my goods to feed the poor, and though I give my body to be burned, but have not love, it profits me nothing" (1 Corinthians 13:3). If I sell everything I have and give it all to the poor, yet I do so with resentment and not out of love—maybe my motive is to been seen by man or to be recognized as a philanthropist. And that doesn't profit me a thing. But if I give out of love, it profits me more than I can possibly imagine.

Giving to Others

The gift of giving is probably exercised more in what we give to others than in what we give to God. And the interesting thing is that what we give to the less fortunate, God considers a gift to Him. "Inasmuch as you did it to one of the least of these My brethren, you did it to Me," said Jesus (Matthew 25:40). Proverbs 19:17 says, "He who has pity on the poor lends to the Lord." If you give even as little as a cup of cold water to a needy little one, Jesus says that you will by no means lose your reward (see Matthew 10:41,42).

We are commanded to give to the poor. In Deuteronomy 15:7,8 God said, "If there is among you a poor man of your brethren, within any of the gates in your land which the Lord your God is giving you, you shall not harden your heart nor shut your hand from your poor brother, but you shall open your hand wide to him and willingly lend him sufficient for his need, whatever he needs."

God has blessed us so much and we thank Him for that. But we must be careful not to close our hearts to those who are in need. We must pray that God would give us a generous heart, that we would receive the gift of giving. Our generosity must go far beyond material things to include time and energy and even ourselves. We are called to do whatever we can to strengthen the weak and minister to those with great needs. In that way we bring glory to God, honoring and glorifying Him by being a conduit of heaven's resources to those who are in need.

God promises to bless you if you will do this. The whole text of Proverbs 19:17 says, "He who has pity on the poor lends to the Lord, *and He will pay back what he has given*" (emphasis added). Would you like to lend some money to God? He pays great interest! God says, "You do that for Me, and I'll do something unbelievable for you. I'll pay you back." Why don't you try it? Lend to the Lord and see what He gives in return.

What Are We to Give?

1. *Give yourself.*

When Paul wrote to the Corinthians about how liberal the Macedonians were in their offerings for the poor in Jerusalem, he said they "first gave themselves to the Lord, and then to us by the will of God" (2 Corinthians 8:5). That's really what God wants—He wants you to *give yourself* to Him. God wants you more than He wants your money or your possessions.

God isn't broke. He doesn't need our money. God said, "Every beast of the forest is Mine, and the cattle on a thousand hills, . . . If I were hungry, I would not tell you; for the world is Mine, and all its fullness" (Psalm 50:10,12). God says to us, "Look, what makes you think I'd ever need to come to you for handouts? I created everything that exists, and I own it all. If I wanted a steak, I have all the cattle I want. Why would I ask you for help?"

We need His help and support, He doesn't need ours. He wants *you* much more than He wants your money or possessions.

2. *Give your talents and time.*

When we talk of giving, too often we think only in terms of money. Surely that's the least of what God wants from us. Unfortunately, so many times when we give our money to God, we believe we have fulfilled our obligation. "After all, I put that five bucks in the plate last Sunday. What more does God want?" What more does He want? He wants you, and He wants your time.

Have you ever thought about giving some of your time to God? Maybe God has given you a talent, a capacity, or an ability that He can use. In fact, I'm sure He has. Whatever talent or capacity you have can be used by God. So give God your time, your energy, and the use of the talents He has loaned to you.

3. *Give your thanks and praise.*

The book of Hebrews speaks about giving to God a "sacrifice of praise, even the fruit of our lips" (see Hebrews 13:15).

Give God the praise and thanksgiving and worship due His name.

Three times in the Bible we are told to "give to God the glory due His name." Six times the Scripture tells us to "give thanks unto the Lord, for he is good, for his mercy endureth forever." Now, I believe the Word of God even if it tells us something only once. If it tells us the same thing twice, then we need to pay special attention. But if God tells us something nine times, we need to pay extra special, heavy-duty attention.

Have you given thanks to God today? Have you given glory to Him this week? Oh, that there would go out from our lips continual thanksgiving to God for His goodness.

The name of God is Yahweh, and we are told that the name of Yahweh is a strong tower which the righteous run into and are safe (Proverbs 18:10). So let's give to the Lord the glory due His name. His name means "the becoming one," and God is an expert at becoming for you whatever your need might be. No wonder we are told to give to the Lord the glory due His name!

The Gift that Grows

As believers, we have one inlet of power, namely the Holy Spirit. Yet this power has several outlets, and one of them is giving. The gift of giving develops and grows. The more you give, the more God gives you to give. You find yourself becoming a channel through which He can funnel His resources. When He finds that the channel is open, He begins to pour out to you so that it might flow from you to others. As the prophet said to King Asa, "The eyes of the Lord run to and fro throughout the whole earth, to show Himself strong on behalf of those whose heart is loyal to Him" (2 Chronicles 16:9).

Do you know that God is looking for people to do what He wants done, that He might make them channels through which He can pour His spirit, His power, His love, and His resources? True wealth is measured not by what we keep, but by what we give away. Jesus said "It is more blessed to give than to receive" (Acts 20:35).

If God has given you the gift of giving, exercise it with simplicity. Be that instrument and channel through which God can flow His resources to meet the needs of others. You'll be blessed more than you can ever imagine. It really is more blessed to give than to receive.

21

An Awesome Responsibility

He that ruleth, [let him do it] with diligence.
—ROMANS 12:8

God hath set some in the church . . . [gifts of] governments.
—1 CORINTHIANS 12:28 KJV

For a society to exist there must be rules, and people who establish and enforce those rules. A society without rules quickly degenerates into a state of anarchy and chaos. People begin living as savages, every person for himself, doing whatever is right in his own eyes.

That is why governments exist. The purpose of government is to ensure domestic tranquility and to establish and enforce laws that will guarantee the common welfare of all members of the society. Good government seeks to eliminate the evil and preserve the good. Man has tried many forms of government throughout his history to achieve these goals.

Some of the earliest forms of government were feudal systems, in which rival leaders ruled over villages or cities. These gradually developed into monarchies, in which kings and queens ruled over more extensive lands and, ultimately, over nations.

The United States was formed as a constitutional republic with a representative form of government. Citizens elect representatives to create the laws by which the nation will be governed.

To this day there are totalitarian forms of government where people are ruled by dictators. Citizens do not have a true say in who will represent them. They may have elections, but the winners have already been selected. There are no real choices.

All these forms of government—as well as all others devised by man—have been unsuccessful. Mankind has proven that he is incapable of governing his fellow man without graft or corruption ultimately destroying every form of government he has created. Man is incapable of ruling with righteousness.

God is the only One who can rule over man in perfect righteousness.

Government in the Old Testament

The first mention of government in the Bible comes in the prophecy of Isaiah: "For unto us a child is born, unto us a Son is given; and the government will be upon His shoulder. And His name will be called Wonderful, Counselor, Mighty God, Everlasting Father, Prince of Peace. Of the increase of His government and peace there will be no end, upon the throne of David and over His kingdom, to order it and establish it with judgment and justice from that time forward, even forever. The zeal of the Lord of hosts will perform this" (Isaiah 9:6,7).

Isaiah's text helps us to recognize that in God's true order the finest and highest form of government is a theocracy (a divine monarchy). When Jesus comes to establish God's government upon the earth, He will arrive as King of kings and as Lord of lords.

In fact, the only form of government God ever endorsed and established was a theocracy. The name *Israel* means "governed by God." Israel was a theocracy; God ruled the nation.

From the very beginning there was a national consciousness that God ruled and reigned over the people of Israel. The tabernacle—the place of meeting God—was always set up in the center of camp. Everyone in all the tribes pitched their tents so they faced the tabernacle. The moment someone came out of their tent, they saw the tabernacle of God. During the day the Israelites saw a cloud over the tabernacle, while at night they saw a pillar of fire. All of this made them keenly aware that they were being governed by God as His people.

God intended that the nation of Israel be different from all other nations; she would not have an earthly king ruling over her. Instead, God was to be her King. This would provide a model to the nations as they saw how blessed were the people ruled by God.

Although God ruled, He made Moses the first human leader of the people. Moses was God's instrument to fulfill His purposes in the lives of the Israelites. Whenever issues arose that needed a decision, Moses inquired of the Lord, and God spoke to him, and gave him the direction and guidance and laws needed to govern the nation's social life.

Under Moses, seventy elders were appointed to act as sub-rulers. People brought their disputes to these elders, who made decisions according to the law of the Lord. When an issue became too difficult for them, the elders brought that issue to Moses, who in turn would go to God for the divine answer.

Under Moses also was Aaron, the high priest and leader of the people in spiritual things. Under Aaron were various orders of the priesthood, men who carried the tabernacle burdens or who conducted the service within the tabernacle.

Throughout ancient Israel a divinely established governmental order ruled. The priests under Aaron; Aaron and the seventy judges under Moses; Moses under God. Our God is a God of order, of government. He establishes order in the universe and among His people.

Government in the New Testament

God has established order within the church as well. Paul says one of the gifts of the Spirit is the gift of ruling (Romans 12:8; 1 Corinthians 12:28). Men are gifted with the ability to rule within the body of Christ through the calling, the power, and the guidance of the Holy Spirit.

At the top in the church hierarchy is Jesus Christ. He is the head of the body, the authority over the church. Of the many disciples who followed Jesus, He chose twelve to be called apostles. These were the men who became the first leaders of the church. This explains why we are told in 1 Corinthians 12 that the Lord has set some in the church, first apostles.

The apostles ordained elders to take care of the spiritual well-being of the church. Elders are to prove themselves capable of ruling in the church by being able to control their own houses. "If a man does not know how to rule his own house, how will he take care of the church of God?" Paul asked in

1 Timothy 3:5. Finally, under the elders are the deacons who handle the material resources of the church.

In this way God set within the church those who are to rule. These leaders are to exercise leadership over the people in matters of the Spirit.

Ruling Is a Gift

God has gifted certain people with the gifts of government. We often say that some particular person is "a gifted leader." He seems to have the kind of personality and demeanor that attracts people to his leadership.

There is always a tremendous need for good leadership. When Moses recognized he was about to pass off the scene, he prayed that God would set a man over the people who would be able to shepherd them well. God responded that He had already made His choice: Joshua, a man in whom the Spirit lived (see Numbers 27:15-23). Though Moses died, the reign of God would continue. There was no diminishing of the nation because the next man was filled with the Spirit and would continue to rule under the guidance and direction of God.

This is the primary qualification for leadership in all ages: a man who has the Spirit, who is governed and led by the Spirit. Nothing can ever substitute for this, and the lack of it is always devastating.

Isaiah tells us, "The leaders of this people cause them to err, and those who are led by them are destroyed" (Isaiah 9:16). That's the sad consequence of poor leadership—people are destroyed. Jesus said, "If the blind leads the blind, both will fall into the ditch" (Matthew 15:14); while Proverbs 29:2 says, "When the righteous are in authority, the people rejoice; but when the wicked man rules, the people groan."

It's a glorious thing when those who are called of God to lead the people of God do so in the wisdom and power of God. Under their spiritual leadership, there grows a marvelous bond of love and service to one another and submission to one another in the grace of Jesus Christ.

Qualifications for Leadership

Who qualifies to be a leader in the church? Paul wrote in 1 Timothy 3:1-4,6:

This is a faithful saying: If a man desires the position of a bishop,[1] he desires a good work. A bishop then

must be blameless, the husband of one wife, tempe-
rate, sober-minded, of good behavior, hospitable,
able to teach; not given to wine, not violent, not
greedy for money, but gentle, not quarrelsome, not
covetous; one who rules his own house well, having
his children in submission with all reverence, . . . Not
a novice, lest being puffed up with pride he fall into
the same condemnation as the devil. Moreover he
must have a good testimony among those who are
outside, lest he fall into reproach and the snare of the
devil.

As Paul lists these qualifications, it seems as if he pretty
much eliminates everybody, even with the very first requirement alone: "blameless."

It is interesting how certain people will jump on any one
of these qualifications and emphasize it over the others. "I'm
sorry, but it seems to me that this person is disqualified for
consideration because he's never invited me over to his house.
He's not hospitable." That's not the way this passage should
be handled. You can get into all kinds of difficulty that way. For
example, Paul says an elder is not to be covetous. Have you
ever looked at your neighbor's fancy sports car and wished it
were yours? That's covetousness, my friend. Would you disqualify yourself because of it? I doubt it.

Paul's list isn't a legalistic sieve through which we strain
out all transgressors. If it were, none of us would make it
through the net, and the church would have no leaders. Instead,
it gives a general picture of the kind of man whom God calls
into leadership; not a perfect man, by any means, but one who
is committed to His Lord and who is growing in grace through
the power of the Holy Spirit. Paul isn't looking for perfection;
he's looking for maturity.

How Are We to Rule?

The Bible gives several rules to those who would exercise
leadership or a role of governing.

1. *Rule in the fear of God.*

As King David lay dying, his last words included this key
command: "He who rules over men must be just, ruling in the
fear of God" (2 Samuel 23:3). No man living without the fear of

God has any right to rule over others. He is not qualified. I guarantee that any man who does not have the fear of God will be a corrupt ruler: he will be crooked and dishonest. No man can exercise leadership over others unless he is conscious that he, himself, is ruled. No man can rule who is not ruled himself.

Nebuchadnezzar, the great king of the ancient Babylonian empire, was acknowledged by God as one of the great leaders in human history. In the dream of a statue described in Daniel 2, God identifies Nebuchadnezzar as the head of gold, superior to all other kings.

But because of his greatness, Nebuchadnezzar discounted God. He thought he was at the top, that he was the final authority. He condemned whoever he chose and he elevated whoever he chose. No appeal to any higher power was allowed; what Nebuchadnezzar said, went. He became proud...and God humbled him. God allowed him to suffer until seven seasons of insanity had passed so that the world might know that the Most High rules in the kingdom of men and that He gives it to whoever He will, even to the basest of men.

The Bible establishes many authorities and chains of command, but always at the top is God. Unless a man is aware that he is governed by God, and is responsible to God, and will have to appear before God, that man is disqualified from having authority. If you give him authority anyway, he will take advantage of it. He will soon pervert his authority to his own benefit and become a tyrant.

No man can rule who is not ruled himself. He must be aware that he is responsible to One who is higher than he, and that one day he will answer to Him.

2. *Rule diligently.*

Proverbs 12:24 says, "The hand of the diligent will rule." I think it likely that this is the verse which prompted Paul to write in Romans 12:8, "He that rules, with diligence" (KJV). Paul says that those who have the gift of ruling are to exercise it with diligence.

Rulers must be diligent to protect themselves against indulging in power trips. They must be careful to see that they do not use their position for their own personal gain. Too often we see such corruption of power among those who rule.

That was Saul's problem in the Old Testament. He fell into the snare that entraps so many rulers, thinking that he was the final authority, that his was the final word. He forgot that he, himself, was ruled by God.

If you've been given a ruling office, it is important to remember that one day you're going to stand before the Judge of the universe and give an account of yourself. Your faithfulness in ruling now will determine what authority you will have in the kingdom to come. Jesus said, "Who then is that faithful and wise steward, whom his master will make ruler over his household, to give them their portion of food in due season? Blessed is that servant whom his master will find so doing when he comes. Truly, I say to you that he will make him ruler over all that he has" (Luke 12:42).

The Scripture promises that we are going to live and reign with Christ over the earth. Some day we will be granted the joyous privilege of ruling with Him when the kingdom of God has come to this earth, and the will of God is finally being done on this planet. The extent of our authority in the coming kingdom will depend on how diligently we exercise rule over those things that God puts in our dominion here.

God took David from ruling over sheep—the lowest job on the totem pole—and made him king over all Israel. At one time Saul, David's predecessor, had recognized his own humble beginnings. But eventually he developed an inflated view of himself, rebelled against the authority of God, and was deposed.

If God has given you a position of rulership, seek the help of the Holy Spirit. Don't abuse your position. Rule with diligence, knowing that you are accountable to God for how you exercise the power He has placed in your hands.

3. *Speak the Word of God.*

Hebrews 13:7 says leaders are to speak to the people the Word of God; and Paul told Timothy simply to "Preach the word!" (2 Timothy 4:2). Rulers are responsible for the spiritual welfare of the people under their care, and the best way to ensure a healthy flock is to preach the Word of God to them.

When rulers do this well, and the people submit to the authority of the Word, then the leaders can "watch for your souls, as they that must give account, that they may do it with joy, and not with grief" (Hebrews 13:17 KJV). I can tell you, it's a lot better to do it with joy than with grief.

An Awesome Responsibility

It is an awesome responsibility to represent God to the people. If you have a role of leadership, you must rule in the fear of God, making certain that you don't misrepresent God to the people. God does not like to be misrepresented any more than you do. That was the sin that kept Moses out of the Promised Land. At the waters of Meribah the people complained, "Moses, we're dying of thirst. We're sorry we ever left Egypt. We've been in this wilderness for 40 years, yet you haven't brought us into the Promised Land. We were crazy ever to listen to you." They were ready to stone Moses.

Moses left them and went in before the Lord, upset and angry by the way the people were treating him. God said, "Moses, go out and speak to the rock that water might come forth." Moses rejoined the people and said, "You rebels! How long do I have to put up with you? Must I smite this rock again to give you water?" And he swung his rod and struck the rock.

God is so gracious, so loving, and so kind that water came gushing out anyway and the people drank and were refreshed. But God said, "Moses—come here, son."

"Yes, Lord?"

"What did I tell you to do?"

"You said to speak to the rock."

"Then how is it that you struck the rock? Moses, you didn't represent Me before the people. You misrepresented Me. You led them to believe that I'm angry with them. They think I'm upset. Therefore, because you failed to represent Me, Moses, I won't allow you to lead them into the Promised Land."

"What? But, Lord—wait a minute! For forty years I've been putting up with these people, just with the hope of..."

"Don't talk to Me anymore about it, Moses. It's a closed issue. Because you failed to represent Me before the people at the waters of Meribah, you will not enter the Promised Land."

That's how important it is that we represent God truthfully.

I wonder how many times when we confront personal frustrations in the ministry—the church isn't growing as rapidly as it should, or there are rumblings in the congregation, or some other problem—that we are upset and angry so we preach through clenched teeth. The people hear us and think, *Ooooh. God's really mad at us today.* Thus we don't accurately represent God to the people.

I wonder if God doesn't get a little upset with us? I wonder if He doesn't say, "Wait a minute! I'm not angry with them; I love them. You're My representative, but from the things you said and the way you said them, now they think I'm angry with them and ready to toss them out. You've misrepresented Me, and I don't like it."

While attending a pastor's conference in Germany, a young girl approached me to talk, obviously agitated. She was attending a church that endorsed what is commonly termed the *shepherding doctrine*. Members of such a church cannot make any decisions on their own, but are required to talk to the "shepherd" of the church concerning every decision. No one is allowed to buy a car or clothes or a pair of shoes unless the shepherd gives them permission to do so. Members are to go to the pastor, who will guide them in the ways and in the things of the Lord.

This doctrine is based on a misuse of Hebrews 13:17, which says, "Obey those who rule over you, and be submissive, for they watch out for your souls, as those who must give an account. Let them do so with joy and not with grief, for that would be unprofitable for you."

This girl was being held in bondage. The leaders of her church said, "If you disobey our church you are disobeying God, and you are going to hell. And if you go to another church you're going to hell because you are rebelling against the authority of God." This poor girl was miserable. She had been attending another church on the sly and she was afraid her pastor might find out and consign her immediately to hell. It was tragic.

I showed her from Scripture where Jesus insisted that those who were called to be leaders must be the servants of all. We aren't to hold people in bondage by threatening them with hell. That isn't like our Lord and that doesn't represent Him truthfully.

Oh, how we must be careful in ruling because, as rulers, we are representing God to the people. We must take care that we don't misrepresent him.

Everyone Has Some Rule

You may not be a pastor of a church or an elder in your congregation, but in some way you are a leader. All of us have some rule. Regardless of who you are, God has placed you in a position of authority over others. You are their guide— directing their activities, telling them when they can go, when they must stay, what they can do, what they can't do. In exercising that rule, it's important that you recognize you are also ruled. We need the kind of rulers who cause people to realize God is the only final Ruler.

Jesus Christ is the head of the body. He's the final authority, and all of our decisions must defer to Him. Jesus is Lord over His church, and we are here only to implement His desires and His wishes. We're not here to rule; we're not here even to make decisions. We're here to find His decisions and to implement His desires.

The only ones who can faithfully do this are those who are filled with the Spirit, who have the gift of government. And, as such leaders seek God through prayer for His direction, His will, and His purposes for the church, we will all be blessed.

22

A Ready Help
in Time of Need

...he who shows mercy, with cheerfulness.

—ROMANS 12:8

As advances in technology enable us to create ever more powerful telescopes, every few years astronomers revise their estimates of the size of the universe. They tell us that our universe is expanding, that the galaxies furthest away from us are receding at incredible speeds.

When I entered high school we were taught that the universe was some 4 billion light years in diameter. By the time I graduated from college they were saying that the universe was some 8 billion light years across. Today they are saying it is somewhere between 12 and 18 billion light years in diameter. So it is expanding at a very rapid rate.

Someone once asked me, "Does it bother you when they come out with these new estimates of the size of the universe?"

"Not at all," I replied. "In fact, it thrills me. God said in Psalm 103:11, 'As the heaven is high above the earth, so great is his mercy toward them that fear him.' He didn't say how high that was, but however high it is, His mercy is that great toward those who fear him. Since the universe is expanding, that must mean His mercy is growing all the time! The expanding universe doesn't bother me; it makes me realize that God's mercy is just that much greater!"

A Merciful God

Mercy is a divine quality, springing from the very character and nature of God. It is an attitude that develops from compassion, from reaching out to help someone in need, and is characterized by kindness and tenderness.

Mercy contrasts with justice. So many times we say of a person, "He got exactly what he deserved." That's justice. But not getting what you deserve is mercy. We all deserve justice, but God gives us mercy. Because God is the source of all mercy and comfort, the mercies of God are a popular topic in the Bible.

The first mention of mercy in Scripture comes in a passage describing how the Lord destroyed the cities of Sodom and Gomorrah. When the angel of the Lord came to get Lot and his family out of the doomed cities, the angels said, "Hurry, we cannot destroy the cities until you are out of here." Lot responded, "Indeed now, your servant has found favor in your sight, and you have increased your mercy which you have shown me by saving my life" (Genesis 19:19).

Lot realized he could have easily been one of the victims destroyed in the two wicked cities. He recognized it was only the mercy of God that separated him from those who perished.

Jacob, too, realized how unworthy he was of God's mercy. He said, "I am not worthy of the least of all the mercies...You have shown" (Genesis 32:10). He was right. Jacob was a conniver. His name means "heel catcher," one who takes advantage of another by devious means. Jacob had deceived and connived his whole life, yet God showed him mercy and made him an ancestor of the Lord Jesus.

As we look at our own lives and see what God has done for us, we realize we don't deserve His mercies, either. Truly the Lord has been good and merciful to us. The blessings God has bestowed upon us are surely not the result of our meriting them. They come because of His mercy.

Many scriptures describe the mercies of God. Second Corinthians 1:3 says, "Blessed be the God and Father of our Lord Jesus Christ, the Father of mercies and God of all comfort." Daniel 9:9 says, "To the Lord our God belong mercy and forgiveness, though we have rebelled against Him." Jeremiah wrote, "Through the Lord's mercies we are not consumed, because His compassions fail not" (Lamentations 3:22). Psalm 116:5 tells us, "Gracious is the Lord, and righteous; yes, our God is merciful." Moses insisted, "The Lord islongsuffering and abundant in mercy, forgiving iniquity and transgression" (Numbers 14:18). Deuteronomy 4:31 says, "For the Lord your

God is a merciful God, He will not forsake you nor destroy you, nor forget the covenant of your fathers which He swore to them." Nehemiah 9:31 tells us, "Nevertheless in Your great mercy You did not utterly consume them nor forsake them; for You are God, gracious and merciful." Micah sums up many of these ideas when he says God "delights in mercy" (Micah 7:18).

God delights in mercy! I don't suppose you'll fully understand that until you're a grandparent. Oh, how I love to intercede for my grandkids. When they are at odds with their parents I'll ask, "May I just take them for a walk?" In that way I deliver the children from a spanking. I delight in mercy; it's glorious.

God is not only full of compassion and great in mercy, but His mercy endures forever. Some 41 times the Bible declares that the mercy of the Lord endures eternally. Psalm 100:5 is typical of these: "For the Lord is good; His mercy is everlasting."

So many people do not believe this. They do not see God as merciful. Their opinions have been formed largely by Satan's lies and they have a monumentally wrong concept of God.

For many years I thought God was angry with me most of the time. I knew what God wanted of me; I knew He wanted perfection. But since I was far from perfect, I imagined that God was constantly angry with me. I never questioned any misfortune that happened to me because I figured it was the judgment of God and I deserved it. If only I had listened to how God describes Himself!

When God met Moses on the mount to deliver the second copy of the Law—Moses had broken the first tablets—the Bible says, "The Lord descended in the cloud and stood with him there, and proclaimed the name of the Lord. And the Lord passed before him and proclaimed, 'The Lord, the Lord God, merciful and gracious, longsuffering, and abounding in goodness and truth, keeping mercy for thousands, forgiving iniquity and transgression and sin" (Exodus 34:5-7). That's the God whom you serve; this is how He describes Himself. He is a merciful God!

Since my younger days, my view of God has changed drastically. Today I know Him as a loving God who eternally delights in mercy. I know He's not mad at me, and I couldn't be happier that He has called me to serve Him!

We're Not Merciful by Nature

The great mercy of God only highlights the ugly fact that we are far from merciful. Mankind is vengeful by nature. We like to get even. We like the idea of "an eye for an eye, a tooth for a tooth." You've heard it said, "To err is human, to forgive divine." It could also be said that to seek revenge is human, but to show mercy is divine.

My problem is that while I want to receive mercy from God, I also want to dispense justice. I don't want people to get away with evil against me. I want justice . . . except, of course, when I'm coming to God about my own failings. Then I want mercy!

Because mercy isn't one of our natural characteristics, it takes a work of God's Spirit in our heart for us to be merciful. God must plant this aspect of His nature in us; it is a gift. Therefore, it is quite proper that the showing of mercy is listed as one of the gifts of the Spirit.

If we are wronged and find ourselves plotting to get even, we need to bring our attitude to the cross and say, "Lord, give me your mercy. Lord, let me show mercy in this situation. Lord, take away from my heart this desire for revenge to get even."

For us to show mercy takes a special work of the Holy Spirit in our lives. And, thus, it is properly listed as a gift.

When Mercy Isn't

Some people seem to have this gift of showing mercy. They give offenders a second and third and fourth chance. It's a gift. They have that capacity of showing mercy. I know one thing for sure: Some people have the gift of mercy and others don't.

When some people show "mercy," they grow real somber, and you can tell that, even as they say they forgive you, they're thinking, *I wish I could pound you into the ground for what you did, but God tells me I have to show mercy. But I don't think I'll ever be able to recover from this.* These people try to make you feel guilty and remorseful, to make you realize the seriousness of your offense.

Many years ago when my father-in-law died, Kay and I went to a funeral home to make arrangements for burial services. A man in a black suit and tie greeted us, wringing his hands and saying, "May I help you?" The poor fellow had chewed off all of his nails and was an emotional wreck. As he talked about the service he kept saying, "Your father—dear, oh my! For such a young child to lose her father." Then he started to cry. We were handling it pretty well until we met this guy! He was trying to show mercy, but he clearly didn't have the gift.

When Job was suffering through all of his trials, his friends came to comfort him—but ended up accusing him. They offered all their theories about the reason for his misfortunes. One said he was a hypocrite; another said he was a liar; and they all said God was punishing him for some secret sin. Finally Job said, "Miserable comforters are you all! You don't show me a speck of mercy. You're no help." And he wished they had never come.

On the other hand, there are times when you've blown it big time and you feel as if your world has come crashing to an end. There doesn't seem to be any reason to try and go on any longer. Then, into your discouragement step friends who really have the gift of mercy. They are so cheerful and confident about the future that they lift you out of your despair.

That's the way people act who have the gift of mercy. They don't show up with a somber face and a low murmur, "Well, I don't know. I suppose we'll try and somehow work this out together. I'll always stand with you, brother."

Those with the gift of mercy say things like, "You know, the Lord is on the throne, and we haven't seen the end of it yet. God's going to bring us through, and we're going to see God's victory. All we have to do is wait upon the Lord and trust in Him, and He's going to bring it together. Yes, you did wrong; but thank God that He's mercifully forgiving, He's kind and He's loving. Let's go on from here. Let's not wallow in the past." They buoy you up and lift you out of discouragement, and you know that you can go on another day. And you look forward to seeing what God might have in store for you.

Mercy Should Be Cheerful

Paul said that those who have the gift of mercy should exercise it with cheerfulness (Romans 12:8). Of course, without God's Spirit empowering us, this is impossible.

Some people have a way of smiling and saying, "Well, that's all right," but are still plotting revenge in their heart.

Usually you can tell they're not really being merciful. Their lack of cheerfulness lets you know they're still burning over whatever wrong had been done to them.

That isn't showing mercy with cheerfulness by a long shot. It is possible to show mercy because God commands it without really having mercy in your heart. Yet that's where God wants it, in your heart. The Spirit wants the attitude of our hearts to match our actions.

If I am helping people in need, then I must do so with cheerfulness. If I am sitting at a hotline, the phone rings, and I think, *Oh, no! I wonder what kind of gross problems this one has?* then I shouldn't be sitting at that hotline. We need to show mercy with cheerfulness, and if we're not doing so then it would be better if we didn't lend a helping hand at all. Only service done to God with a willing heart, full of love, earns a reward.

Those with the gift of mercy are eager to do so cheerfully because God has been so compassionate to them and has blessed them so much. Their hearts leap at the chance to reach out in mercy to others. Showing mercy is a thrill and a delight. A person with the gift of mercy loves to plug into a need to help someone in their time of trouble. They can't help but show mercy with cheerfulness.

Mercy Leads to Forgiveness

Mercy is a parallel trait to forgiveness; to show forgiveness is to show mercy. Therefore the things that are said about forgiveness are also true concerning mercy.

Jesus tells us to be careful how we judge others, for the same measure of judgment we use with others will be applied to us. If we are harsh and judgmental, we will face a harsh judgment. If we are merciful, we shall receive mercy (see Matthew 7:1,2). James said, "For judgment is without mercy to the one who has shown no mercy" (James 2:13).

In His model prayer, Jesus included this petition: "And forgive us our debts, as we forgive our debtors." At the end of the prayer Jesus paused to emphasize this petition. "For if you do not forgive men their trespasses, neither will your Father forgive your trespasses," He said (Matthew 6:15). This means Jesus made our forgiveness dependent upon our being forgiving. Some of you theologians may want to argue this point, but don't do it with me—talk to Jesus. He's the One who said it.

The Lord's basic point was this: Having received forgiveness from God, we should forgive others. A parable in Matthew 18 highlights this principle.

A servant borrowed what amounted to 16 million dollars from his master. When the servant begged for more time to repay it, his master forgave him the whole debt. Yet that servant tracked down someone who owed him 16 dollars, grabbed him by the throat, and threatened that if he didn't immediately repay, he'd be thrown into debtor's prison. When the man asked for more time, this servant tossed him in jail.

The servant's friends saw what happened and reported it to their master. Furious, the master hauled the wicked man before him and said, "Tell me—how much did you owe me?" "About 16 million dollars," the servant replied. "And didn't I forgive your debt?" the master demanded. "Yes," replied the servant. "Well, what is this I hear about you having a fellow servant thrown into debtor's prison because of a 16-dollar debt?" the master roared. Then he ordered his men to take the man and throw him into prison until he had paid back the entire amount.

Jesus used extreme amounts so we'd get the idea. God has forgiven us so very, very much—an enormous debt of sin. God wiped it out. Because of what His Son did on the cross, God said to us, "I forgive you." Yet we are so prone to hold bitter feelings against a fellow servant because of some little wrong done to us. Maybe someone didn't smile when we walked by and we think, *I'll get you, man.* That's what the Lord is talking about here. If we have been forgiven such a huge debt, who are we to harbor petty grievances against our brothers?

Something is wrong when we say, "I'll forgive you, but I can't forget what you did." That's like saying, "I'll bury the hatchet, but I'll leave the handle exposed so that if I need it again I'll be able to grab it in a hurry." That isn't true forgiveness, nor is it true mercy. And it certainly is not what we want God to do with us. So when you forgive, forget. That's true forgiveness and that's real mercy.

The Positive Side of Mercy

We shouldn't get the idea that showing mercy is merely a negative action; it isn't merely restraining oneself from judgment. The gift of mercy should lead a person to positive action.

How many times do we recall in the New Testament where people cried to Jesus for mercy? The blind man called out, "Jesus, Son of David, have mercy on me!" (Mark 10:47). This wasn't a request for forgiveness or a plea to forestall judgment. He was asking Jesus to have pity on him, to have compassion toward his needs. Remember the ten lepers who cried out, "Jesus, Master, have mercy on us!" (Luke 17:13), the Syro-Phoenician woman who begged for her daughter, " Have mercy on me, O Lord" (Matthew 15:22), and the father with the demon-possessed son who called for mercy (Matthew 17:15)? In each case, Jesus was moved with compassion to reached out and help these suffering people.

Mercy is the driving force behind the Covering Wings ministry, a group that takes blankets around Christmastime to homeless people so that they can cover themselves on the cold winter nights. It is mercy and compassion for the unborn child that drives Operation Rescue. Mercy is what causes these people to stand in front of abortion clinics to voice their objection to the horrible national crime of allowing life to be taken within the womb. The good Samaritan had mercy on the Jew who had been victimized by the robber.

When you are motivated by mercy, you see a need and your heart is moved and touched, so you reach out. It is mercy that extends a helping hand to someone in trouble or who is distressed. This is the positive side to showing mercy.

Showing Mercy: A Divine Command

We should note that we need to show mercy—whether we have the gift or not. It's not an option; it's a command.

Jesus commanded us in Luke 6:36, "Be merciful, just as your Father also is merciful." We're to take on this characteristic of God's nature. As a child of God, you are to be merciful just as your Father is merciful. God is our example in showing mercy, and we're to be like our Father. He sets the standard for us.

Micah 6:8 says, "He has shown you, O man, what is good; and what does the Lord require of you but to do justly, to love mercy, and to walk humbly with your God?" And in Zechariah 7:9 the Lord said, "Execute true justice, show mercy and compassion everyone to his brother."

Just as our own forgiveness is related to our being forgiving, Jesus tied our showing mercy to our receiving mercy. Many of the graces God bestows upon us are tied to our bestowing those same graces on others. In the Sermon on the Mount, Jesus said, "Blessed are the merciful, for they shall obtain mercy" (Matthew 5:7). This is also borne out in the Old Testament. Second Samuel 22:26 says, "With the merciful You will show Yourself merciful; with a blameless man You will show Yourself blameless."

We are so merciful when it comes to ourselves, and we always stand ready to justify what we have done. That's just part of human nature. But so often, when we see someone else doing the very thing we have done, we become harsh and critical. We are ready to call the lynch mob and string them up. "Do you know what they did?" we accuse.

We forget that in failing to show mercy to others, we are setting the standard by which God will one day judge us. That's why I like to be very merciful. When I stand before God, I want Him to be very merciful to me. Remember James 2:13? "For judgment is without mercy to the one who has shown no mercy." When you stand before God, you will receive the same kind of mercy that you showed to others. If you haven't shown mercy, then He will judge you without mercy. Do you want to face that? Not me! That is why being merciful is so important to me.

We serve a merciful God and, as He plants His nature in us, we become more like Him. We become more merciful.

A Touch of God's Heart

Mercy is a gift of the Spirit. Through the gift of mercy we are given a little touch of the heart of God. God's compassion for the world, His concern for the poor and the needy, becomes our own when He puts this gift in our heart. He allows us to be the instrument of expressing His love and desires to people in distress.

It is always an exciting and thrilling experience to realize that God is using me to accomplish His purposes and His work. I marvel that God would use me to be the instrument of His mercy toward others. And I realize that all this is made possible only through His infinite mercy.

If God has given you the gift of mercy, exercise it with cheerfulness. Realize how privileged you are to be God's instrument to bring His compassion and mercy to others. Let Him fill you with His love so that you, in turn, can shower it on others. And as the years go by, you'll come to appreciate Psalm 103:11 more and more because, no matter how large the universe grows, you'll understand that His mercies are larger still.

"As the heavens are high above the earth, so great is His mercy toward those who fear Him."

How Should We Respond to the Holy Spirit?

23

The *Real* Baptism of Fire

John answered, saying to them all, "I indeed baptize you with water; but One mightier than I is coming, whose sandal strap I am not worthy to loose. He will baptize you with the Holy Spirit and with fire.

—LUKE 3:16

Some time ago I ran across an autobiographical account by the great American evangelist Charles Finney. I am thrilled each time I read his description of the special work God did in his life one evening long ago:

> Just before evening the thought took possession in my mind that as soon as I was left alone in the new office I would try to pray again, that I was not going to abandon the subject of religion and give it up. And therefore, although I had no longer had any concern about my soul, still I would continue to pray.
>
> By evening we got the books and furniture adjusted and I made up in the open fireplace a good fire, hoping to spend the evening alone. Just at dark Squire Wright, seeing that everything was adjusted, bade me goodnight and went to his home. I accompanied him to the door and as I closed the door and turned around, my heart seemed to be liquid within me. All my feelings seemed to rise and flow out. And the utterance of my heart was, I want to pour out my whole soul unto God.

The rising of my soul was so great that I rushed into the room back of the front office to pray. There was no fire and no light in the room and nevertheless it appeared to me as if it were perfectly light. As I went in and shut the door after me, it seemed as if I met the Lord Jesus Christ face to face. It did not occur to me then, nor did it for sometime afterwards, that it was wholly a mental state. On the contrary, it seemed to me that I saw him as I would see any other man. He said nothing, but he looked at me in such a manner as to break me right down at his feet.

I've always since regarded this as a most remarkable state of mind, for it seemed to be a reality. I fell down at his feet and poured out my soul to him. I wept aloud like a child, and I made such confession as I could with my choked utterance. It seemed to me that I bathed his feet with my tears and yet I had no distinct impression that I touched him, that I recollect.

I must have continued in this state for a good while, but my mind was too much absorbed with the interview to recollect anything that I said. But I know as soon as my mind became calm enough to break off from the interview, I returned to the front office and found that the fire that I had made of large wood was nearly burned out.

But as I turned and was about to take a seat by the fire, I received a mighty baptism of the Holy Spirit—without any expectation of it, without ever having the thought in my mind that there was any such thing for me. Without any recollection that I had ever heard the thing mentioned by any person in the world, the Holy Spirit descended on me in a manner that seemed to go through me, body and soul. I could feel the impression like a wave of electricity going through and through me. Indeed, it seemed to come in waves and waves of liquid love, for I could not express it any other way. It seemed like the very breath of God. I cannot recollect distinctly, but it seemed to fan me like immense wings.

No words can express the wonderful love that was shed abroad in my heart. I wept aloud with joy and love. I do not know but I should say I literally bellowed out the unutterable gushings of my heart. The waves came over me and over me one after another until I recollect I cried out, "I shall die if these waves continue to pass over me." I said, "Lord, I cannot bear anymore." And yet I had no fear of death.[1]

Finney's account of his own experience of the baptism with the Holy Spirit is wonderful, but it also raises some important questions. What exactly is the baptism with the Holy Spirit? Is it the same thing as conversion? Is it a subsequent event to regeneration? Is it always accompanied by special manifestations, or can it be a more subdued experience? How do you receive it?

Because these questions are so vitally important to every believer, it is critical that we spend some time considering each one.

What Is the Baptism with the Spirit?

In Luke 3:16, John the Baptist says of Jesus, "I indeed baptize you with water; but One mightier than I is coming, whose sandal strap I am not worthy to loose. He will baptize you with the Holy Spirit and with fire." In John 1:33, once again, John the Baptist says of Jesus, "I did not know Him, but He who sent me to baptize with water said to me, 'Upon whom you see the Spirit descending, and remaining on Him, this is He who baptizes with the Holy Spirit.'"

Acts 1:4 describes how Jesus was assembled with His disciples when He commanded them that they should not depart from Jerusalem, but should wait for the Promise of the Father which "you have heard from Me; for John truly baptized with water, but you shall be baptized with the Holy Spirit not many days from now."

These verses teach us that there is an experience properly called the baptism with the Holy Spirit. But what exactly is it?

Is It the Same as Regeneration?

The Bible teaches that the baptism with the Holy Spirit is separate and distinct from regeneration. It is one thing to be born of the Spirit; it is yet another to be baptized with the Holy Spirit. Several passages confirm this to us.

In John 20:22, we read that Jesus breathed on His disciples and said to them, "Receive the Holy Spirit." The laws of biblical interpretation insist that the obvious meaning is usually the correct one. So, if Jesus breathed on His men and said, "Receive the Holy Spirit," the obvious meaning is that they received the Holy Spirit at that point—the Holy Spirit began to indwell them.

Not everyone accepts this interpretation, however. Some say that Jesus' words were only symbolic. They believe that regeneration and the baptism of the Holy Spirit are one and the same experience, and that the Master's words in John 20:22 only preview what was to come at Pentecost.

Yet there is no scriptural warrant for such an interpretation. Nothing in Scripture indicates that the disciples did not receive the Spirit in John 20. In fact, it's hard for me to believe that when Jesus says, "Receive the Holy Spirit," nothing happens.

And when you consider the record, it becomes clear that something *did* happen in John 20. Earlier Jesus had said to Peter, "When you are converted, strengthen your brethren," and after John 20, we find Peter doing exactly that. He began to take a leadership role in the church and became one of her primary spokesmen. So it seems clear that Peter did in fact receive the Spirit in John 20.

Yet it wasn't until *after* this event that Jesus promised His disciples the baptism of the Holy Spirit. In Acts 1:4,5 Jesus told His men to wait in Jerusalem for the Promise of the Father, "for John truly baptized with water, but you shall be baptized with the Holy Spirit not many days from now." The promise was fulfilled on the day of Pentecost. That means the baptism with the Holy Spirit occurred some time after the disciples' conversion, and subsequent to their receiving the Holy Spirit as an indwelling presence.

Another Objection Answered

Some interpreters put together two Pauline passages in an attempt to prove that regeneration and the baptism with the Spirit always occur at the same time. While they do not claim regeneration and the baptism are the same thing, they do maintain that they are indistinguishable to human eyes.

First, these critics point to 1 Corinthians 12:13, which says we were all baptized by the Spirit into one body. The baptism of the Spirit, these critics say, is what makes us part of the body of Christ.

In Matthew 3:11, John is prophesying the coming of Jesus, and declares, concerning Him, that He would baptize them with the Holy Spirit and fire. John was baptizing people in water. John was the baptizer, water was the element, and repentance of sin was the issue.

In 1 Corinthians 12, the Holy Spirit is the baptizer and the issue is initiation into the body of Christ. The promise was that Jesus would be the baptizer, the Holy Spirit would be the element, and the issue would be power to witness.

Second, those who deny that the baptism of the Holy Spirit is separate from regeneration usually quote from Ephesians 4, where Paul encourages the church to keep the unity of the Spirit. "There is one body and one Spirit, just as you were called in one hope of your calling; one Lord, one faith, one baptism; one God and Father of all, who is above all, and through all, and in you all," he writes (4:4-6). After pointing out that there is only one baptism, the argument is made that the one baptism is the baptism of the Spirit into the body of Christ.

But this interpretation misses the point of the Ephesian passage. Paul's thrust is that there is only a single body of Christ—there are not many such bodies. Paul was warning us about the type of factionalism that we see so often today between warring denominations.

Paul was saying, "No, no. There's only one body, the body of Christ. There is only one baptism." There isn't a Lutheran baptism and a Presbyterian baptism and a Methodist baptism and a Baptist baptism; you can't divide the body of Christ like that. There is only one Lord and only one baptism.

Therefore, it is a mistake to pair Ephesians 4:5 with 1 Corinthians 12:13 in an attempt to disprove the validity of the baptism with the Spirit as a separate event subsequent to conversion. There is an experience distinct from regeneration that is properly called the baptism with the Holy Spirit.

Three Key Prepositions

We still have yet to describe what this baptism with the Spirit is and does. To help us understand it, let's take a look at three Greek prepositions which are used to describe relationships with the Holy Spirit.

In John 14, Jesus is encouraging a discouraged bunch of disciples. He promises to send them a Comforter—the Spirit of truth—who would abide with them forever, "whom the world cannot receive, because it neither sees Him nor knows Him; but you know Him, for He dwells with you and will be in you" (John 14:17).

Note that Jesus said the Holy Spirit was dwelling "with" His men, or "alongside" of them. The Greek preposition here is *para*. Yet soon the Spirit would be more than "with" the disciples; soon He would dwell "in" them. Here the preposition is *en*. I believe the disciples went from *para* to *en* in John 20, when Jesus breathed on them and said, "Receive the Holy Spirit."

The same two prepositions characterize your own experience. Prior to your conversion, it was the Holy Spirit who convicted you of your sins. It was the Holy Spirit who revealed to you Jesus Christ as the One who could take away your sin, who convinced you to accept Jesus as your Lord. The moment you accepted Jesus as the Lord of your life, the Holy Spirit came into you and began to indwell you. You went from *para* to *en*.

Not every believer, however, has the baptism with the Holy Spirit. In Acts 1:8 Jesus said to His men, "You shall receive power when the Holy Spirit has come *upon* you." This is the third Greek preposition, *epi*—the Spirit comes "upon" you or "over" you. (I personally prefer the idea that He "overflows" you.)

This *epi* empowers the believer for service. It is an outflowing of the Spirit, a flowing forth from my life of the *dunamis*, the dynamic, the power of God's Spirit, working through my life and touching those around me. In Acts 1:8 Jesus said, "You shall receive power [*dunamis*] when the Holy Spirit has come upon [*epi*] you."

It is one thing to have the Holy Spirit "with" you (*para*), another thing to have the Spirit "in" you (*en*), but something even more to have the Holy Spirit "upon" you (*epi*). Allow me to illustrate the difference.

If I should place an empty glass next to a large pitcher of water, this pitcher would be *para*, "with" the glass. If I start pouring the water from the pitcher into the glass, the water is now "in," *en*, this pitcher. As the glass fills with water and I continue to pour water into it, the glass begins to overflow. The water is now "upon" or "overflowing," *epi*, the glass. You started out with the *para*, moved to the *en*, and wound up with the *epi*.

So it is with the Holy Spirit in our lives. He is first "with" us, He begins to dwell "in" us, but as the Lord continues to pour out His Spirit "upon" us, He begins to overflow from us.

While many Christians have the Holy Spirit in them, the Holy Spirit is not flowing forth out of their lives. They need to experience the *epi*, this baptism with the Holy Spirit.

The Power to Serve

So many Christians have the Spirit all bottled up inside. The Spirit does not flow forth from their life, and they seem content to be nominal Christians, to hang around but never to overflow. Yet it is God's desire, purpose, and will that our lives overflow with the Spirit.

When Peter stood up on the day of Pentecost and preached the message of Jesus Christ to the people, the Holy Spirit brought conviction to their hearts and they cried out, "Men and brethren, what shall we do?" (Acts 2:37). They recognized their sin and what they had done wrong. Peter answered, "Repent, and let every one of you be baptized in the name of Jesus Christ for the remission of sins; and you shall receive the gift of the Holy Spirit" (Acts 2:38). The "gift" Peter was talking about is the *epi*, the overflowing of God's power for service. He then concluded, "For the promise is to you and to your children, and to all who are afar off, as many as the Lord our God will call" (Acts 2:39).

Note that Peter made no indication that this gift of the Holy Spirit would cease with the death of the last of the apostles. In fact, just the opposite seems true. This promise of the gift of the Holy Spirit is "to you and to your children, and to all who are afar off, as many as the Lord our God will call." That means the promise is for us, today, wherever we live and whatever our backgrounds.

I am convinced that the greatest need in the church today is a renewal of teaching on the subject of the Holy Spirit. Only then will you and I be empowered to go into the world as effective witnesses for Jesus Christ. The only hope for our nation today is a spiritual awakening that begins in the church with a fresh movement of the Holy Spirit upon the lives and hearts of the saints of God. And that takes the *epi*, the baptism with the Holy Spirit.

The Baptism of the Spirit in Acts

Acts 2 describes how God fulfilled His promise to baptize His children with the Holy Spirit. As the disciples were waiting in an upper room, suddenly a sound from heaven like a mighty rushing wind filled the house. At the same time tongues of fire appeared and rested upon each of them, and all the disciples were filled with the Holy Spirit and began to speak with other tongues.[2]

In Acts 8, a great revival broke out under the preaching of Philip. Many believed and were baptized. When the apostles at Jerusalem "heard that Samaria had received the word of God, they sent Peter and John to them, who, when they had come down, prayed for them that they might receive the Holy Spirit. "For as yet He had fallen upon [*epi*] none of them. They had only been baptized in the name of the Lord Jesus" (Acts 8:14,15). Although these believers had been baptized in the name of Jesus, they had not yet received this gift of the Holy Spirit. When Peter and John laid their hands on them and prayed for them, they received the Holy Spirit.

Acts 9 tells us that Paul, who was then known as Saul of Tarsus, was on his way to Damascus to imprison those who were calling on the name of the Lord. Suddenly a light brighter than the noonday sun knocked Paul to the ground, and he heard a voice saying to him, "Saul, Saul, why are you persecuting Me?" He responded, "Who are You, Lord?" and the answer came, "I am Jesus, whom you are persecuting." Then he asked, "Lord, what do You want me to do?" (Acts 9:1-6).

I do not see how anyone can question whether Paul was converted at that moment on the road to Damascus. When a man submits himself to the Lordship of Jesus Christ, that is a definite sign of conversion. It is also a definite sign of the Holy Spirit coming into that person's life. No man can call Christ "Lord" except by the Holy Spirit (see 1 Corinthians 12:3), yet here Paul is saying, "What would you have me to do, *Lord?*" Jesus told him to go into town where he would find out. A blinded Saul was led into Damascus and taken to the house of a man named Judas who lived on Straight street, the main road in town.

A certain disciple named Ananias then had a vision in which the Lord told him to seek out Saul. After a brief argument with God, Ananias obeyed, found Paul, and said, "Brother Saul, the Lord Jesus, who appeared to you on the road as you came, has sent me that you may receive your sight and be filled with the Holy Spirit'" (Acts 9:17). Note that Paul's filling with the Holy Spirit was subsequent to, and distinct from, his conversion on the road to Damascus.

In Acts 10, Peter was sent to the house of a centurion named Cornelius, who had assembled many of his friends at his house. As Peter began to declare the truth of Jesus Christ, the Holy Spirit fell upon (*epi*) all who were hearing the Word. The Jews who came with Peter were surprised that the gift of the Holy Spirit was poured out upon the Gentiles. In this case, it appears that the Gentiles' conversion and their filling with the Spirit was a simultaneous experience.

Later, as Peter was explaining what had happened, he made it clear he wasn't accepting any responsibility for it. "As I began to speak, the Holy Spirit fell upon them, as upon us at the beginning," he said. "Then I remembered the word of the Lord, how He said, 'John indeed baptized with water, but you shall be baptized with the Holy Spirit'" (Acts 11:15,16). In essence, Peter said, "I just started talking to them, and while I was speaking the Holy Spirit fell on them. I didn't do anything— it just happened. Then I remembered how Jesus said He would baptize us with the Holy Spirit."

In Acts 19, Paul had come to Ephesus, where many people had believed through the ministry of Apollos. But something was lacking. Maybe it was a lack of joy. They said they were Christians, but you would never know it by looking at their faces; they seemed so sober and almost angry with the world. Or perhaps it was a lack of love, or a cutting, critical spirit. Or maybe Paul detected a lack of fervency—they were neither hot nor cold, but just lukewarm.

Whatever it was, Paul detected something lacking in the Ephesians' experience and relationship with the Lord. He was determined to identify it so he asked them, "Have ye received the Holy Ghost since ye believed?" (KJV). In other words, "Have you had this subsequent relationship? Did you receive the Holy Spirit?"[3]

They responded, "We've never even heard of the Holy Spirit." They were totally ignorant. "The Holy Spirit? What's that?" Then Paul asked, "How were you baptized? Were you baptized in the baptismal formula that Jesus commanded—in the name of the Father, the Son, and the Holy Spirit?" They replied, "No. We were baptized with John's baptism." John's baptism was a baptism of a repentance from sin, not a baptism into Christ. So right then they were baptized in the name of Jesus Christ. And when Paul had laid his hands upon them, the Holy Spirit came upon (*epi*) them, and they spoke with tongues and prophesied (see Acts 19:1-6). Once more, this baptism was an experience subsequent to conversion.

Different Experiences, Same Event

As we have just seen, the book of Acts records a wide variety of experiences, methods, and ways by which people received the gift of the Holy Spirit. Consider this brief review:

- In Acts 2, a noise from heaven that sounded like a mighty, rushing wind filled all the house. Cloven tongues as of fire sat upon each of the disciples and they all began to speak in other tongues as the Spirit gave them the ability.

- In Acts 8, the gift of the Holy Spirit was imparted by the laying on of hands by Paul and John. No special manifestations are mentioned.

- In Acts 9, the Holy Spirit was imparted to Paul by Ananias, "a nobody", a common believer from Damascus.

- In Acts 10, Peter's message was interrupted when the Holy Spirit fell upon the Gentiles, who began to speak in tongues.

- In Acts 19, Paul laid his hands on the people in Ephesus, and they spoke in tongues and prophesied.

Note that no two of these experiences in Acts are identical. The closest parallel is perhaps Acts 2 with the experience at the house of Cornelius—but even here there was no mighty, rushing wind and no cloven tongues of fire.

This reminds us that God is not bound by a particular method or by a particular way of doing things. God can act as He wants, and we are wrong in trying to pattern our experience after those of someone else—no matter how great that experience seems.

Remember Finney's account of his own baptism with the Spirit recounted at the beginning of this chapter? His experience was wonderful and glorious, but our own experience may be quite different from his. That's just the way God works.

Be Ready and Open

I suggest that you be open to whatever and however God wants to work in your life. Don't look for a particular sensation or reaction or response. Allow God to work however He desires in the imparting of this glorious gift to you.

It may be that the baptism will come through the laying on of hands by a pastor or one of the laymen in your church, as it did with the apostle Paul. Or it may be that no one will lay their hands on you, as was the case in Acts 2, where the disciples were all sitting and waiting. I've heard of people who were baptized while standing or lying on the floor or in bed. It doesn't matter: God isn't bound to one particular way of doing things.

So be open. Don't try to pattern God. Just receive the gift of the Holy Spirit, and experience His dynamic power in your life to be what God wants you to be. Tap into His power, and be a true witness of Jesus Christ in this world.

How desperately we need this power today! We need it for survival. We are living in the perilous days foretold by the Scriptures, when the love of many would wax cold. We need so urgently to wait upon God until we overflow with His Holy Spirit. Only then will the church again become a powerful witness to a world that so desperately needs the Savior.

24

Ask and You
Shall Receive

Repent, and let every one of you be baptized in the name of
Jesus Christ for the remission of sins; and you shall receive
the gift of the Holy Spirit. For the promise is to you and to
your children, and to all who are afar off, as many as the
Lord our God will call.

—ACTS 2:38

The feast holiday of the year had come. The disciples were waiting in an upper room in Jerusalem according to the command of Jesus, looking for the promise of the Father. Perhaps they wondered how God would pour out his Spirit upon all flesh.

At last the promise of God was fulfilled. The Holy Spirit descended upon the 120 waiting disciples with a sound like a mighty, rushing wind and it filled the house, and cloven tongues of fire sat upon each of them. They were all filled with the Holy Spirit and began to speak in tongues.

This supernatural phenomenon drew a crowd of people who were wondering what had happened. Some mocked, "Oh, they're just drunk." But Peter stood up and called for the people to listen. "These men are not drunk, as you suppose," he said. "It's only nine o'clock in the morning. But this is what was spoken by the prophet Joel: 'And it shall come to pass in the last days, says God, that I will pour out of My Spirit on all flesh; your sons and your daughters shall prophesy, your young men shall see visions, your old men shall dream dreams.

And on My menservants and on My maidservants I will pour out My Spirit in those days; and they shall prophesy.' "

When Peter had concluded his message concerning Jesus Christ—His death, burial, resurrection, ascension into heaven, and the sending of the Holy Spirit—the people were convicted and cried out, "Men and brethren, what shall we do?" Peter replied, "Repent, and let every one of you be baptized in the name of Jesus Christ for the remission of sins; and you shall receive the gift of the Holy Spirit. For the promise is to you and to your children, and to all who are afar off, as many as the Lord our God shall call" (see Acts 2:1-39).

A Promise for Everyone

Peter's words assure us that the promise of the gift of the Holy Spirit is for all believers in all generations. Throughout the history of the church, this is God's promise to all His children. He wants to bestow upon us the gift of the Holy Spirit.

By definition, a gift cannot be deserved or earned. God does not give the gift of the Holy Spirit as a reward for being good and faithful, or for achieving a high degree of holiness. Regardless of your present state of spiritual development—whether you've just started down the path or you've been on it for a long time—you can receive the gift of the Holy Spirit. It's available to you right now, no matter how advanced or incomplete your spiritual development might be. It's a gift that must be received.

This is where a lot of people get hung up. They think they must somehow become worthy of the Holy Spirit, that they must earn His power and His blessing. I myself struggled with this idea for a long time.

During my youth, many preachers and evangelists drilled into me that the Holy Spirit would not possess an unclean vessel. Since He is a *Holy* Spirit, I was told, you must become holy to receive Him. The testimonies I often heard people give about how they received the Holy Spirit confirmed this teaching to me. The testimonies frequently went something like this: "I was seeking God for the Holy Spirit, praying and tarrying. For months I waited upon God, crying out to God, seeking the Holy Spirit. Finally, I took the cigarettes out of my pocket, laid them on the altar and said, 'God, I'll even give up my cigarettes.' Then God filled me with the Holy Spirit." Or someone else would say, "When I promised God I'd never take another drink, then He filled me with the Holy Spirit."

My problem was that I never smoked cigarettes or drank, so I couldn't take out a pack or a bottle and lay them on the altar. So I would try to figure out, "What is it, Lord, that I need to give up? Chewing gum? Oreo Cookies? I'll quit whatever I have to, Lord." So I laid the cookies and the chewing gum on the altar...but still nothing happened.

We seem to feel that we must be worthy, that we have to deserve this gift. Yet because we know we are unworthy and undeserving, we disqualify ourselves for the blessing. We don't expect to receive the gift because we know we don't deserve it; after all, He fills only holy vessels.

But that's all backward. The truth is that the Holy Spirit comes into your life to help you *become* holy. Not the other way around! Think how false it would be to say to someone, "Look, if you want to get saved, go out and clean up your act. Quit all of the rotten stuff you've been doing. Get your life right with God, because God doesn't want to save you in the mess you're in. Get yourself straightened out and then come to the Lord." I know of a lot of people who believe this. "I'll get saved once I clean up my act," they say.

But that would be like saying, "We're going to get married as soon as we have enough money." If you stick to that plan, you're going to remain single all of your life! In the same way, if you try to get yourself cleaned up before you submit to the Lord, you'll never get saved.

The Holy Spirit is given to enable you to overcome the flesh life. You don't have to get yourself holy to be fit for His habitation. The only way you get holy is by allowing Him to fill you with His holy presence. Peter said we would receive the *gift* of the Holy Spirit. Jesus also called the Holy Spirit a gift (see Acts 1:4). And the only way to possess a gift is to receive it. The gift of the Holy Spirit must be received by faith.

The Necessity of Faith

In the book of Galatians, Paul asked a rhetorical question about faith and the Holy Spirit. He wrote, "Did you receive the Spirit by the works of the law, or by the hearing of faith?" (Galatians 3:2). The obvious answer is that they had received the Holy Spirit through faith. They heard about the gift of God, and by faith, they received it. They didn't earn it; they didn't work for it; it wasn't a reward for attaining some special degree of holiness or righteousness. Rather, when they heard the word of God they believed it, and so received the gift.

Receiving the Spirit is like believing in Jesus Christ for salvation. It is a gift of God to be received by faith. It is not something that you deserve or earn, and it is not a reward for good works. It is God's gift to us, a gift of grace to be received by faith.

And what is faith? The writer of Hebrews says, "Now faith is the substance of things hoped for, the evidence of things not seen" (11:1). Faith is the substance of things *hoped* for, the evidence of things *not* seen. Yet somehow, when it comes to receiving the Holy Spirit by faith, we want to see some evidence.

Many people are hindered in asking for the Holy Spirit because they expect or desire some kind of supernatural evidence that God has answered their prayer. Just believing in the promise of God doesn't seem to be enough; they want God to send a sign. They're looking for skyrockets, for blazing, fiery letters that light up the horizon and say, *"Go to Africa!"*

When I went to seminary I had a problem. The application form asked for a description of my call of God into the ministry, and I didn't have a great story to tell. So many students described sensational calls, visions, recurring dreams, voices, crosses in the sky. I didn't have any of those things. It was hard for me to describe my call because it was only a still, small voice: "Do you want to invest your life in things of the temporal or things of the eternal? Do you want to heal man's bodies through medicine—a temporal healing at best—or do you want to heal man's spirit, which is eternal healing?" All I had was that thought, a challenge in my mind. Yet I followed through on it, went to school, and entered the ministry.

It's interesting to me that now, more than four decades later, I'm still in the ministry, while a lot of those who described dramatic calls and visions are selling used cars. Remember, the Spirit of God often works in very natural ways. He isn't always in the fire, in the earthquake, in the hurricane. He often speaks in a still, small voice.

I think there is a lot of Thomas in all of us. Thomas was the disciple who said, "I will not believe until I can see the print of the nails in His hands and put my hand into His side. I'm not going to believe until I see for myself." When Jesus later appeared to the disciples, He turned to Thomas and said, "Go ahead and touch My hands if you'd like. Go ahead and feel My side. And don't be unbelieving, but believe." Thomas replied, "My Lord and my God!" Jesus answered, "Because you have seen, you believe. But blessed is he who believes even though he has not seen" (see John 20:24-29).

I think something similar happens when we plead for a sign from heaven to prove that God has filled us with His Holy Spirit. Sometimes, in His mercy, God does give us that sign—but then He says to us, "You've had the holy tingles and you believe. But blessed are they who believe without the holy tingles."

We are to receive the gift of the Holy Spirit by faith. There may be tingles or there may not. The gift of the Holy Spirit is received by faith apart from evidence. Certainly evidence will come, but the evidence isn't the proof. Faith receives *without* evidence.

A Trick of the Enemy

Whenever you take a stand of faith, understand that the devil will be right there to challenge it. Whether you have believed God for healing or for salvation or for receiving the gift of the Spirit, you can be sure Satan will challenge you. That is one of his favorite tricks.

If you've taken a stand of faith for salvation, the next time you get angry Satan is going to whisper, "Aha! You see? You're not really saved. Look how mad you got."

If you've taken a step of faith for healing, he's going to multiply your symptoms. You'll feel worse than you ever felt. He'll get you looking for evidences, for signs of your healing.

It's the same way in receiving the gift of the Spirit. If you believe the Lord for the gift of the Spirit, be sure that Satan will come along to challenge your step of faith. That is why we must not only exercise faith in receiving God's gift, but we must maintain that initial step of faith. Remind yourself that you received God's gift. Go back in your mind to the day you took God at His word, and rehearse God's promise and the action you took based on His promise. Every time Satan comes to challenge you, say, "Hey, look—God is true."

Always, without exception, the real question in our Christian life is, Who are we going to believe? Are we going to believe the truth of God or are we going to believe the lie of Satan? You say, "Well, that's not hard." You don't think it is?

God said to Adam and Eve, "You can eat of all the trees in this garden. Freely eat of them—except that tree in the middle there. You're not to eat of that. In the day that you eat of that, you will surely die."

Satan slithered along one day and said to Eve, "My, what a beautiful place. Lovely trees. Wonderful! Can you eat of all of them?"

"Well, yes," she answered. "All except that tree in the middle. We can't eat of that."

"What do you mean?" Satan demanded. "That fruit looks more delicious than all the rest. Why would God say you can't eat of that? He must not like you. I'll bet He knows that that one has the best fruit of all. That tree can make you as wise as God. You see, that's the tree of knowledge. He's afraid you'll be as wise as He is and try to take over. Look how beautiful it is."

"But God said that if we eat of that we'll surely..."

"No, you can't believe that! I mean, isn't He a God of love? How could a God of love put anybody to death? You won't die."

Suddenly Eve was faced with a choice. Would she believe the word of God or would she believe the lie of Satan? The devil lies so convincingly; he sounds so logical. How could a God of love destroy someone He created and loved? Eve had the choice to believe God's truth or Satan's lie, and we've been paying for her choice ever since.

All the way along in our Christian experience, as step-by-step we begin by faith to conquer and take territory from the enemy, Satan is there to challenge us and to speak a lie. "You just conjured that up in your own mind," he whispers. "It isn't really happening. It isn't really working." And too often we agree, "It's true, I have been rather miserable of late. I guess it really isn't working."

The whole fight boils down to this: Do we believe the truth of God? God said, "You shall receive the gift of the Holy Spirit." Now, do we believe that, or do we believe the doubts Satan plants in our mind? We know we will receive the gift because God said we would. The question is, will we doubt what God has said?

The Evidence Mounts

When I say we shouldn't look for evidences of the baptism with the Spirit, don't think I'm suggesting that there will never be any evidence in your life of the touch of God's Spirit. As you walk in the Spirit and allow Him free rein in your life, you will begin to see the power of God at work in your life. The beautiful thing is that many times you won't even notice it for a long time.

For many years as a child of God, I fought vainly against several ugly and horrible characteristics of the flesh—things that blighted my testimony and which brought me to despair. I was unable to cure myself or to help myself, even though I struggled and tried. Yet God, through the power of His Holy Spirit, delivered me from them...and I didn't even know it had happened for five or six years!

Self-inflicted pain caused by my own stupidity used to tick me off more than almost anything else. I would leave a cupboard door open and then stand up, banging my head. It hurt like everything and it made me so angry; I would lose my temper every time. What a beautiful thing it has been to see God work in this area of my life. In fact, many times now I'll bang my head and, when I don't react, the kids think it didn't hurt. It hurts like crazy, but I no longer have the angry outbursts that used to accompany it. I just say, "Yeah, it hurt. So I'm stupid. So?"

When God is working in your life, you'll see the evidence; it will come. God will give you insight. He'll begin to reveal things to you, to warn you of a flaw in a person's character or show you how someone was trying to deceive you. You'll begin to see the evidences of the Spirit of God and His gifts at work in your life.

As you walk in the Spirit and develop in your relationship with Him, it is quite possible you will begin to enjoy all kinds of glorious, supernatural experiences. Sometimes you will respond with weeping; at other times there will be tremendous joy and an overwhelming love. You will enjoy exciting experiences that will thrill you to the core of your being. You'll see the power of God at work in your life, and you'll witness the various manifestations of the Spirit.

Our faith must never be predicated on our experience but in God's Word which we believe by faith. We aren't to look for ecstatic experiences. We are called to believe God and act on His Word. In that way we will find ourselves wanting more of God and desiring Him to have more of us.

Receive the Gift

The Holy Spirit is a gift that must be received. Jesus said to His disciples, "Receive the Holy Spirit." The apostle John said that those who believed on Jesus should "receive" the Spirit. When Peter and John went to Samaria to greet the new believers there, they "prayed for them that they might receive the Holy Spirit."

Of course, no one begs for a gift; you simply receive it. The Holy Spirit is God's gift to you to enable you to overcome sin, to be conformed to the image of Jesus Christ, and to transform you into a powerful witness for the Lord. The Holy Spirit is not given to you so that you might have an ecstatic spiritual experience. Rather, He is given to you so that you might have the power to live for Jesus.

But you must *ask* for the Holy Spirit. Jesus said, "If a son asks for bread from any father among you, will he give him a stone? Or if he asks for a fish, will he give him a serpent instead of a fish? Or if he asks for an egg, will he offer him a scorpion? If you then, being evil, know how to give good gifts to your children, how much more will your heavenly Father give the Holy Spirit to those who ask Him" (Luke 11:11-13)!

What's the procedure here? To whom does the Father give the Holy Spirit? He gives the Spirit to His children who ask. You don't have to reach some exalted standard of holiness nor must you do something extraordinary. No, just *ask*. It's a gift. Ask, and then receive by faith the promise of God.

God is not going to force on you something that you do not want. You must desire what He has to give. God will not violate your free will. You must ask the Lord in faith for the gift of the Holy Spirit. This is a petition you can make in full confidence. John tells us that if we ask for anything according to God's will, we can know that God hears us, and that He will grant us our request (1 John 5:14). Therefore, when you ask God for this gift of the Holy Spirit, you can be utterly confident that you are asking according to His will. It was Jesus Himself who instructed us to ask for this gift!

If you have not already asked to receive this gift, I urge you right now to pray in faith that God would give it to you. You could pray something like the following:

> Lord, I thank You for this promised gift. I receive now the gift of Your Spirit in my life, along with the power to transform and to change me. I ask that Your power might flow forth from my life to help and to strengthen others around me. Bless them

through me by bestowing on them Your love and Your power. In Jesus' name I pray, Amen.

That's all there is to it—but realize that Satan will challenge such an important step of faith. Whenever necessary, say, "Look, the Lord said that I would receive this gift by faith, and I have accepted God's Word. By faith, I have received the gift of the Holy Spirit. It's mine. So take your lies elsewhere."

Blessings for Those Who Thirst

Jesus said, "Blessed are those who hunger and thirst for righteousness, for they shall be filled" (Matthew 5:6). I wonder: Do you hunger and thirst after the things of God? Do you long for a rich spiritual life? Do you desire freedom and deliverance from the power and bondage of your flesh? Can you, like David, say, "As the deer pants for the water brooks, so pants my soul for You, O God" (Psalm 42:1)? Do you thirst for the living God?

"Blessed are those who hunger and thirst for righteousness." Why are they blessed? What is the promise? "For they shall be filled." Now, that's the promise; that's what God said. Can you take God at His Word? Will you believe the Word of God? Or will you believe things like, "Oh, not you, man. He wouldn't fill *you*. You're too far gone. The flesh has too great a hold on you. God can't set you free. Oh, sure, He can free others—but not you. Yours is a special case. You've gone too far."

What will you believe? Will you accept the truth of God or the lie of Satan? I assure you that you have absolutely no reason to believe the lie of Satan; he's a liar and the father of all lies. But you have every reason in the universe to believe God. God cannot lie, and if God has declared it, then you can bet your life on it. You can stand on it, and trust in it.

As you ask the Lord to fill you with His Spirit, receive Him by faith, then thank Him for His magnificent gift. How ungrateful it would be if you went on your way without expressing your appreciation for such a glorious gift. So often it is precisely when people give thanks to God that they experience some of the most supernatural, glorious ecstasies of His power.

The gift is yours. It's free. God has given it to you. Why don't you ask for it, then receive it in faith? Let Him take your hands and use them to touch the needy, the afflicted, the sick, the suffering. Let Him use your voice to share His love and His truth. Let Him use your heart to love the world around you. Ask Him to fill you until you overflow—and then rejoice as He uses your life as an instrument in His hands to accomplish His good purposes in a needy and desperate world.

25

A Torrent
of Love

*If anyone thirsts, let him come to Me and drink. He who
believes in Me, as the Scripture has said, out of his heart
will flow rivers of living water.*

—JOHN 7:37,38

Imagine that you are a child of about eight or nine,
living in ancient Israel long before the Romans came to destroy
your nation. A special time of year has arrived, and your parents ask you to do something a little odd. They want you to
move out of your comfortable house and live for eight days in
a flimsy, tiny, temporary shack made out of palm fronds.

At night when you go to bed you can look up through
spaces in the thatched roof and see the stars. As you lie there in
the blackness, looking up and wondering at the pinpricks of
light, you exclaim, "Oh, Daddy! I can see a star up there." And
your father replies, "Yes, honey. Our fathers lived out under
the stars for 40 years, and God protected them and preserved
them." As the night creeps on, a cold wind picks up and whis-
tles through the space between the thatches in the walls of
your flimsy shack, chilling you to the bone. You can't sleep and
you cry out, "Oh, Daddy, the wind is blowing on me. I'm
cold!" And your father answers, "I know, honey. And we must
remember that our Father, God, was with our fathers for 40
years as they slept out under the sky with the wind blowing on
them—and yet God preserved them."

After eight days of living as your ancestors did, you're more than ready to return to your real home. But in those eight days, you learned a great deal about how God cares for you today—just as He did for your fathers so long ago. And you also learn that you'll be repeating your own "wilderness wandering" next year, when the feast of tabernacles rolls around once more.

The Feast of Tabernacles

The feast of tabernacles was also known as Succoth ("booth"), or the feast of booths. The feast commemorated God's miraculous preservation of the nation of Israel during the 40 years the people wandered in the wilderness, living under the elements of nature. It is conservatively estimated that some 1.6 million people came out with Moses from Egypt. This feast commemorated that wonderful miracle.

God commanded His people to build little booths beside their homes during this feast. Generally, they would make these booths out of palm thatches, and the family would move out of the house and into these booths during the feast.

For the first seven days of the eight-day feast, the temple priests in Jerusalem would march in procession down many steps with large water jugs on their shoulders to the pool of Siloam in the Kidron Valley. There they would fill their jugs and make a solemn procession back up the steps and into the temple courtyard where thousands of people would be gathered to worship God. As the priests entered the courtyard, the people would break forth in singing the Hallel Psalms—the songs that begin and end with Hallelujah ("praise God").

As the people sang and worshiped God, the priests poured out the water on the pavement. As the water splashed on the big stones, everyone was reminded how God brought water out of the rock when their fathers were dying of thirst in the wilderness. They remembered how Moses took the rod and struck the rock according to the commandment of God, and how life-giving water came gushing out the rock. All this spectacle was to remind the Israelites of God's divine preservation of their fathers during their 40-year wilderness wandering. It was all very symbolic and very moving.

Now on the last day, the great day of the feast, the priests did not make a procession to the pool of Siloam nor did they pour out water on the pavement. This too was significant, for it acknowledged that God had kept His promise to their fathers. He preserved them in the wilderness and brought them into a land flowing with milk and honey—a well-watered land where they no longer needed water to gush miraculously out of rocks. The activities of the eighth day proclaimed that God had fulfilled His promises in bringing the Israelites to their land.

It was on this day, as the people were gathered to worship God—at the same time the water was poured out on the pavement during the seven earlier days of the feast—that Jesus stood and cried to the thousands of worshipers in the courtyard: "If anyone thirsts, let him come to Me and drink."

The fact that Jesus was standing was significant. According to Jewish practice, when a rabbi was teaching he would sit while his pupils would stand. Only when a teacher was going to make a special proclamation would he stand. The fact that Jesus stood and spoke meant He was heralding an important truth to the people. "If anyone thirsts," He cried out, "let him come to Me and drink."

Jesus wasn't speaking of physical thirst or even man's emotional need for love, for security, or to be needed. Rather, He was talking about the human thirst for God. Deep down in the spirit of every man resides an unquenchable need for God. Inside of every one of us our spirit is crying out, yearning for a meaningful relationship with God. We are incomplete without Him.

You might say God created us with an inner vacuum. Nature abhors a vacuum and seeks to fill it. If we don't fill this vacuum with God, we will try to fill it with something else. That is the bedrock reason behind the problems in our society. Man tries to fill this vacuum with physical and emotional experiences instead of with the Living God. But because the vacuum can be filled only with God, the thirst only grows greater and more desperate.

Only one thing can satisfy the cry of the human spirit, and that is a meaningful relationship with God. Dr. Henry Drummond, in his book *The Natural and the Supernatural*, declares that even the very protoplasm of man reaches out for Father God. The need and thirst and belief in God seems to be encoded in our DNA.

The heart of every person on the globe senses a deep lack of fulfillment, a sense that there's got to be more to life. This is a universal thirst that affects everyone. You've been built with it; it was created in you. Romans 8:20 tells us that the creature was made subject to emptiness by design of the Creator Himself. God created us with this emptiness so that we might reach out to Him, and find a meaningful relationship with Him. It is the only way to fulfillment.

That is why Jesus cried out, "If anyone thirsts, let him come to Me and drink." This is the essence and the heart of the gospel in a very brief and beautiful form. Jesus is the answer to man's thirst. He is the only One who can satisfy our thirst for God. He is the only One who can bring fulfillment and completion. He is in essense saying, "In the deepest part of your being you need God. Come to Me!"

And what did He say would result from accepting His offer? "He who believes in Me, as the Scripture has said, out of his heart will flow rivers of living water." Probably Jesus was making a reference to Isaiah 44:3, in which God promised, "For I will pour water on him who is thirsty, and floods on the dry ground; I will pour My Spirit on your descendants, and My blessing on your offspring."

The original Greek text here is far more dynamic and intense than the King James Version indicates. The word translated *flow* in Greek is actually the word *gush*, while the word translated *rivers* is the Greek term for *torrent*. So a better translation would be, "Out of his innermost being there will gush torrents of living water." The King James might cause us to picture a gentle stream trickling quietly through the woods, but the original Greek pictures a mighty deluge cascading down a mountain gorge. It depicts the flood stage of a river rampaging through a canyon. "There will gush torrents of living water," Jesus says.

At this point, John departs from the Savior's words to comment, "But this He spoke concerning the Spirit, whom those believing in Him would receive; for the Holy Spirit was not yet given, because Jesus was not yet glorified" (John 7:39). The evangelist therefore makes it clear that Jesus meant the Spirit would be like a torrent of living water flowing out of the life of believers in Christ.

Released for Service

So why is this important? Why is it crucial for you to realize that the Spirit wants to flow forth from you as a mighty, gushing torrent and not merely as a gently bubbling stream?

It's glorious that God's Spirit blesses us with joy and beauty and a deep consciousness of God, but the Lord is never satisfied with the subjective work of the Spirit within us. He never intended that the Spirit be kept bottled up within us to bless us. His objective is always that you and I be the instruments through which the Holy Spirit might flow forth to the needy world around us. It is crucial for our service to God that the Spirit be released as a mighty, gushing torrent.

Years ago, at a conference, I heard a speaker declare that the greatest capacity of man was his ability to contain God. He was preaching on 2 Corinthians 4:7, where Paul says, "We have this treasure in earthen vessels," and was describing the glory of our bodies being the temple of the Holy Spirit. He made a very inspiring, powerful presentation and I was stirred and moved that my body should be the temple of the Holy Spirit.

But as you read on in the Scriptures, you discover that the greatest capacity of man is *not* being a vessel that can contain God; rather, it's being a vessel *through which* God can be poured out to the world around us. That's the real glory!

The ultimate work of the Spirit is not merely to transform and change and empower us that we might be blessed. His ultimate work is empowering us to serve, to become effective in bringing Jesus Christ to others. God's Spirit wants to use you and me to bring the love of God to others. He wants His Spirit to flow like a torrent of living water out of our lives and into the lives of those who have yet to quench their thirst at the fountain of God.

The book of Acts is the story of what happens when the Spirit of God flows out in dynamic power from the lives of believers. Through the anointing and the power of the Spirit, Peter preached and bore witness to the resurrection of Jesus Christ from the dead—and conviction gripped the hearts of 3,000 men, all of whom committed their lives to Jesus Christ.

When the Spirit flows out in dynamic power from the lives of believers, entire communities are changed. The world is turned right-side up. When the apostles came to ancient Thessalonica, some alarmed citizens ran to the judges and said, "These who have turned the world upside down have come here too" (Acts 17:6). Their evaluation was in error. The world is upside down; the apostles were turning it right-side up. That's what happens when the Spirit of God begins to flow forth out of the lives of yielded believers.

We are called not merely to be a vessel to contain God's Spirit, but to become a channel through which the Spirit can flow to the thirsty world around us.

A Torrent of Love

As the Spirit flows forth from our lives, what is it that flows forth? What should be manifested?

Paul answered that question by saying, "the fruit of the Spirit is love" (Galatians 5:22). When a person is overflowing with the Spirit, what rushes out is God's divine love. The love of God should be flowing out of our lives like a mighty torrent of living water.

The Greeks had several words for love. One spoke of physical love, another of emotional love, and yet another of spiritual love. In English, our single word *love* has to cover everything. We use it to describe our affection for our grandkids and our fondness for peanuts. Now, I love both peanuts and my grandkids, but you'd better believe I'm talking about two different kinds of love. I could get along without peanuts; I couldn't get along without my wife or my children or my grandkids.

The Greek word for love within the family was *storge*. *Phile* usually described love between friends, while love in the physical realm was *eros*. But there is a love that exceeds all of these. To describe this deepest kind of love the New Testament had to take a little-used word and give it whole new meaning. It used this word to define a dimension of love that cannot be found apart from Christ and the Spirit. This word describes the love that God has for us, the love God places in our hearts, the love that we, through the Spirit, have for each other. It describes the kind of love that flows forth from our life when we are filled with the Spirit. It's the word *agape*.

Now, whenever you add a new word to your vocabulary, it is necessary that you define that word so people will know what you are talking about. Thus, *agape* is defined for us in two places in the New Testament.

In 1 Corinthians 13:4 Paul tells us that "*Agape* suffers long and is kind." Not only is love longsuffering, but it is kind even after it has suffered for a long time. A lot of times we say, "I've taken it and taken it and taken it, and I'm up to here, and now I'm going to do something about it." That is not *agape*. After *agape* has taken and taken and taken, it is still kind.

Agape does not envy. It doesn't parade itself. It's not puffed up. Are you envious? Do you parade yourself? Are you puffed up? If so, you don't have the fruit of God's Spirit blossoming from your life.

Agape doesn't behave in an arrogant or rude manner. It is not provoked and it thinks no evil. *Agape* does not rejoice in iniquity, but does rejoice in the truth. *Agape* bears all things, believes all things, hopes all things, and endures all things. *Agape* never fails.

That's Paul's definition of *agape*. That's the kind of love that God wants to flow forth from your life like a river of living water. That is the kind of love that will bear witness to the world that indeed you are a child of God. By this sign shall all men know that you are His disciple, that you love—*agape*—one another (see John 13:35).

If you were to replace each appearance of the word *agape* in this passage with the name of Jesus, you'd notice that the passage flows easily. Jesus suffered long and was kind. Jesus did not envy, did not parade Himself, did not behave Himself in an arrogant or rude way. He believed all things, hoped all things, endured all things. Jesus never failed. See, the text just flows.

Now try putting your own name in there. How far can you get before you gulp? "Chuck suffers long and is kind." How far do you need to go? Yet this is what the Spirit desires for each of us.

In Galatians 5:22,23, Paul gives us a second definition of *agape*. He begins, "The fruit of the Spirit is *agape*," and then lists eight other terms: joy, peace, longsuffering, kindness, goodness, faithfulness, gentleness, and self- control. Many times I have heard someone say there are nine fruits of the Spirit, but that is not what Paul wrote. He said the fruit (singular) of the Spirit is *agape*. All the other eight terms merely show a different aspect of love.

What about "joy"? The consciousness of *agape* is joy. When God's love fills your heart and flows forth from you, the consciousness of your state brings unutterable joy. The Bible uses the term *joy unspeakable* to describe what is indescribable. That's the affect of *agape*.

What about "peace"? That's love's nature. When *agape* love characterizes your life, you enjoy a deep peace. You're not worried or concerned about what Betty is saying about you, or what that group is doing over there. You have a deep peace fostered by the *agape* in your heart.

"Longsuffering" is the attitude of love. It says, "Oh, let them go ahead. What difference does it make?" It's patient. I have a dog that's more longsuffering than a lot of people I've met. My grandkids come over to the house and crawl all over him and pull his ears and his tail, but he just takes it. He's so longsuffering. I admire my dog. I wish more people were like him.

"Gentleness" or "kindness" is another aspect of love's nature. There is a reason why our Savior is sometimes called "the gentle Jesus." He was filled with the Spirit and *agape* flowed out from his inner being and gently touched everyone He met.

"Goodness" is the effect of love. I believe love is the highest motive for goodness. I was tempted to many wrong things when I was growing up: I was tempted to smoke like my friends, speak profanities, and take what didn't belong to me. But I did none of that—and not just because I didn't have the opportunity! I knew that if my mother found out what I had done, it would break her heart. My love for my mom and her love for me was a strong bond that kept me out of a lot of trouble. Mutual love was a strong factor in keeping me pure and on the right track.

"Faithfulness" is the result of God's love within my life. His love creates trust that I wouldn't otherwise have. I become someone who is truly trustworthy.

"Meekness" is the demeanor of love. As Paul said, it doesn't parade itself. It doesn't seek its own way.

"Temperance" or "self-control" is the safety-valve of love. It isn't extreme, it keeps itself under control. Those who are filled with *agape* don't fly off the handle or get swept up in some ungodly fervor.

Agape is the kind of love that the Spirit produces in your life. Each one of these eight traits of love should serve as a mirror in front of your face. As you read these words, you either say, "Yes, that's me," or "Oops! Missed that one."

The genuine evidence of the Holy Spirit within your life is *agape* love. So many times people are looking for evidences of the Holy Spirit in the realm of speaking in tongues or in words of prophecy or in words of knowledge. But if these things are done without love, they are unprofitable. Without *agape*, any other manifestation of the Spirit becomes invalid. Although you may speak with other tongues, if you do not have *agape*, it is no more meaningful than taking lids from a communion set and banging them together.

The one thing we should seek more than all else—more than any other manifestation of the Holy Spirit—is that this *agape* love would gush forth from our lives to touch others in the name of Jesus. The fruit of the Spirit is love.

What Flows from Your Life?

As believers, we enjoy the tremendous privilege of having the Holy Spirit indwell us. We know the glory of having our bodies as the temple of the Holy Spirit. We see the wonderful work of the Holy Spirit in our lives as He conforms us into the image of Jesus Christ.

But this outflow of the Spirit from our lives is something different. "Out of your innermost being will gush torrents of living water," Jesus promised.

I don't care what you call this: the baptism of the Holy Spirit, the gift of the Holy Spirit, the filling of the Holy Spirit. It doesn't matter what terminology you might choose. What's important is the underlying reality.

My questions to you are, Does this describe what is going on in your life? Does this describe your relationship with the Holy Spirit? Can you say, "Yes, praise God, there is flowing forth from my life a torrent of love and power as a result of the Spirit overflowing my life." The question is not, Are you baptized or filled or do you have the gift of the Holy Spirit? The question is, Do overflowing torrents of living water gush from your life?

If this doesn't describe your relationship with the Holy Spirit, then may I suggest that God has something more for you than what you've yet experienced? And should you not desire everything that God has for you? Should you not seek the promise of God—a life overflowing with the power and the love of the Holy Spirit?

I, for one, need and desire all the help I can get and all the resources God has provided for me. As Paul prayed for the Corinthians that they would not come short in any spiritual gift, so is my prayer for you. Don't choose to come short of anything God wants to do in your life.

Allow the mighty dynamic of the Spirit to be released in your life. Allow Him to touch your family through you, to touch your neighbors, to touch those you work with, to touch everyone you contact. Then you will see God's love flowing from your life, offering living water to quench the raging thirst of this spiritually parched world.

The Ultimate Experience

I find it fascinating that some modern-day philosophers are discussing what they call "the ultimate experience." Although the general idea of the ultimate experience can be described, a specific ultimate experience is beyond words. It's an experience beyond anything a person has ever known, so no vocabulary exists capable of describing it. Words simply fail.

Imagine that tomorrow you walked into a group of your philosophical friends and said, "Last night, it happened. I received the ultimate experience." If they replied, "Tell us about it," you would know they were ignorant. You can't describe the ultimate experience because it is the ultimate experience and no vocabulary can articulate it.

One of the philosophers involved in these discussions was Julian Huxley. He believed the ultimate experience was possibly death while on an LSD high, so he proceeded to test his theory. He reportedly died high on LSD but wasn't able to tell us about it. No doubt it was the ultimate experience for him (at least it was his last one). So many students took their own lives in response to Huxley that philosophy professors throughout Germany had to assure their classes that no one knew for sure that suicide really was the ultimate experience.

The Genuine Article

Those of us who have been born again and filled with the Spirit know that the Christian life really is the ultimate experience. Yet it's hard to describe to a person with no spiritual understanding. The Bible says, "The natural man does not receive the things of the Spirit of God, for they are foolishness to him; nor can he know them, because they are spiritually discerned" (1 Corinthians 2:14).

It's like trying to relate to a deaf man the beauty of a symphony. He lacks the faculties by which to enjoy the music. Or try to describe to a blind man the brilliant colors of a sunset on a partly cloudy day. Words are inadequate.

So it is that the natural man lacks the faculties by which to understand and appreciate the things of the Spirit. That is why we have difficulty in expressing to unbelievers the joy and the peace we have been given. Nothing in their experience can relate to it; they have no base for grasping the things of the Spirit. In fact, spiritual things are foolishness to them. They look at you and scratch their head and say, "I just don't get it. He's weird. He goes around smiling when they're repossessing his car. Look, they're towing his car away right now—and the guy's just smiling. He's crazy."

No, not crazy. And not stupid, either. It's just that someone who has been born into the family of God, and who is walking in the fullness of the Spirit, doesn't have to worry about cars anymore. Why fret about cars when the universe and all that's in it is part of your inheritance? Why get upset when the Spirit of the Living God dwells in you forevermore? Why be anxious when you're a dearly beloved child of the King of kings and Lord of lords?

Yes, the Christian life really is the ultimate experience. But it is so only for those who allow God free rein in their lives. It is so only for those who invite God to do everything for them that He wants to do. It is so only for those who say no to the flesh and yes to the Spirit. It is the ultimate experience only for those who allow God to bring forth much fruit in their lives.

Fruit Comes Through Relationship

Fruit is the natural product of relationships. Jesus said, "I am the true vine, and My Father is the vinedresser. Every branch in Me that does not bear fruit He takes away; and every branch that bears fruit He prunes, that it may bear more fruit" (John 15:1,2). God isn't looking for the works of our flesh. God wants the fruit that sprouts from our lives because of our vital relationship with Him.

The glorious thing about fruit is that it doesn't have to strain or exert strenuous effort to exist. All it has to do is remain attached to the vine. As long as it is in relationship, it produces fruit. A branch cut off from the vine will die.

Years ago I was conducting a summer camp in Williams, Arizona. In front of the dining hall stood a large bell and next to the bell grew an apple tree. My problem was that the camp was always held in July and August but the apples were never ripe by then. Yet they always looked delicious.

One morning I cut off a tree limb filled with several green apples. I took the branch to a camp session and started describing to the kids how I decided to take this branch home so that when its apples ripened, I could enjoy them. The kids giggled and shouted, "Those apples will never get ripe!"

"What do you mean, they won't get ripe?" I asked. "Look at them! They look great! And, boy, I can't wait until September when they get ripe. Maybe I will even make an apple pie."

"Those apples will never ripen!" they snickered.

"Well, of course they will," I replied.

"No, stupid!" they laughed. "You cut the branch off!"

So it is. Even little kids know that when a branch is cut off from its source of life, it will never produce fruit.

It's the same way in your spiritual life. You will never develop if you are cut off from the life of the Spirit. Just as the branch draws its nourishment and energy from the vine, so do you from the Spirit. It is through the Spirit that God's life flows through you. It is in the realm of the Spirit that you come into contact with God.

C.H. Spurgeon, a great British preacher of the last century, knew this very well. It was he who said,

> I believe, brethren, that whenever the church of God declines, one of the most effectual ways of reviving her is to preach much truth concerning the Holy Spirit. After all, He is the very breath of the church. Where the Spirit of God is, is power. If the Spirit be withdrawn, then the vitality of the godliness begins to decline and we are backbiting. Let us turn to the Spirit of God crying, "Quicken thou me in thy way."
>
> If we sorrowfully perceive that any church is growing lukewarm, be it our prayer that the Holy Spirit may work graciously for its revival. Let us return to the Lord. Let us seek again to be baptized into the Holy Spirit and into fire, and we shall yet, again,

behold the wonderful works of the Lord. He sets before us an open door and if we enter not, we ourselves are to be blamed.

Spurgeon is right. If we enter not, we ourselves are to be blamed. God invites us in. He has provided everything we need for life and godliness. He has piled the table high with delectable morsels of every kind—every one chosen with care and love by His own discriminating eye.

Child of God, enter in. The ultimate experience awaits you. So what if you can't fully explain it to those outside? The idea is not to explain it, but to enjoy it.

There's room at His table for everyone!

Notes

CHAPTER 11

1. Some of today's skepticism, unfortunately, is well-founded. A great deal of charlatanism surrounds modern claims of divine healing. When a person is terminally ill, when the doctors have given up hope and say, "There's nothing we can do. Your loved one probably has 30 days on the outside..." we feel so desperate that we will grasp at any straw. Intelligent people who desperately desire to prolong a loved one's life will try anything and seek out anyone who holds out hope. Too many times healing meetings are nothing but hype. These frauds take advantage of people's desperate desire to see their loved ones walking again and restored to perfect health.

CHAPTER 12

1. It's interesting how Bible critics like to explain away this miracle. They say it was not really the Red Sea, but the Sea of Reeds, which is only about two feet deep. Oftentimes a strong east wind blows over a period of days, driving the sea back and leaving a place to cross. They contend that after just such an occurrence, a place was left for Moses and the children of Israel to cross. Thus it was not really a supernatural event. Yet this version requires Pharaoh's army to be drowned in two feet of water! I ask you, Which would be the greater miracle?

CHAPTER 13

1. One rule concerning prophecy seems to apply only to women of the Corinthian church. Paul instructed them, "If a woman prays or prophesies with her head uncovered, she dishonors her husband." He suggested that the women cover their heads. But then he says that there was no such rule in all the churches, so he seems to be dealing with a local situation in Corinth. At this time, Paul was speaking about chain of command—how the wife is subject to the husband, the husband is subject to the Lord, and the Lord to the Father.

Now, Corinth, a busy seaport filled with sailors, was an extremely wicked city, associated with total debauchery. It was known for its wild revelry, drunkenness, and partying. To say that a person lived like a Corinthian meant that the person was debauched.

At the top of the hill above Corinth was a huge temple to Aphrodite, the female goddess of love. In the evening, a thousand priestesses of Aphrodite—all prostitutes—would come down into the city. To identify themselves as priestesses, they would not wear veils. Consequently, an unveiled woman of Corinth was thought to be a prostitute.

With this in view, perhaps this is why Paul said if a woman prayed or prophesied and didn't wear a veil, it dishonored her husband: "Every woman who prays or prophesies with her head uncovered dishonors her head" (1 Corinthians 11:5). This rule was applied only to the women of Corinth who publicly exercised the gift of prophecy in church. But because his advice was limited to Corinth, Paul added "We have no such custom, nor do the churches of God" (11:16).

CHAPTER 15

1. Some argue that the last twelve verses of Mark are forgeries and should not be considered part of his gospel. These scholars say that because these verses do not appear in two of the oldest manuscripts we have—the Codex Sinaiticus and the Codex Alexandrinus, which both belong to the Alexandrian family of manuscripts and date back to between A.D. 420–460—they must have been inserted by a later copyist.

However, it is interesting to note that several early church fathers (such as Irenaeus, who lived from A.D. 140–202, and Hippolytus, who lived from A.D.170–235) quoted from the last twelve verses of Mark's Gospel. Such good evidence suggests that this portion of Mark *was* included in the original manuscript, but somehow got deleted from the Codex Sinaiticus and the Alexandrinus.

2. We could add a fourth purpose for tongues as given in 1 Corinthians 14:22: "a sign to unbelievers." But it is uncertain to what Paul refers here. This is a difficult passage because it seems to contradict itself in the context: "Therefore tongues are for a sign, not to those who believe but to unbelievers. It is difficult because in verse 23 Paul said, "Therefore if the whole church comes together in one place, and all speak with tongues, and there come in those who are uninformed or unbelievers, will they not say that you are out of your mind?"

That seems to be totally contradictory. First he tells us tongues are meant as a sign for unbelievers, then he says if the church is gathered and an unbeliever comes in and hears us all speaking in tongues, he'll call us crazy. So, if it's a sign to the unbeliever, then it's a sign that we're crazy! That's the problem. There are four basic ways to deal with this problem.

A. The British canon J.B. Phillips, who translated the New Testament into modern conversational English, took the liberty of changing verse 22 to read, "That means that tongues are a sign of God's power, not for those who are unbelievers, but to those that already believe." He changed the text itself (which he explains in a footnote). He felt bound to conclude from the sense of the next three verses that we have here either a slip of the pen on the part of Paul, or more probably a copyist's error. By changing the translation, he definitely removes the apparent contradiction. But I'm not certain he is correct, or that this is the only possible way of interpreting what Paul is saying.

B. The context of the passage is the prophecy of Isaiah, where God said He would speak to His people through stammering lips and other tongues, yet for all of this they would not believe. Therefore, the gift of tongues was a sign not for believers, but for those who do not believe. In this interpretation, the sign to the unbelievers is not to bring them to belief, but to signal God's judgment upon them.

C. Some talk about the sign gift of tongues versus the pure language. In this case, the gift of tongues is a sign to the unbeliever, as in Acts 2 when the

Holy Spirit first came upon the church. These Jews believed in God but did not believe in Jesus Christ. When they heard the disciples speaking in various dialects the wonderful works of God, many were convicted by the Spirit and some 3,000 of them were added to the church that day. Tongues and the message of Peter brought them to salvation on the day of Pentecost.

D. Still others teach that speaking in tongues is the primary evidence of the baptism of the Holy Spirit. Those who accept this teaching do not believe that they have been filled or baptized with the Holy Spirit until they have spoken in tongues. Thus, tongues become a sign to the unbeliever *who does not believe he has been filled with the Spirit until he has spoken in tongues*, not to the unbeliever *in Jesus Christ*.

So which view is correct? You can't settle on any one of them and say, "This is absolute." There are too many possibilities, and a wide variety of choices. All of them cannot be correct, of course, and perhaps none of them are. The jury is out on this one.

3. Only since the turn of the century, when there was again a renewal of the work of the Holy Spirit within the church (the birth of the Pentecostal movement with the accompanying gifts of the Spirit, such as speaking in tongues), have certain fundamentalists (who deny the validity of the supernatural work of the Spirit today) begun to interpret "that which is perfect" (1 Corinthians 13:10) to mean "the full canon of Scripture." Until that time, the phrase had always been understood to refer to the second coming of Christ.

According to this new interpretation, after John had written the book of Revelation and the canon was complete, the gifts of the Spirit were no longer needed or necessary. The gifts of word of knowledge or prophecy or of speaking in tongues were eliminated, because the church no longer needed such supernatural revelation. The church had the complete Word of God and didn't need the "sign gifts" any longer.

To bolster their argument, they point out that the word "perfect" in the phrase "that which is perfect" is in the neuter in Greek, and thus must be a reference to the Word rather than to Jesus at His second coming.

Let's examine these arguments.

First, such a teaching necessarily implies that tongues were used as a teaching tool in the early church—a belief the Bible does not bear out. As Paul points out in 1 Corinthians 14, tongues is a gift used by individual believers to aid in communicating their worship, praise, thanksgiving and prayer to God. It was *never* used as a means of spreading or teaching the gospel.

Second, it should be noted that Bible scholars always have understood from the context that "that which is perfect" is a reference to the coming again of Jesus Christ. If you will check in Thayer's *Greek New Testament Lexicon* or the Corinthian commentary of G. Campbell Morgan, you will find that the older church saints always understood 1 Corinthians 13:10 as a reference to the coming again of Jesus. When He returns, these things that are in part will be done away. At that time we will know, even as we are known. Then we will see Jesus face-to-face, no longer dimly as through a mirror.

To check this interpretation we could ask: At this moment, do we know *even as we are known*? I know I don't, and I've never met anyone else who did. Do we see Jesus face-to-face instead of as in a dim mirror? Peter didn't, and neither did his readers ("though now you do not see Him" 1 Peter 1:8); John didn't, but said that when we did, we would be like Him (1 John 3:2). No one doubts that I'm not like Him—not just yet. Which means I can't have seen Him face-to-face. Which means "that which is perfect" can't have arrived. Which means "that which is perfect" cannot refer to the completed canon of Scripture.

Third, the argument that because the word "perfect" is in the neuter, it must refer to the Word and not to Jesus, is very weak. It is well known that the word "spirit" (as in "Holy Spirit") is always in the neuter. Yet we know that the Holy Spirit is the third person of the Godhead. In the same way, the word "perfect" can refer to the coming of Jesus without compromising His personhood.

[Some critics pair "that which is perfect" with James' phrase "the perfect law of liberty" (James 1:25) and conclude that both phrases refer to the Scriptures. While it is true that the word translated "perfect" in both verses is the Greek term *teleion*, and that the verse in James does refer to the Scriptures, this proves nothing. The same word (*teleion*) is used to describe God Himself (Matthew 5:48); God's will (Romans 12:2); the work of patience (James 1:4); mature Christians (Ephesians 4:13); and a host of other things. It is arbitrary to pair James 1:25 with 1 Corinthians 13:10 simply because the same term appears in each. This is no argument at all.]

I am convinced that the context of 1 Corinthians 13:10 makes the traditional view the only proper interpretation. "That which is perfect" can only refer to the time of the second coming of our Lord. To try to make it mean anything else the interpretation must be forced away from that which is plain and obvious. The general rule is that the obvious meaning is usually the correct meaning.

CHAPTER 16

1. The events recorded in Acts 2 cannot be considered a record of the gift of the interpretation of tongues, for at least two reasons. First, those who heard the disciples "speaking in our own tongues the wonderful works of God" (verse 11) were not yet believers. The gifts of the Spirit, of course, are given only to believers—members of the body of Christ. Second, as far as the record tells us, the men who understood the disciples' utterances in tongues never declared their interpretations to anyone else. While they understood what was said, they kept it to themselves.

CHAPTER 18

1. Many men are gifted both as teachers and as evangelists. In the Calvary Chapel movement I think of Greg Laurie, Mike MacIntosh, and Raul Reis. These fellows not only have a teaching ministry, but they are evangelists. As teachers, these men have a pastor's heart. And through their shepherding a congregation, they gain a greater knowledge of what evangelism should be and do.

CHAPTER 21

1. The bishop was an overseer, a ruler or a governor within the body of Christ. The word "bishop" comes from the Greek term *episcope*. The Episcopalian church takes its name from this term, and follows this form of

government. Paul also speaks of the "elders." The Greek word is *presbuteros*; from which we get the word "presbyterians"—so-called because their form of government is rulership by a board of elders.

CHAPTER 23

1. J. Gilchrist Lawson, *Deeper Experiences of Famous Christians*, (1911), 248.

2. The phrase "filled with the Holy Spirit" in Acts seems to be used interchangeably with the phrase "baptism of the Holy Spirit."

3. Some Greek scholars say the phrase should be translated, "Did you receive the Holy Spirit *when* you believed" rather than "*since* you believed." But it really doesn't matter how you translate it. In either case, it carries the same implication. That is, the receiving of the Holy Spirit is subsequent to believing; one can believe without receiving this filling or baptism of the Holy Spirit. However the phrase should be translated into English it has the same affect. This baptism or infilling with the Spirit occurs subsequent to believing.

OTHER RESOURCES BY CHUCK SMITH:
BOOKS

LIVING WATER

This book captures the message of God's ability to change lives through His Holy Spirit. The reader will grow deeply in the knowledge and understanding of the Holy Spirit; His grace, His love, His power, and His gifts. 297 pages. **Study guide available**.

WHY GRACE CHANGES EVERYTHING

Through remarkable insight gleaned from the Bible and his own life, Pastor Chuck unfolds the mystery of grace. The reader will be refreshed and encouraged by the depth of God's grace toward us. 218 pages. **Also available in Spanish.**

THE MAN GOD USES

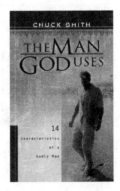

Do you want to be used by God? In his warm personal style, Chuck Smith examines the personal characteristics of the people God used in the Book of Acts. "The Man God Uses" will lead you into a deeper spiritual walk, while helping you to understand God's plan for your life. 144 pages.

TO ORDER CALL 1-800-272-WORD (9673)

SIX VITAL QUESTIONS OF LIFE

Pastor Chuck considers biblical answers to six vital questions asked by the Apostle Paul in Romans 8:31-39. As you study these questions, ponder them in your heart, and consider the biblical rationale, you can be certain your relationship with God will be transformed! 80 pages.

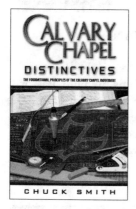

CALVARY CHAPEL DISTINCTIVES

Calvary Chapel values both the teaching of God's Word, as well as the work of the Holy Spirit. It is this balance that makes Calvary Chapel a distinct and uniquely blessed movement of God. 250 pages.
Also available in Spanish.

NEW TESTAMENT STUDY GUIDE

Master the New Testament quickly and easily using this verse-by-verse overview. Includes Introductions, explanations, study questions, Greek word origins, biblical maps, charts, and diagrams. 208 pages.

WRITE P.O. BOX 8000, COSTA MESA, CA. 92628

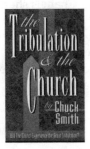

**THE TRIBULATION AND
THE CHURCH**
Will the church of Christ experience the
Great Tribulation? This book expounds
upon biblical prophecy and future events
while looking at the role of the church.
72 pages.

**THE GOSPEL
ACCORDING TO GRACE**
A clear and enlightening
commentary on the Book of
Romans. Chuck Smith reviews
Paul's epistle, one of the most
important books in the Bible, on a
verse-by-verse basis. 231 pages.
Study guide included!

EFFECTIVE PRAYER LIFE
This practical study in prayer will equip
and help you to have a more effective
and dynamic prayer life. An excellent
resource for personal growth and group
discipleship. 99 pages.

TO PLACE AN ORDER E-MAIL INFO@TWFT.COM

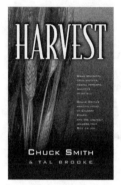

HARVEST
Pastors from ten Calvary Chapels share how God broke through the barriers of evil, pride, and anger to carry out His plan. Many insights into evangelizing and trusting God's Word make this book a valuable resource for every believer. 160 pages.

**STANDING UP IN
A FALLEN WORLD**
Based upon the book of Daniel, this book by Chuck Smith inspires today's young adults to take a stand for righteousness, and to seek to overcome this fallen world and its evil ways. 102 pages.
Study guide available.

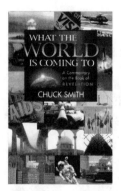

WHAT THE WORLD IS COMING TO
This book is a complete commentary on the book of Revelation and the scenario for the last days. Our world is coming to an end fast, but you don't have to go down with it! 215 pages.

VISIT OUR WEBSITE: WWW.TWFT.COM

1 JOHN NOTES
Excellent for pastors or students! Taken from Chuck Smith's personal study notes, this can be used as an outline for Bible study groups, Sunday school classes, or individual studies. First John is explored verse-by-verse, with cross-referencing to other books of the Bible. 66 pages.

ANSWERS FOR TODAY
A compilation of popular questions & answers regarding the rapture, God's plan, false doctrines, carnality, healing, and many others. 183 pages.

CHARISMA VERSUS CHARISMANIA
Chuck Smith explores the "charismatic experience," a theological controversy that has existed for years. A wonderful book for those seeking to find a balanced relationship with the Holy Spirit. 146 pages.

TO ORDER CALL 1-800-272-WORD (9673)

COMFORT FOR THOSE WHO MOURN

In this pamphlet, Pastor Chuck shares the glorious hope we have in the resurrection of Jesus Christ and how we can find comfort through Him during a time of loss. 15 pages.

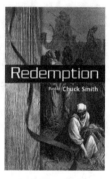

REDEMPTION

In this clear and easy-to-read commentary, Pastor Chuck explores and explains the concept of our redemption in Christ using as background the story of Ruth and her "Goel" or savior, Boaz. 16 pages.

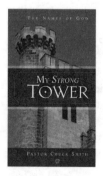

MY STRONG TOWER

What are the names of God? Starting with Proverbs 18:10, Chuck Smith takes a close look at the names of God mentioned in the Old & New Testaments. 24 pages.

WRITE P.O. BOX 8000, COSTA MESA, CA. 92628

THE SEARCH FOR MESSIAH

Written by Dr. Mark Eastman & Chuck Smith, this book is a gateway of discovery for the serious pilgrim in search of the Messiah. The skeptic will be challenged and the Christian deeply enriched. 276 pages.

CALVINISM, ARMINIANISM & THE WORD OF GOD

This pamphlet discusses the facts upon which these two doctrinal stands are based, and compares them to the Word of God. 20 pages.

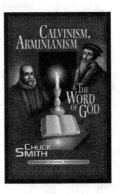

HOW CAN A MAN BE BORN AGAIN?

Pocket-sized and perfect for witnessing, this pamphlet explains what it means to be born again and why it is crucial if you want to see the kingdom of God. Includes a sinner's prayer and follow-up suggestions. 24 pages.
Also available in Spanish.

BIBLE STUDY BY CHUCK SMITH:
M P 3

**PASTOR CHUCK SMITH
THROUGH THE BIBLE
C-2000 SERIES ON MP3**
Using an MP3 format, The Word
For Today has compiled Pastor
Chuck Smith's entire C-2000
series on a set of 8 CD's. You can
now fit the complete audio of
Pastor Chuck's Old and New
Testament Bible commentaries
into your pocket.

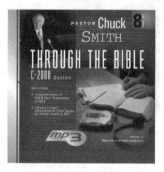

*You can play these CD's on your computer or an MP3 player.
Macintosh & Windows compatible.*

SOFTWARE
Windows 95/98/2000/NT
Macintosh PowerPC
• Adobe Acrobat Reader 4.0 • RealPlayer 8

MP3 PLAYER REQUIREMENTS:
• Must be able to play 32KB files.

Bonus Materials:
• A Bible Search Engine
• Pastor Chuck's Personal Sermon Notes
• Internet Accessible Bible & Programs
• Incredibly, 4 of Pastor Chuck Smith's Books!

AUDIO RESOURCES
By Chuck Smith:

THE BOOK OF REVELATION
These messages will help the listener understand one of the most enigmatic and prophetic books of the Bible. Pastor Chuck explains and dissects Revelation, chapter by chapter—the only book of the Bible that declares a blessing on those who read, hear, and keep it!

PROPHECY UPDATE
What are the implications of the recent events in Israel? Are the pieces of the puzzle finally coming together, leading to a one-world government? Pastor Chuck examines these issues in a timely series.

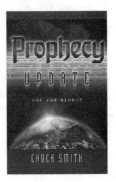

SIGNS OF HIS COMING
This series examines current events as they relate to end times. Drawing from Bible studies in the books of Daniel, Matthew, Revelation, and Zechariah; Pastor Chuck explains prophecy in light of today's changing world.

TO ORDER CALL 1-800-272-WORD (9673)

PROPHECY UPDATE 2005
Pastor Chuck Smith's prophecy update recorded live at Calvary Chapel Costa Mesa. Bonus messages include the coming invasion of Israel, identity theft, rampant immorality, and the war in Iraq.

ISRAEL: A SPECIAL TREASURE
This series studies the richness of the Hebrew culture and homeland; from their feasts to their covenants with God. Ten biblical studies by Pastor Chuck Smith, Chuck Missler, Brian Brodersen, Dave Hunt, and David Hocking.

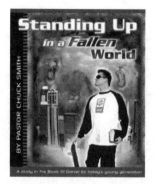

STANDING UP IN A FALLEN WORLD
Based on the Book of Daniel, these audio teachings were recorded during a youth camp. Each study contains a powerful message for today's young generation.
Study guide available.

WRITE P.O. BOX 8000, COSTA MESA, CA. 92628

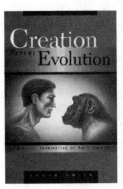

CREATION VS. EVOLUTION
Pastor Chuck Smith hosts a collection of biblical studies that focus on the validity of Creation and the scientific evidence that backs it up. Joining Pastor Chuck are guest speakers; Chuck Missler, Roger Oakland, Dr. Mark Eastman and Dr. Henry Morris.

DEFENDING THE FAITH
A series to equip believers to defend the Christian faith. Subjects include prophecy, cults, Islam, Mormonism, evolution, New Age, and more. Speakers include: Chuck Smith, Dave Hunt, Dr. Mark Eastman, Ed Decker, Paul Carden, Roger Oakland, and Justin Alfred.

THE WISDOM OF THE AGES
Pastor Chuck Smith, Dr. Henry Morris, and Dave Hunt discuss the most reliable Bible translations, the basis for our Bible, as well as the inerrancy, sufficiency, and authority of the Scriptures.

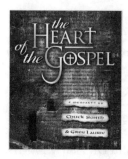

THE HEART OF THE GOSPEL
Have you ever wondered what it means to be born again or why Jesus' resurrection is crucial to the Christian faith? A great resource to share your faith with others. By Pastors Chuck Smith & Greg Laurie.

MY REDEEMER LIVES
This collection contains 14 Old & New Testament Bible studies. It covers the death and resurrection of Jesus Christ: From the fulfillment of prophetic Scriptures to the proof of the resurrection. Pastor Chuck Smith & Dr. Mark Eastman

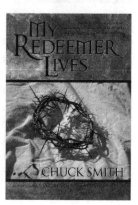

WHY? Evangelistic CD & Tract
Hands down the easiest way to witness the Gospel of Jesus Christ! Comes complete with a powerful message by Pastor Chuck teaching the "Passion of Christ," a song by Danny Donnelly, and a persuasive tract with an invitation to accept Jesus as Savior.

VISIT OUR WEBSITE: WWW.TWFT.COM

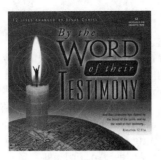

BY THE WORD OF THEIR TESTIMONY

Hear the miracle of redemption through 12 different testimonies: Chuck Smith, Raul and Sharon Ries, Jon Courson, Corrie Ten Boom, Greg Laurie, Joni Eareckson-Tada, Mike and Sandy MacIntosh, Skip Heitzig, & more.

WHEN STORMS COME

A variety of Bible studies by Pastor Chuck Smith designed to bring encouragement to those who are struggling with life's burdens. The listener will learn that God may not always deliver us from the storm, but He is faithful to be with us as we go through it.

PASTOR CHUCK SMITH'S MOST REQUESTED BIBLE STUDIES

12 of the most requested Bible studies by Pastor Chuck. Some messages included are: Faith that prevails; How can a man be born again; Trusting in lies, and How long 'til the end.

TO ORDER CALL 1-800-272-WORD (9673)

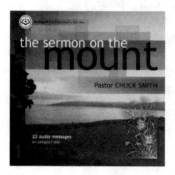

SERMON ON THE MOUNT
IN-DEPTH COMMENTARY SERIES
One of the most important
sermons Jesus ever preached,
Pastor Chuck gives an expansive
explanation for principles
concerning Christian living; i.e.,
the Beatitudes, Anger Lust,
Judging, etc.
Study Guide available.

THE PERSON OF
THE HOLY SPIRIT
IN-DEPTH COMMENTARY SERIES
This set explains who the Holy
Spirit is and how He works.
12 messages.

THE GIFTS OF
THE HOLY SPIRIT
Covers such subjects as
miracles, healing, prophecy,
faith and speaking in tongues.
19 messages.

Study guide available.

WRITE P.O. BOX 8000, COSTA MESA, CA. 92628

For information about additional products,
receiving a free product catalog,
or to be added to our e-mail list
for product updates,
please contact

THE WORD
FOR TODAY

P.O. Box 8000, Costa Mesa, CA 92628
800-272-WORD (9673)
www.twft.com • E-mail: info@twft.com